WOMEN REFRAME
AMERICAN LANDSCAPE

The book accompanies *Women Reframe American Landscape: Susie Barstow & Her Circle / Contemporary Practices*, the two-part exhibition organized by and debuting at the Thomas Cole National Historic Site in Catskill, New York, May 6 – October 29, 2023 and traveling to the New Britain Museum of American Art in New Britain, Connecticut, November 16, 2023 – March 31, 2024.

Published by:
Thomas Cole National Historic Site
218 Spring Street
Catskill, New York 12414
U.S.A.
www.thomascole.org

Hirmer Publishers
Hirmer Verlag GmbH
Bayerstrasse 57–59
80335 Munich
Germany
www.hirmerpublishers.com

Authors and Editors: Nancy Siegel, Kate Menconeri, and Amanda Malmstrom
Consulting Editor: Annette Blaugrund
Assistant Editors and Researchers:
Sofia Thieu D'Amico and Kristen Marchetti
Transcriber: Vicente Cayuela

Copy editing and proof reading: Jane Michael
Design: Lucia Ott
Senior Editor at Hirmer Publishers:
Elisabeth Rochau-Shalem
Project Manager at Hirmer Publishers:
Rainer Arnold

Lithography and pre-press:
Reproline Genceller, München
Printing and binding: Grafisches Centrum Cuno
Paper: Gardamatt Art 170 g/m^2

Printed in Germany

ISBN 978-3-7774-4039-2

Cover and title image credits:

left: Ebony G. Patterson, *...the wailing...ushers us home...and there is a bellying on the land...* (detail), see p. 60

right: Susie M. Barstow, *Untitled* (detail), see p. 21

back and p.50: Saya Woolfalk, *Self-Portrait (Words by Sojourner Truth)* (detail), see p. 99

p. 4: Anna Plesset, *Value Study 1: A View of the Catskill Mountain House / Copied from a picture by S. Cole copied from a picture by T. Cole / 1848* (detail), see p. 95

p. 10: Susie M. Barstow, *Wooded Interior* (detail), see p. 30

p. 74: Jaune Quick-to-See Smith, *Unhinged (Map)* (detail), see p. 64

p. 86: Tanya Marcuse, *Woven № 33* (detail), see pp. 96/97

WOMEN REFRAME AMERICAN LANDSCAPE

Susie Barstow & Her Circle   Contemporary Practices

Nancy Siegel,
Kate Menconeri,
and Amanda Malmstrom

THOMAS COLE NATIONAL HISTORIC SITE

HIRMER

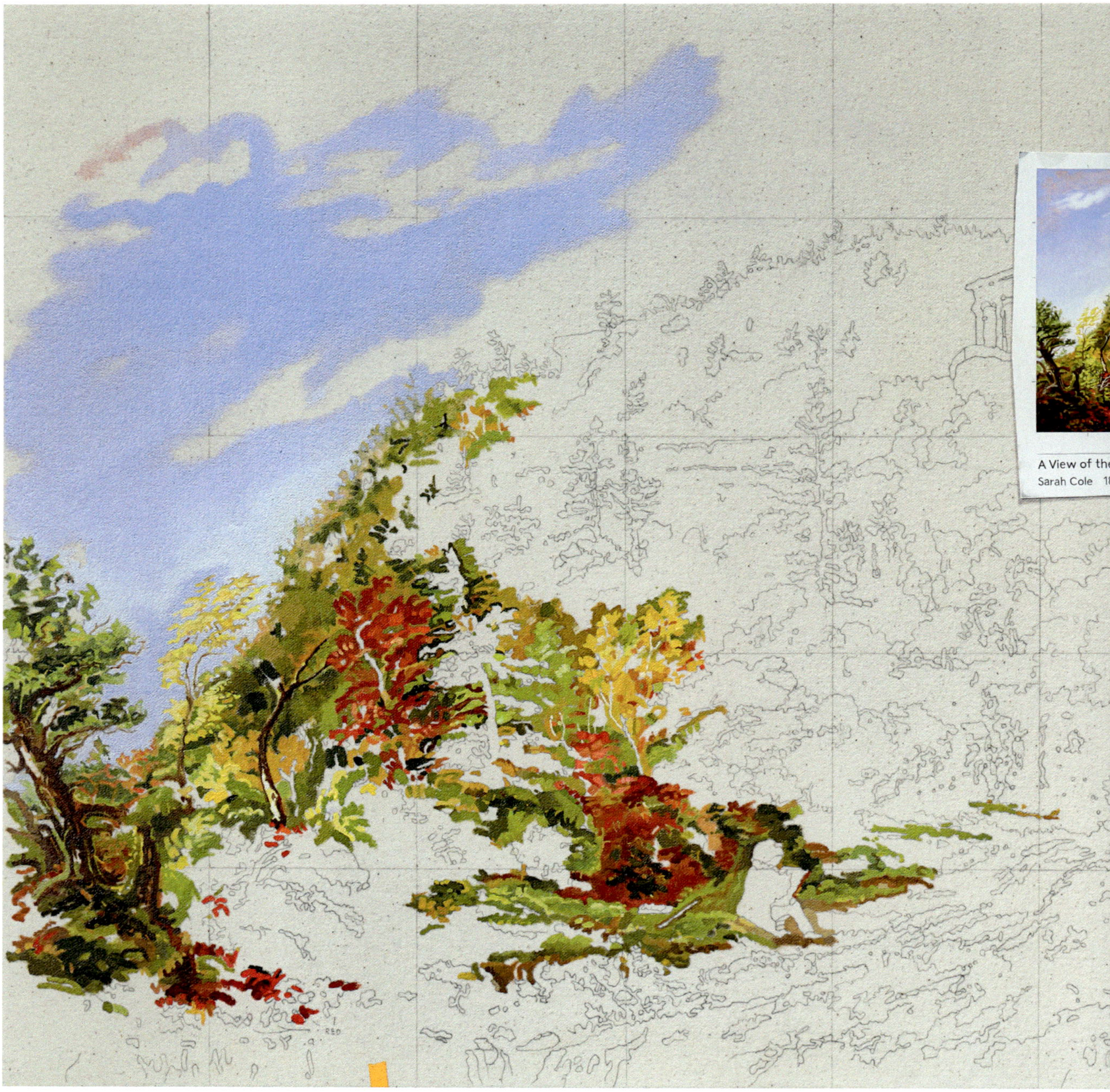
A View of the
Sarah Cole

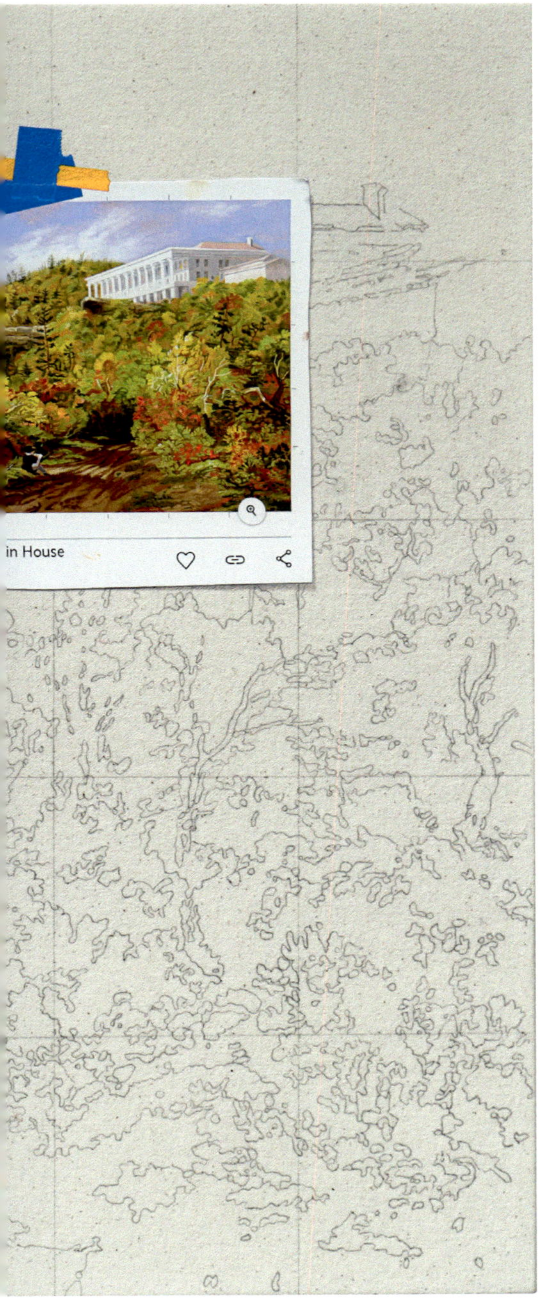

TABLE OF CONTENTS

This book makes reference to broad and shifting definitions of the term "American landscape." It is important to recognize and honor all lands as the ancestral homes of their Indigenous caretakers. It is with gratitude and humility that we acknowledge that at the Thomas Cole National Historic Site, we are learning, speaking, and gathering on the ancestral homelands of the Muhheaconneok or Mohican, who are the Indigenous peoples of this land. Despite tremendous hardship in being forced from here, today their community resides in Wisconsin and is known as the Stockbridge-Munsee Community. We pay honor and respect to their ancestors past and present as we commit to building a more inclusive and equitable space for all. We respect the enduring relationships that exist between these peoples and the land and waterways.

FOREWORD

Elizabeth B. Jacks

While still in his early 20s, the emerging artist Thomas Cole set out to redefine landscape paintings as "something more than mere imitations of nature." In a highly revealing set of letters, Cole pushes back against his wealthy patron Robert Gilmor's insistence that "Above all things...truth in drawing the scenes of our own country is essential." The question that Gilmor perhaps had not considered is what is meant by "truth?" Depictions of land were primarily seen as objective documentation, with the White male viewpoint as a given. Two centuries later, our urgent task is to enable the hidden, forgotten, and deliberately erased truths about America to be seen and heard. The land is a fertile vessel for all of these.

In 2010 the Thomas Cole Site teamed up with two visionary scholars who were on a trailblazing mission to bring women artists of the 19th century to the fore: Nancy Siegel and Jennifer Krieger. Together we organized an exhibition here in the Main House entitled *Remember the Ladies: Women of the Hudson River School*, quoting Abigail Adams writing to John Adams in 1776: "...in the new Code of Laws which I suppose it will be necessary for you to make I desire you would Remember the Ladies and be more generous and favourable to them than your ancestors." Interestingly, the primary reaction of the exhibition's visitors was surprise. "These paintings are all by women?" they asked incredulously. The artworks seemed to be indistinguishable from those of their male counterparts, so why then were they excluded from the recent explosion of books and exhibitions on nineteenth-century landscape painting? As the first museum exhibition to focus solely on these women, *Remember the Ladies* broke new ground, but today we are asking new questions. What if we didn't hold up men's paintings as the standard by which all other art is judged? If depictions of land are indeed subjective, how could such a limited subset of humanity possibly speak for all of us?

To our delight and good fortune, the brilliant and perceptive Dr. Siegel is again working with us on a groundbreaking exhibition, having completed years of research on the extraordinary life and work of Susie Barstow. The curators Nancy Siegel, Kate Menconeri, and Amanda Malmstrom provide the thoughtful, courageous answer to the seminal feminist art historian Linda Nochlin's call to action fifty years ago to make sure that women's voices are heard. The voices they have amplified with this publication and exhibition are a revelation, shifting the very earth beneath our feet. I have never been more proud and excited to present an exhibition as this one, the cornerstone of our year-long initiative, *Women, Land, + Art,* bringing women to the forefront of our work at this historic site. It is primarily women who have owned, operated, and preserved these buildings and grounds over the last two centuries, some as artists, others formerly enslaved, and all performing a critical role in crafting history. Bringing forward the outstanding work of the intrepid artist Susie Barstow feels not only important and overdue but also greatly empowering to women today.

The Board of Trustees, led by our indefatigable chairman Lisa Fox Martin, and our exceptionally intelligent and passionate staff, inspire me every day with their creativity and dedication. One of the reasons that this place continues to engage us so forcefully is that there are few things more consequential than our relationship with land. Considering humankind's current direction, it is tempting to despair, but making a work of art is itself an act of hope, choosing action over inaction. The words of the artist Sarah Cole come to mind, when her brother Thomas was feeling low: "You speak rather despondingly about your paintings, you should not do so...In a little while you will find that the art will return to you...The lights and shadows of this life are like the lights and shadows in your own pictures. The one makes the other more beautiful."

ACKNOWLEDGEMENTS

The curators join the Director and the Thomas Cole National Historic Site to extend our profound thanks to the visionary artists and writers who are the heart of this project: Candice Hopkins and Jolene Rickard, Teresita Fernández, Guerrilla Girls, Marie Lorenz, Tanya Marcuse, Mary Mattingly, Ebony G. Patterson, Anna Plesset, Wendy Red Star, Jean Shin, Jaune Quick-to-See Smith, Cecilia Vicuña, Kay WalkingStick, and Saya Woolfalk. And, to the nineteenth-century artists: Susie M. Barstow, Julie Hart Beers, Fidelia Bridges, Sarah Cole, Charlotte Buell Coman, Eliza Pratt Greatorex, Mary Josephine Walters, and Laura Woodward—this is only the beginning; we have more stories to tell.

We are further indebted to Ken Barstow, Jerry Barstow, and the extended Barstow family who made so much of Susie Barstow's narrative possible, and to all of the generous lenders and liaisons who made the exhibition possible, including: Albany Institute of History & Art and Douglas C. McCombs; American Antiquarian Society; Dr. Trissa Babrowski and Sundeep Mullangi; Ron Berg; Max Berry and Pamela Berry; Birmingham Museum of Art; Stephen Brody; Allan E. Bulley, Jr.; Electronic Arts Intermix; Teresita Fernández Studio and Chelsea Ramirez; Garth Greenan Gallery and Gilles Heno-Coe and Hugh O'Rourke; Georgia B. Gosnell; Harriet Beecher Stowe Center and Elizabeth Burgess; Ann Huebner; Hales Gallery and Stuart Morrison; Hawthorne Fine Art and Jennifer Krieger; Lehmann Maupin Gallery and Alexis Rose; Susan Livingston; G. Daniel Massad and Scott H. Eggert; Monique Meloche Gallery and Alyssa Brubaker; The Newark Museum of Art and Patricia Laughlin Bloom; Patron Gallery and Julia Fischbach; Deborah Pollack; Sargent's Daughters and Allegra LaViola, Sofia Love, and Christine Nyce; Elizabeth and Alfred Scott; Suzanne H. Arnold Gallery at Lebanon Valley College; Paul Stuka; The Art Museum of West Virginia University and Bob Bridges; Thomas Tolska and Marilyn Tolska; and Hilary Peery Vesell. We are also grateful to work with Hirmer Publishers and thank the staff and our talented colleagues, especially Rainer Arnold, Lucia Ott, and Elisabeth Rochau-Shalem, for their patience, expertise, and innovation.

In addition to those noted above, the curators would like to acknowledge that this publication and exhibition would not be possible without the soaring vision and unwavering dedication of Elizabeth B. Jacks, Executive Director at the Thomas Cole National Historic Site, who first invited Nancy Siegel and Jennifer Krieger to present *Remember the Ladies: Women of the Hudson River School* in 2010 and who has always been an advocate and support to women and our work. Additionally, we are grateful to the TCNHS Board; the incredible staff; Annette Blaugrund, consulting editor who has been an inspired and indefatigable colleague, mentor, and publication manager who oversaw our partnership with Hirmer Publishers; and Sofia Thieu D'Amico and Kristen Marchetti, Assistant Editors and Cole 2023 Fellows, for their intelligent and dedicated research, which has been vital to realizing every aspect of the publication and exhibition. We are also indebted to Heather Bruegl, for her vital contribution to the timeline included within, as well as leading our organization to embrace a fuller story, one that centers Indigenous history and knowledge. We also thank Vicente Cayuela for his valued work and help in transcribing interviews and conversations featured within this publication, as well as 2020–2023 Cole Fellows: Isabelle Bohling, Brooke Krancer, and Bethany Wynne, for their important contributions along the way.

All projects are realized and shaped by many people and numerous conversations. In addition to the artists, writers, lenders, and TCNHS staff, we are indebted to colleagues who have introduced us to artists and/or ideas that have meaningfully shaped this project. Sincere gratitude and admiration goes out to Marilyn Dunn, Nicole Hayes, Mary-Kay Lombino, Josie Lopez, Denise Markonish, Lisa Sanditz, Kiki Smith, Rebecca Solnit, Shannon Vittoria, Alan Wallach, Jessica Wilcox, and Paula Wisotzki.

This book accompanies the two-part exhibition organized by and debuting at the Thomas Cole National Historic Site in Catskill, New York, May 6 – October 29, 2023 and traveling to the New Britain Museum of American Art in New Britain, Connecticut, November 16, 2023 – March 31, 2024. We would like to thank our exhibition partners at the New Britain Museum of American Art, with special thanks to Brett Abbott and Lisa Hayes Williams for their curatorial vision and shared commitment to this project.

The **Thomas Cole National Historic Site** in Catskill, NY preserves and interprets the historic artist's home and studios of Thomas Cole (1801-1848), the founder of the Hudson River School of painting, a unique movement in American art and landscape. The nationally-recognized historic site is an affiliate of the National Park Service and operates as a forward-thinking nonprofit organization embracing change and continually pursuing authenticity and resonance through innovative offerings that are relevant today. The Cole Site's activities include historic and contemporary art exhibitions, guided tours, printed publications, online programs, activities for school groups, free community events, lectures, and public programs. Located on six acres in the Hudson Valley, the site includes the 1815 Main House; Cole's 1839 Old Studio; the artist's designed, reconstructed New Studio; and gardens. For details visit: www.thomascole.org.

Women Reframe American Landscape:
Susie Barstow & Her Circle / Contemporary Practices

is made possible by
The Warner Foundation

The exhibition is supported by a grant from the National Endowment for the Arts and Empire State Development's I LOVE NEW YORK program under the Market NY initiative.

Additional support is provided by
Wyeth Foundation for American Art and
Tavolozza Foundation.

The exhibition and publication are also supported by Jennifer Krieger and Eric Siegel, Maurice D. Hinchey Hudson River Valley National Heritage Area, The Coby Foundation, Ltd., Marshall Field V., Allan E. Bulley, Jr., Greene County Legislature through the Greene County Cultural Fund, National Trust Insurance Services, LLC, Suncommon, The Bank of Greene County Charitable Foundation, New York State Council on the Arts with the support of the Office of the Governor and the New York State Legislature, and the Kindred Spirits Society of the Thomas Cole National Historic Site.

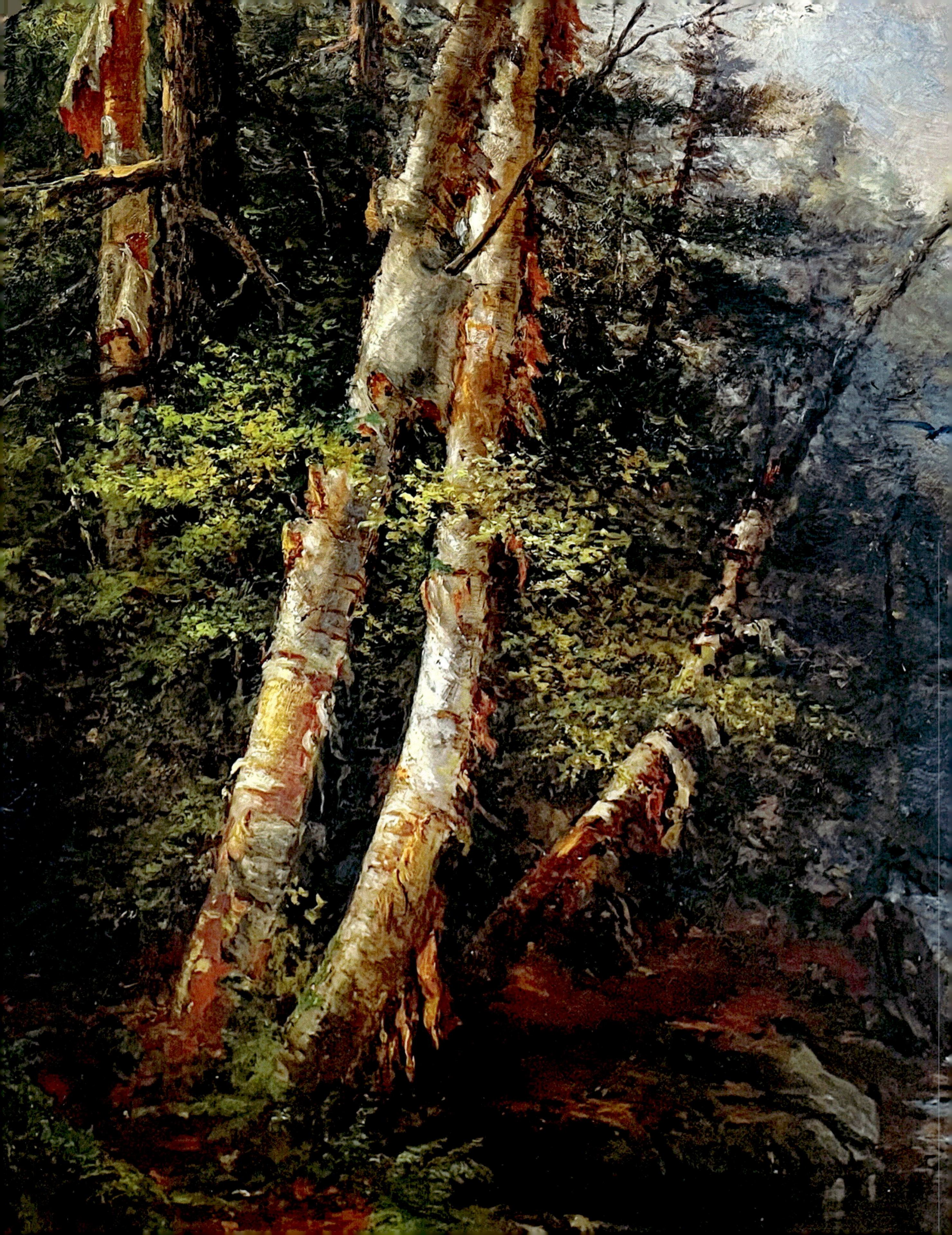

SUSIE M. BARSTOW: REDEFINING THE HUDSON RIVER SCHOOL

Nancy Siegel

For almost two centuries, Thomas Cole—the founder of the first American school of painting, as he is often labeled—has come to personify the Hudson River School. However, recent scholarship has provided us with an increased awareness of the breadth and depth of numerous artists who, like Cole, explored and painted the American landscape from the 1820s to the end of the nineteenth century. In fact, by the middle decades of the century, increasing numbers of women not only aspired to paint professionally but also achieved personal and financial success as artists, resulting in part from broader educational curricula, the instruction they acquired at home and abroad, and passionate determination to experience nature's wonderland directly.[1] Among the professional landscape painters at mid-century who hiked, sketched, and exhibited their work were the artists Julie Hart Beers, Fidelia Bridges, Charlotte Buell Coman, Eliza Greatorex, Mary Josephine Walters, and Laura Woodward. A common thread uniting them was Susie M. Barstow (fig. 1), whose landscapes showcased picturesque qualities, a romantic sensibility, and well-balanced compositions earning her fame and prominence in her day (fig. 2). Barstow and her female colleagues, painting in the style of the Hudson River School, routinely traveled to immerse themselves in American scenery. They wrote poetically of their adventures and captured on canvas the beauty and awe they encountered out of doors, inspired by the landscape just as were Thomas Cole, Asher Durand, and Frederic Church—the male canon of the Hudson River School. These nineteenth-century women artists, including Barstow, shared not only a deep engagement with the themes of American land and the natural world but also an assertion of their place within an art world that too often failed to offer the same opportunities and visibility to female artists as their male counterparts. Working *en plein air* or from the comfort of their studios, Barstow and her circle consistently exhibited and sold their paintings competitively in the most prestigious academies and galleries of New York. The professionalization of their work, beyond the decorative and mechanical fields of engraving, situates these women among the many whose lives, careers, and creative practice necessitate a redefinition of who and what the Hudson River School was and is.

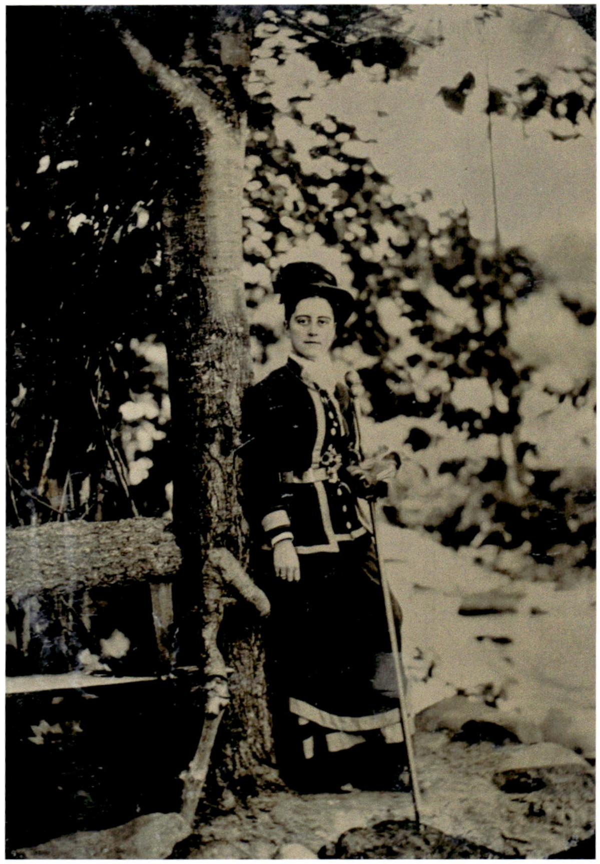

Fig. 1 Unidentified Photographer, Portrait of Susie M. Barstow, ca. 1870, tintype, 5½ × 4 in., Private Collection, Photograph: Dennis DeHart

Originating at the Thomas Cole National Historic Site in Catskill, New York, *Women Reframe American Landscape* is a two-part exhibition including *Susie Barstow & Her Circle* and *Contemporary Practices,* which expands the narrative sur-

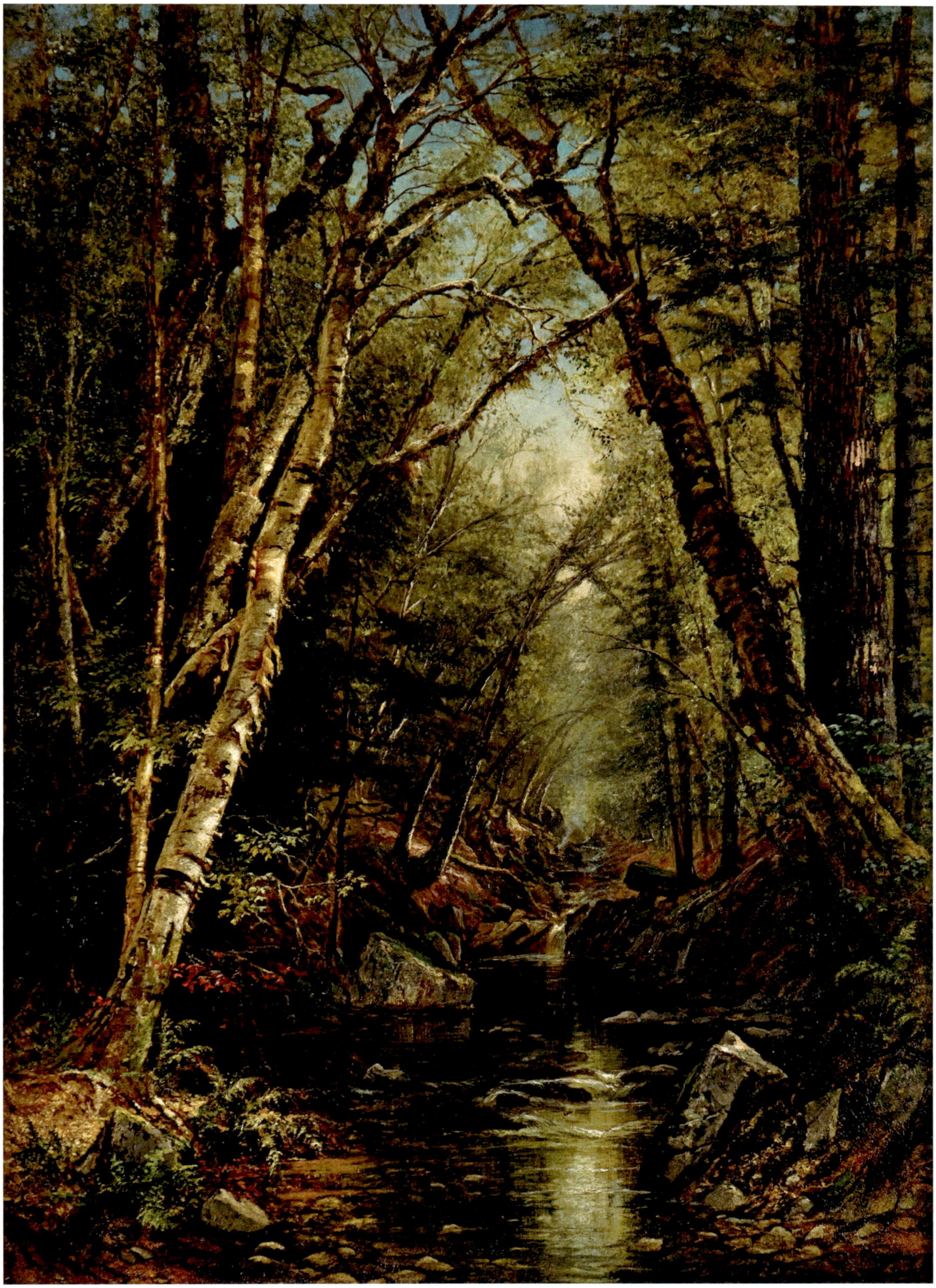

Fig. 2 Susie M. Barstow, *Landscape*, 1865, oil on canvas, 30 × 22 in., Betsy and Al Scott Collection

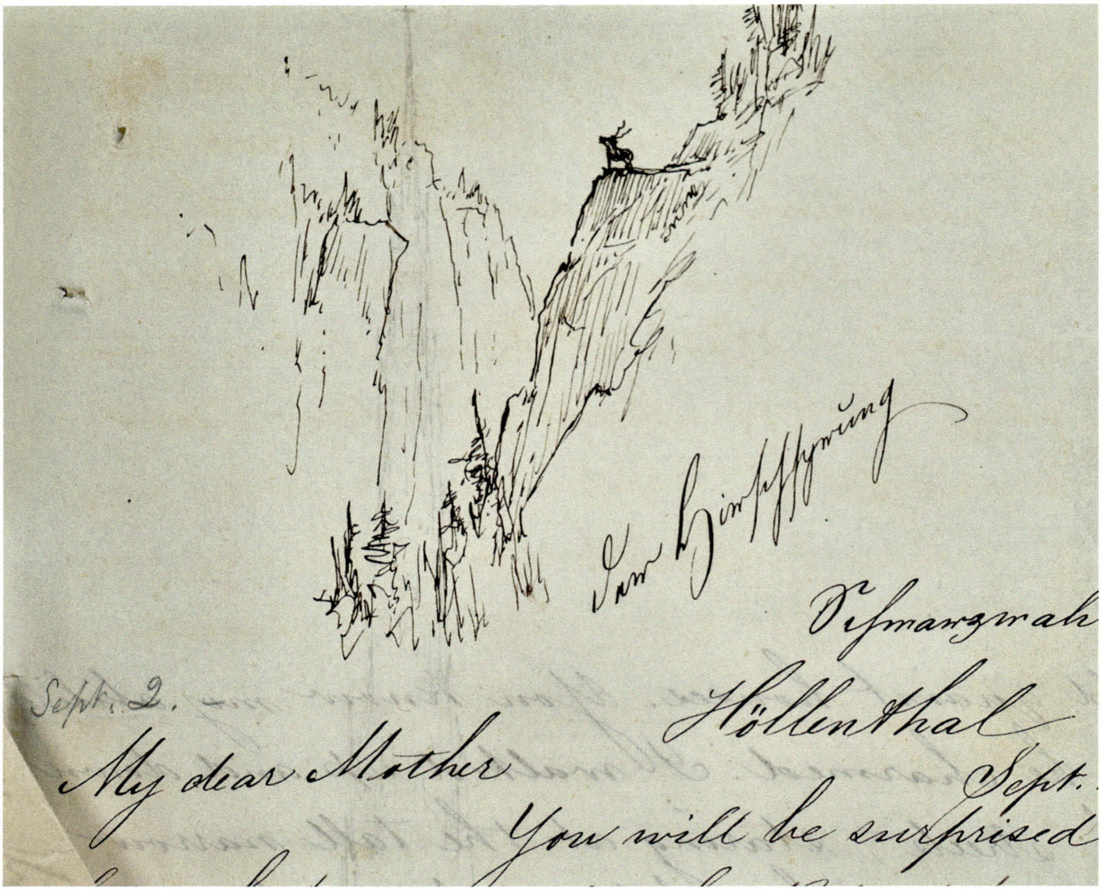

Fig. 3 Susie M. Barstow, Sketch on letter from Höllenthal, September 2, 1880, 8⅞ × 5½ in. (full sheet), Private Collection, Photograph: Dennis DeHart

rounding nineteenth-century women landscape painters and places them in conversation with contemporary artists. Through diverse voices, this exhibition revisits and builds upon the national success of the 2010 exhibition *Remember the Ladies: Women of the Hudson River School*, the first exhibition devoted solely to American women landscape painters of the Hudson River School. Addressing/redressing the historical gap that has traditionally written women out of this genre, *Susie Barstow & Her Circle* is not only the first retrospective of Barstow's work, but is also the first retrospective by any woman landscape painter of the Hudson River School. On the one hundredth anniversary of Barstow's death, this in-depth exploration of her paintings, watercolors, and drawings, as well as pages from her journals, letters (fig. 3), photographs (fig. 4), and related ephemera (fig. 5), provides a visually stunning deep dive into the life and artistic practice of a prolific nineteenth-century artist who deserves an important place in the history of art and landscape in America.[2] From the mid-nineteenth century through the first decades of the twentieth, a comprehensive biography unfolds, replete with extensive visual analyses and historical context through which to position Barstow well within New York's artistic community.

Fig. 4 Unidentified Photographer, *Portrait of Susie M. Barstow*, ca. 1870, Rawson 255 & 257 Fulton St., Brooklyn, 6½ × 4¼ in., Private Collection, Photograph: Dennis DeHart

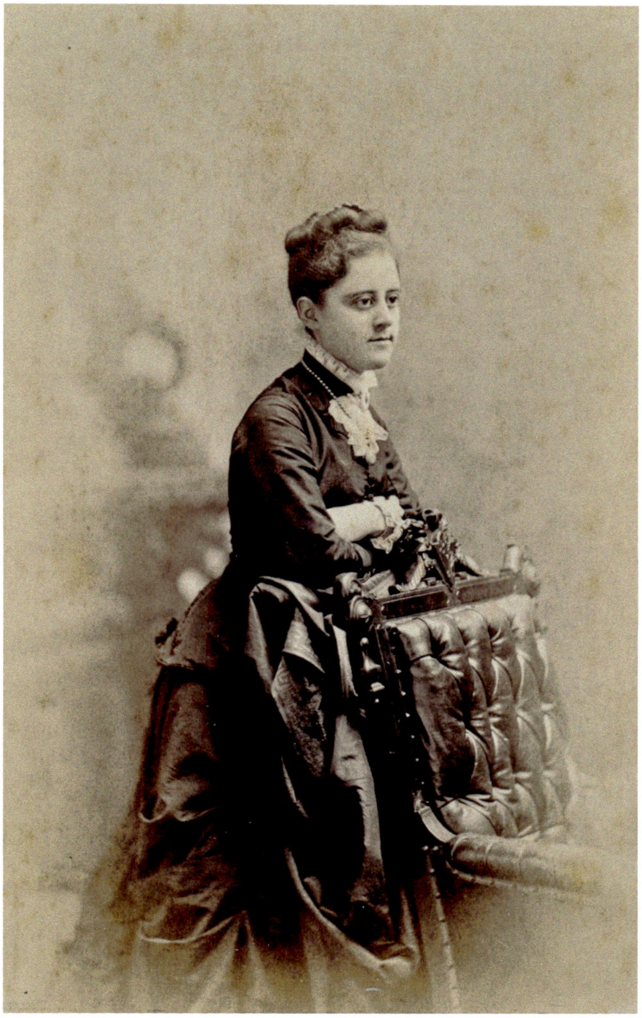

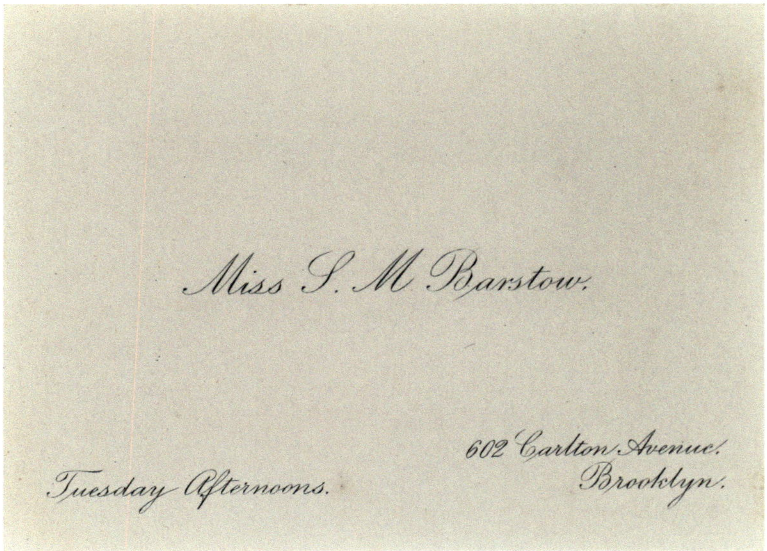

Fig. 5 Susie M. Barstow's Calling Card, ca. 1891, 2¾ × 3¾ in., Private Collection, Photograph: Dennis DeHart

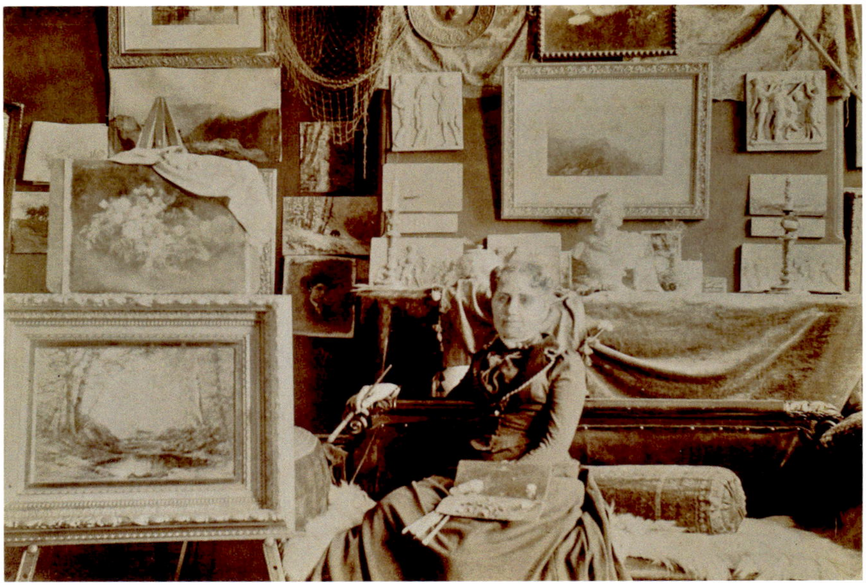

Fig. 6 Susie Barstow Skelding, Susie M. Barstow in her Brooklyn Studio, 1891, 5 × 7 in., Private Collection, Photograph: Dennis DeHart

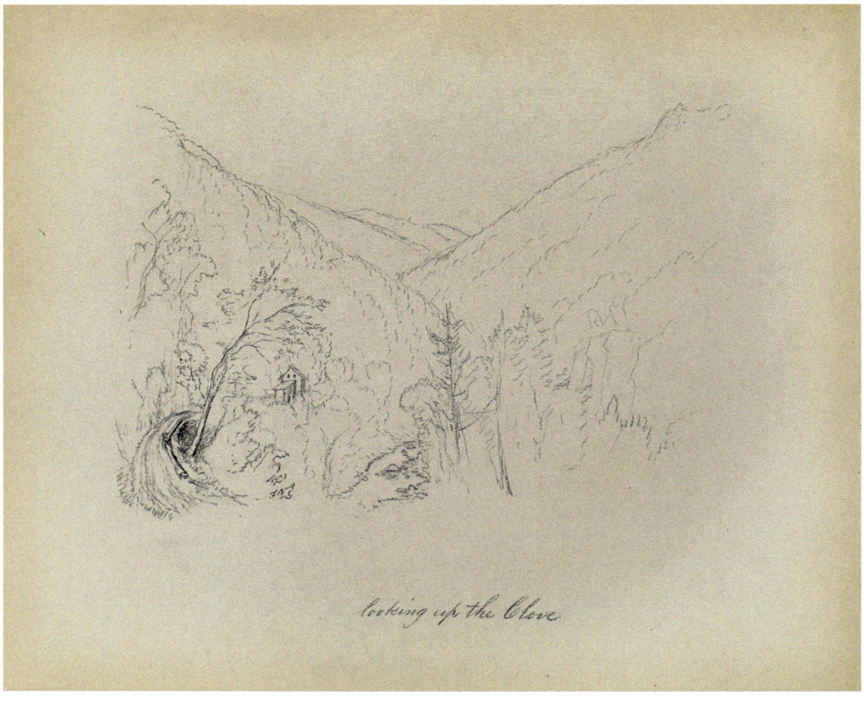

Fig. 7 Susie M. Barstow, *Looking Up the Clove*, ca. 1865, pencil on paper, 9 ⅛ × 11 ½ in., Private Collection, Photograph: Dennis DeHart

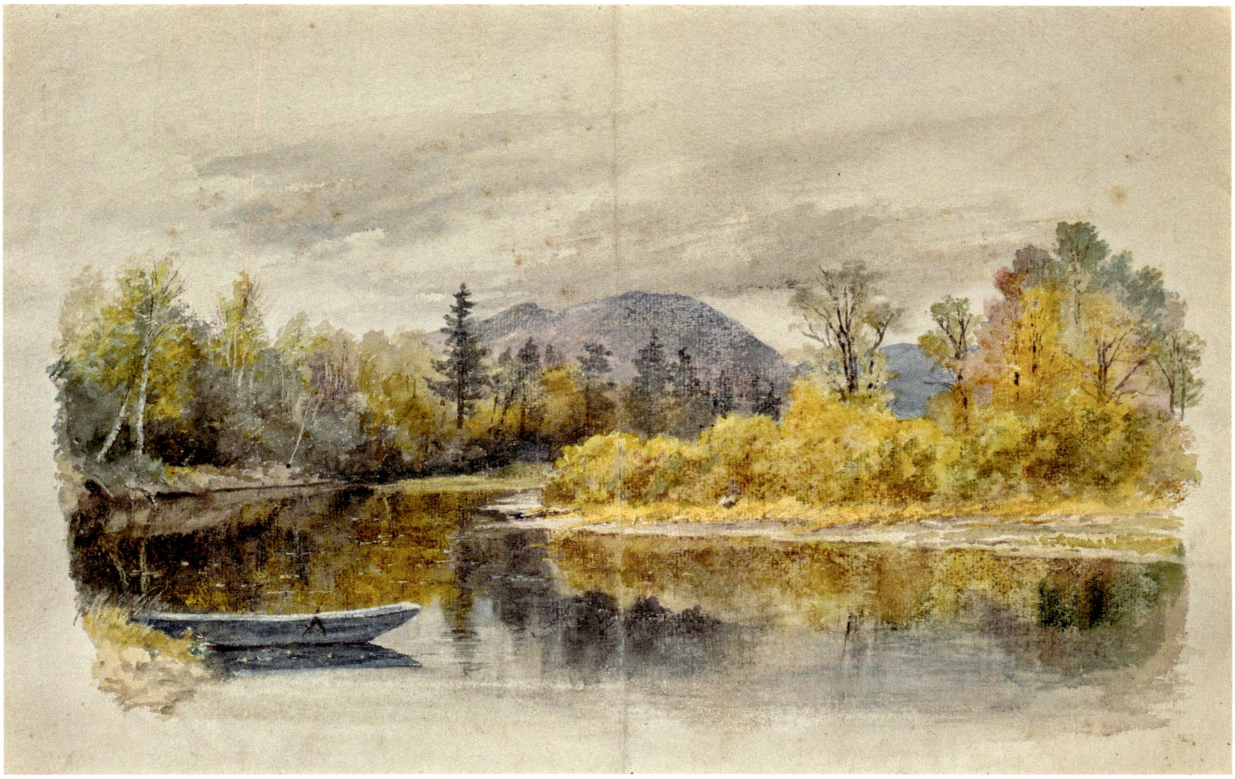

Fig. 8 Susie M. Barstow, *White Mountains with Canoe*, ca. 1880, watercolor on paper, 12 ⅛ × 19 ⅝ in., Private Collection, Photograph: Dennis DeHart

Susanna (Susie) Moore Barstow (1836–1923) was raised in the upper-middle-class family of a well-respected tea merchant. She maintained a studio in Brooklyn (fig. 6) that was certainly well known to many and described by one art critic, in unintentionally pejorative language, as Miss Barstow's "dainty little studio."[3] Barstow frequented the Catskills (fig. 7), the Adirondacks, the White Mountains (fig. 8), and the lakes and mountains of Maine for inspiration (fig. 9) often in the company of her partner, Florence Nightingale Thallon (fig. 10), a fellow artist with whom she often lived and traveled for nearly two decades. Barstow made multiple trips abroad to study art in Germany, Switzerland (fig. 11), and Italy, as well as a trip around the world in 1901 to Japan, China, India, and Egypt with Thallon. Susie was also an inveterate hiker. The 1889 issue of the *White Mountain Echo* noted that Barstow had climbed up to 110 peaks, including "all the principal peaks of the Catskills, Adirondacks, and White Mountains, as well as those of the Alps, Tyrol, and Black Forest, often tramping twenty-five miles a day, and sketching as well, often in the midst of a blinding snowstorm."[4] *The Brooklyn Daily Eagle* repeatedly characterized Barstow as "one of the best-known Brooklyn artists," and when she died, she was described in her obituary as a "prominent landscape artist, whose paintings won her wide renown" and as a "woman of keen intellectual attainments."[5]

Well read, well educated, and well traveled, Barstow was a notable figure in the field of American landscape painting. A darling of the New York press, she was interviewed often. Her ideas about the

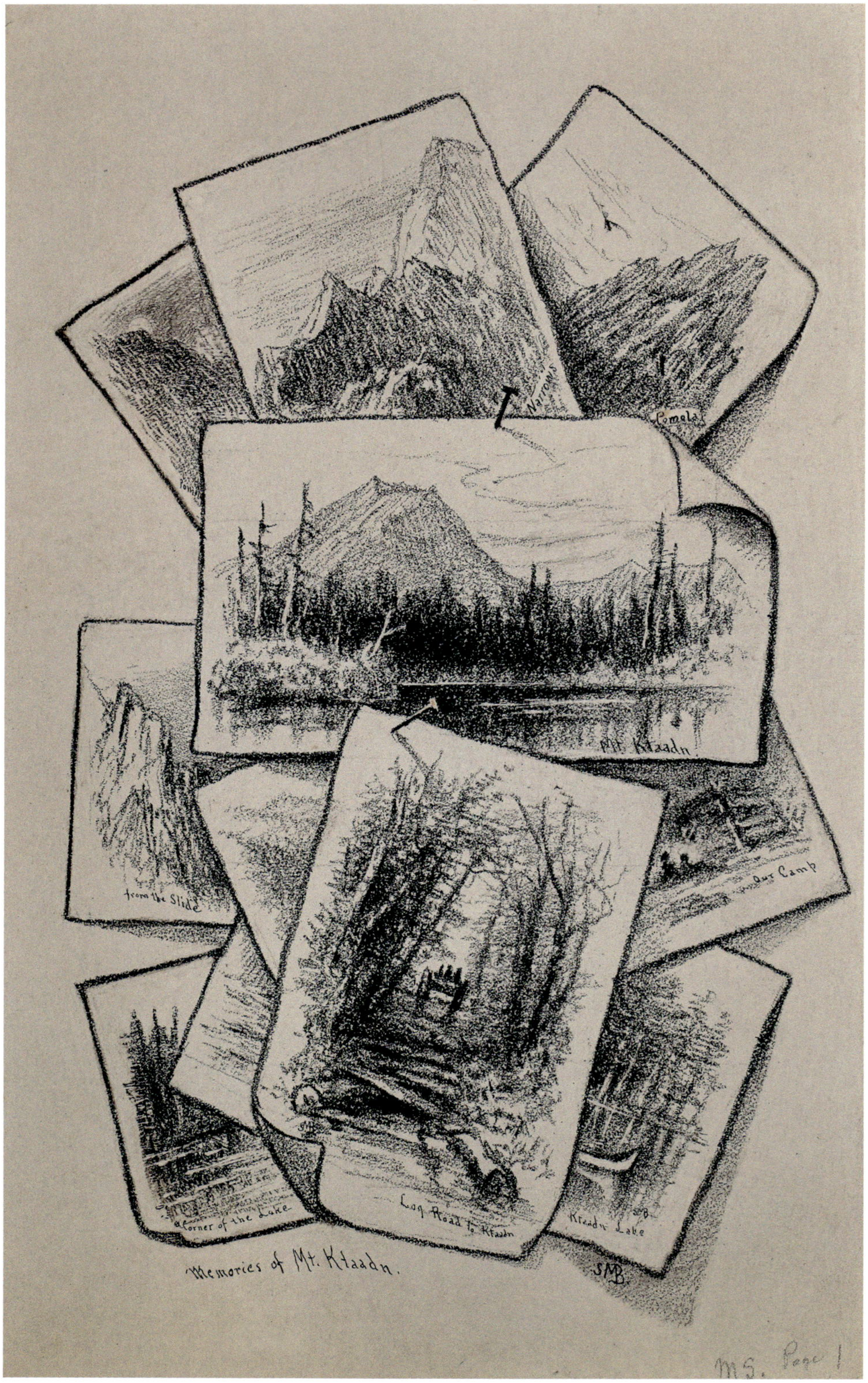

Fig. 9 Susie M. Barstow, *Memories of Mt. Ktaadn* [sic], ca. 1892, pencil on paper, 9 ⅞ × 5 ⅞ in., Private Collection, Photograph: Dennis DeHart

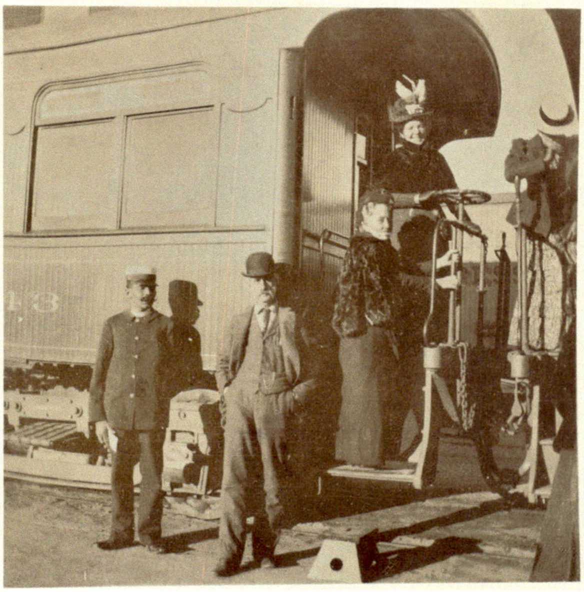

Fig. 10 Unidentified Photographer, Susie M. Barstow and Florence N. Thallon on a train in San Diego, October, 1899, $3\frac{3}{8} \times 3\frac{3}{8}$ in., Private Collection, Photograph: Dennis DeHart

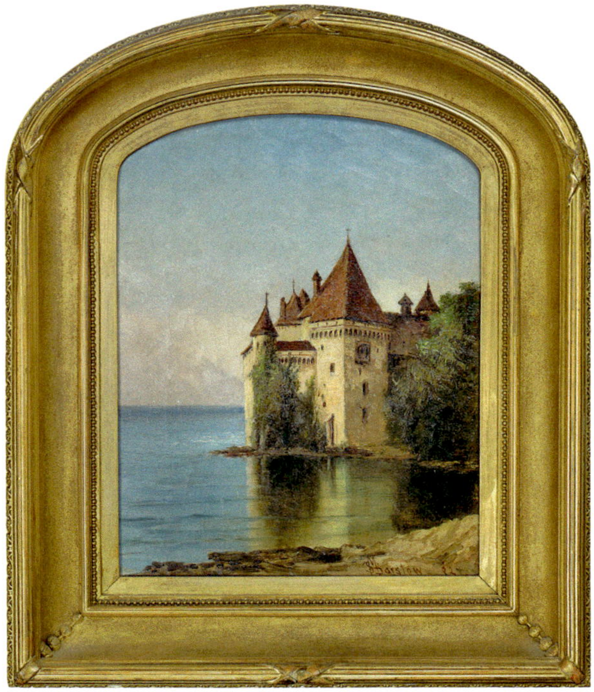

Fig. 11 Susie M. Barstow, *Chillon Castle, Lake Geneva*, 1881, oil on canvas, 20×18 in., Barstow Family Trust Collection, Photograph: Chrome Digital

value of experiencing nature directly were often published, and she lectured widely on the topic. In a lecture on the American landscape, Susie recalled details from a visit to the Catskill Mountains:

> When I was a child I visited the Catskill Mts. As we saw them from the river on a hazy summer afternoon they lay like a delicate cloud – so delicate and dreamlike that it seemed as if a breath would blow them away. I hardly dared to look away from them fearing they might vanish. As we approached, their forms became more distinct but always vapory and unreal, seeming to belong to another world than the river and its wooded shores and villages. Then we landed at Catskill and began to drive toward the mountain. Absorbed by the beauty of the wayside flowers, of field, brook, of forests with their wealth of ferns, the Mts. now hidden seemed still as far away – until the road became so steep that, to my delight, we were allowed to walk, and ther[e] I first realized that we were on the Mt. and the vapory mists of dreamland had become enormous crags.[6]

Building upon her outdoor experiences, Barstow taught and traveled with female students to give them instruction *en plein air* in the northeastern landscape (fig. 12) and advocated for progressive ideas such as women's suffrage and access to study the nude male model as part of women's late nineteenth-century academic training. Barstow was on the earliest committees for the establishment of the Brooklyn Museum of Art and was a well-respected member of the faculty at the Brooklyn Institute. She donated work to support

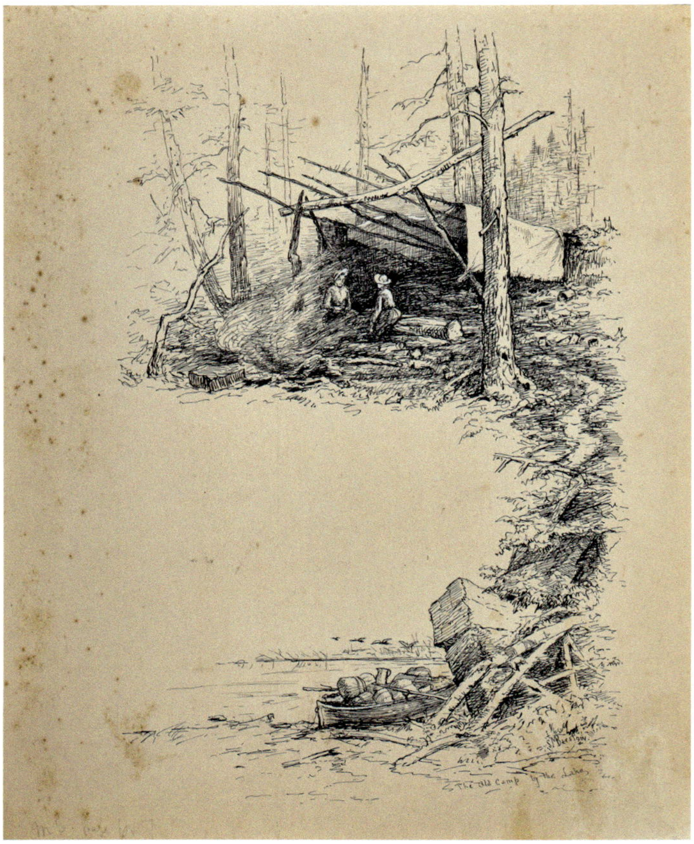

Fig. 12 Susie M. Barstow, *The Old Camp by the Lakes,* ca. 1870, pen and ink on board, 12⅛ × 10⅛ in., Private Collection, Photograph: Dennis DeHart

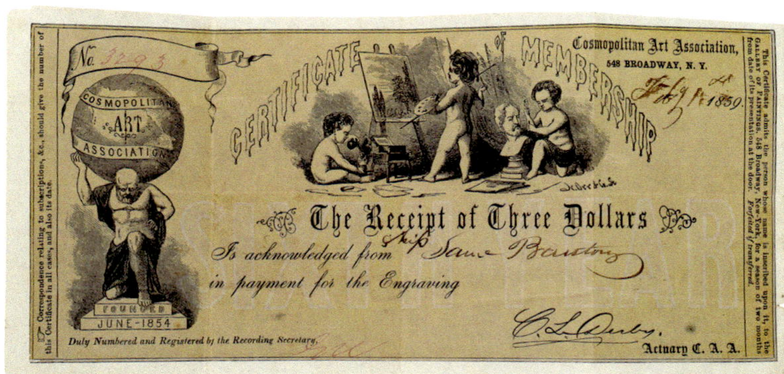

Fig. 14 Susie M. Barstow's Certificate of Membership in the Cosmopolitan Art Association, 1859, 4 × 8⅝ in., Private Collection, Photograph: Dennis DeHart

the efforts of the Sanitary Commission during the Civil War and again to the American Red Cross during the First World War. As a professional artist, she exhibited at major venues alongside male colleagues and realized comparable prices for her paintings. Furthermore, she commanded the physical landscape of the Hudson Valley, the White Mountains, the rigorous terrain of Yosemite, the Alps—actually, any mountain range she encountered that offered stunning vistas and marvelous views—all the while altering her long skirts and hiking garb so as not to be encumbered on these rugged explorations. Susie Barstow was undaunted (fig 13).

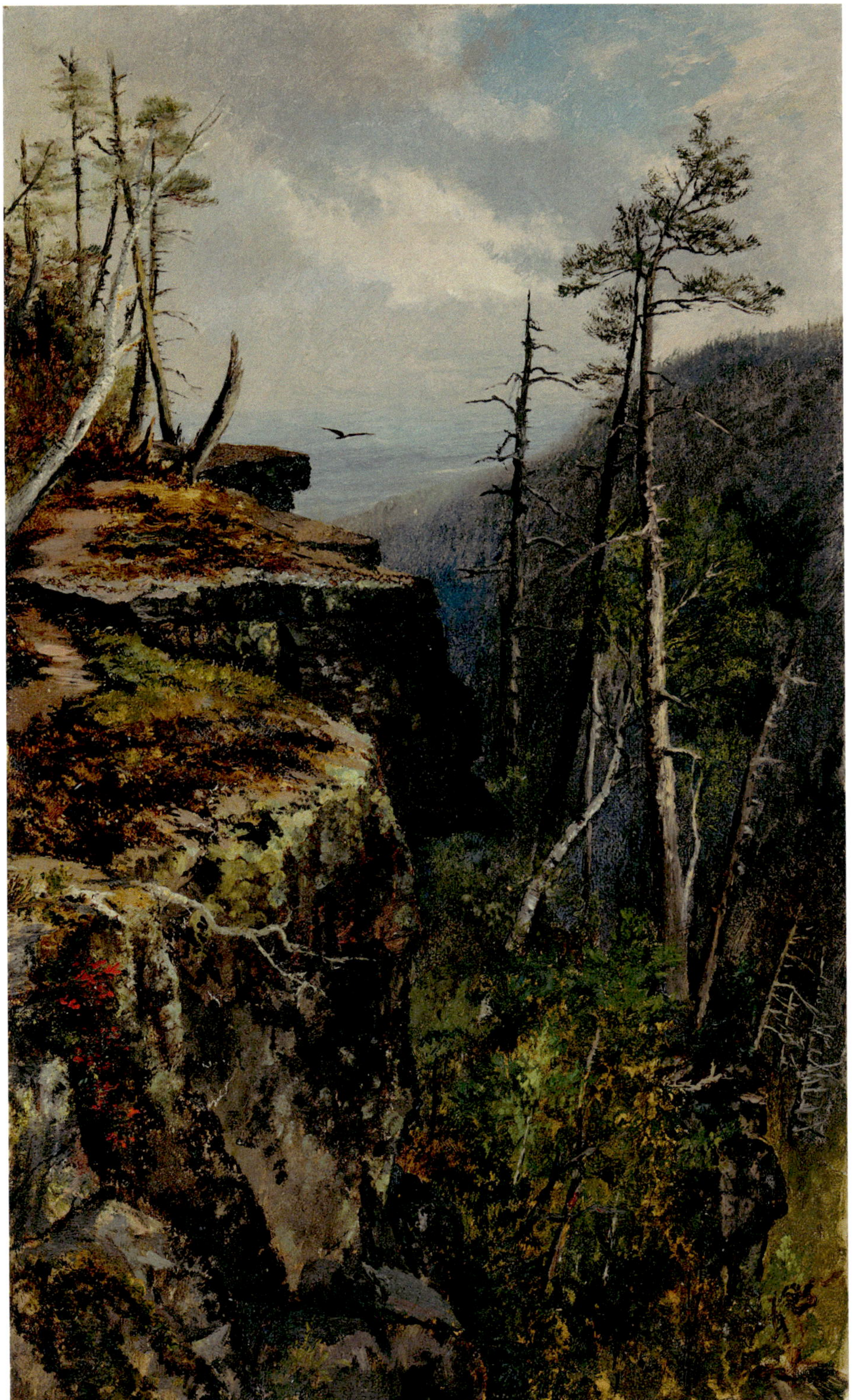

Fig. 13 Susie M. Barstow, *Untitled*, ca. 1880, oil on canvas removed from stretcher, 21 × 13 in., Barstow Family Trust Collection, Photograph: Chrome Digital

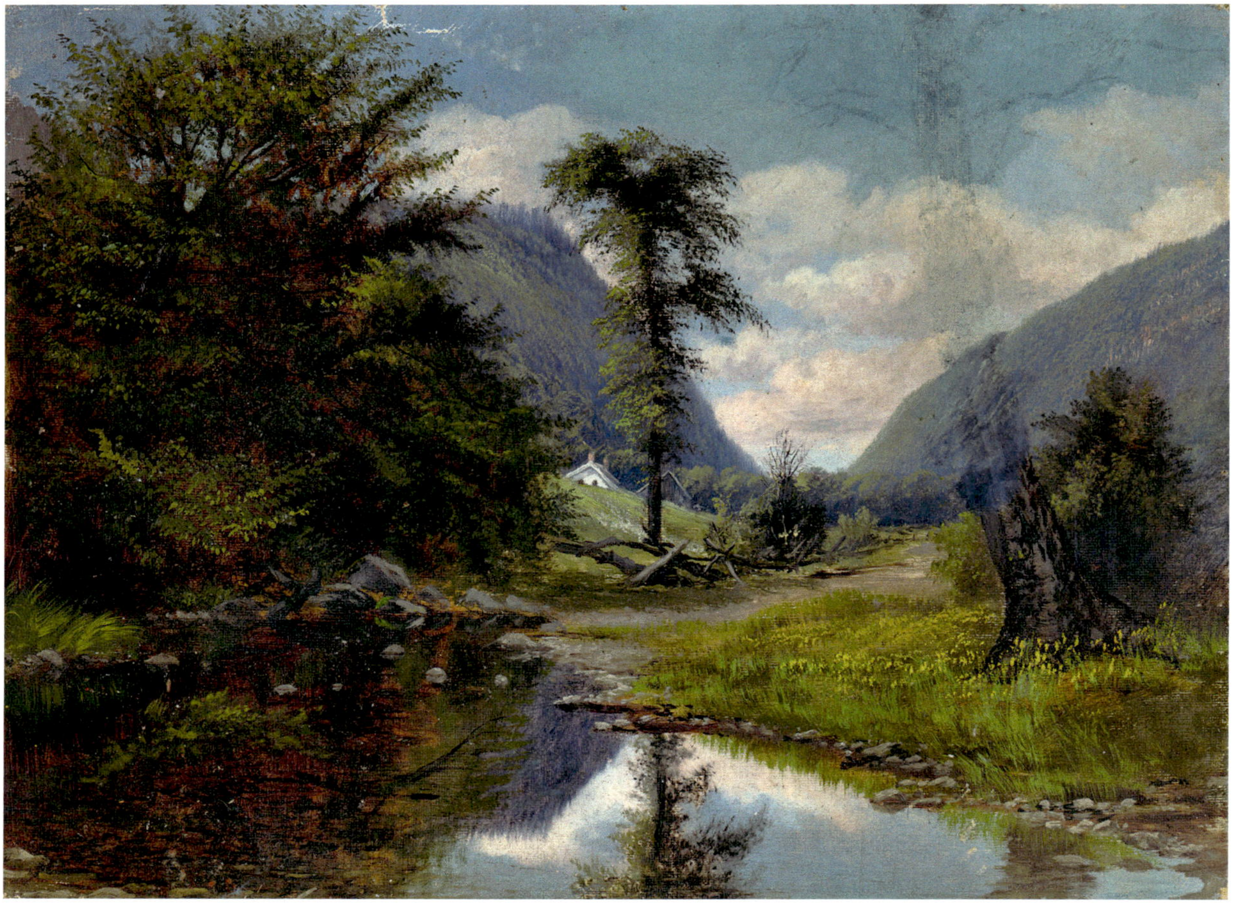

Fig. 15 Susie M. Barstow, *Landscape with Fading Tree*, ca. 1870s, oil on canvas, 10 × 13½ in., Barstow Family Trust Collection, Photograph: Chrome Digital

After attending the Rutgers Female Institute (1853) and the Cooper Union (1861), Barstow began exhibiting her work in her twenties and joined the important art organizations of her day, such as the Cosmopolitan Art Association (fig. 14). The early style of her painting can be characterized as that of the Hudson River School—romanticized, site-specific compositions with secluded depictions of nature's beauty (fig. 15). Barstow's paintings, however, are not the grandiose panoramic visions of Thomas Cole, Frederic Church, and Albert Bierstadt which reflected the art market of the 1830s to the 1860s. Theirs was a time of great exploration and nationalism, marked by a quest to situate the deity well within the American landscape—a time when wealthy men were compelled to purchase the largest canvases possible in an attempt to rival the European tradition of art and patronage. Barstow and fellow artists including Jervis McEntee, James Hart, and John William Casilear for example, were part of the second wave of the Hudson River School—an era after the Civil War in which reconstruction and economic growth fueled the art market, spurring increased demand for smaller, intimate scenes of the American landscape (figs. 16, 17). Artists such as Barstow responded enthusiastically to this call for parlor-sized compositions from a new and vibrant middle

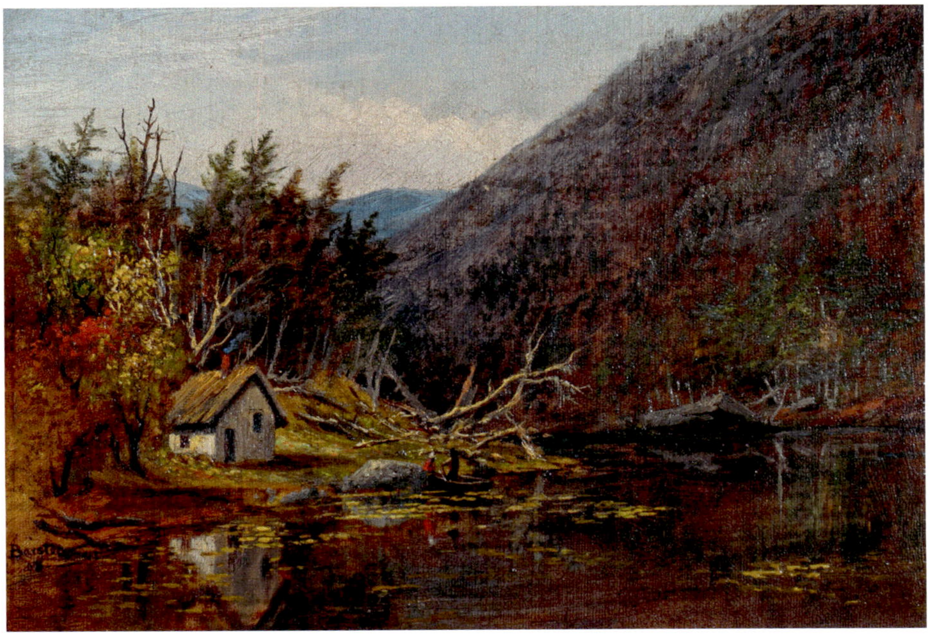

Fig. 17 Susie M. Barstow, *Untitled*, 1868, oil on canvas, 6 ¾ × 9 ¾ in., Thomas Cole National Historic Site, Catskill, NY, Gift of Raymond Beecher, TC.2012.2

class of collectors who were eager to adorn their walls with scenes of the Catskills and the Green and White Mountains, with their unspoiled rivers, lakes, streams, and wooded scenery—landscape as it still existed, seemingly untouched by progress or war, reflecting a nostalgic taste for the myth of a more peaceful past.

The prime of Barstow's career occurred between the 1870s and the end of the nineteenth century (fig. 18), artistically a span of time in which scholars have claimed the Hudson River School had fallen out of fashion, with more avant-garde European influences being favored. Barstow, however, understood popular taste, and her painterly style evolved continuously across the nineteenth century. Stylistically, though, landscape painting itself was experiencing a shift. While some were purchasing works in the now conservative mode of the Hudson River School, critics and collectors alike were praising an emerging style in which truth to nature was reconsidered (fig. 19). Channeled through the influence of Barbizon artists such as Jean-Baptiste-Camille Corot and

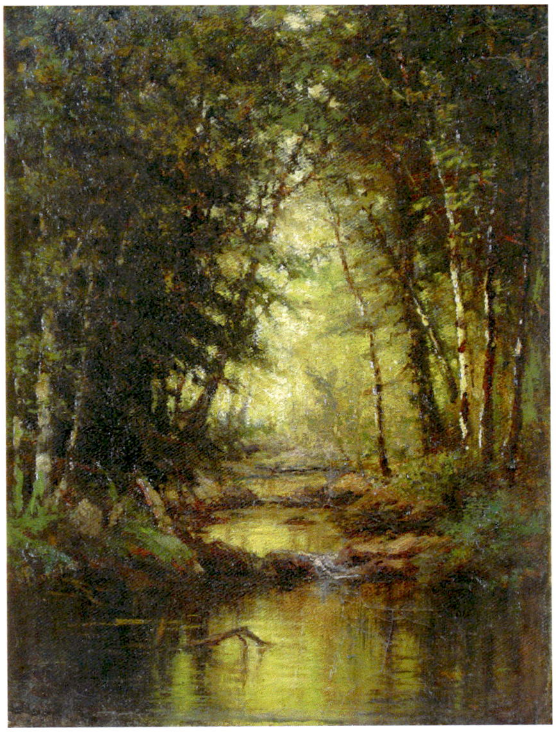

Fig. 16 Susie M. Barstow, *Sunshine in the Woods*, 1886, oil on canvas, 9 ½ × 7 ½ in., Paul Stuka Collection, Photograph: Hawthorne Fine Art, New York, NY

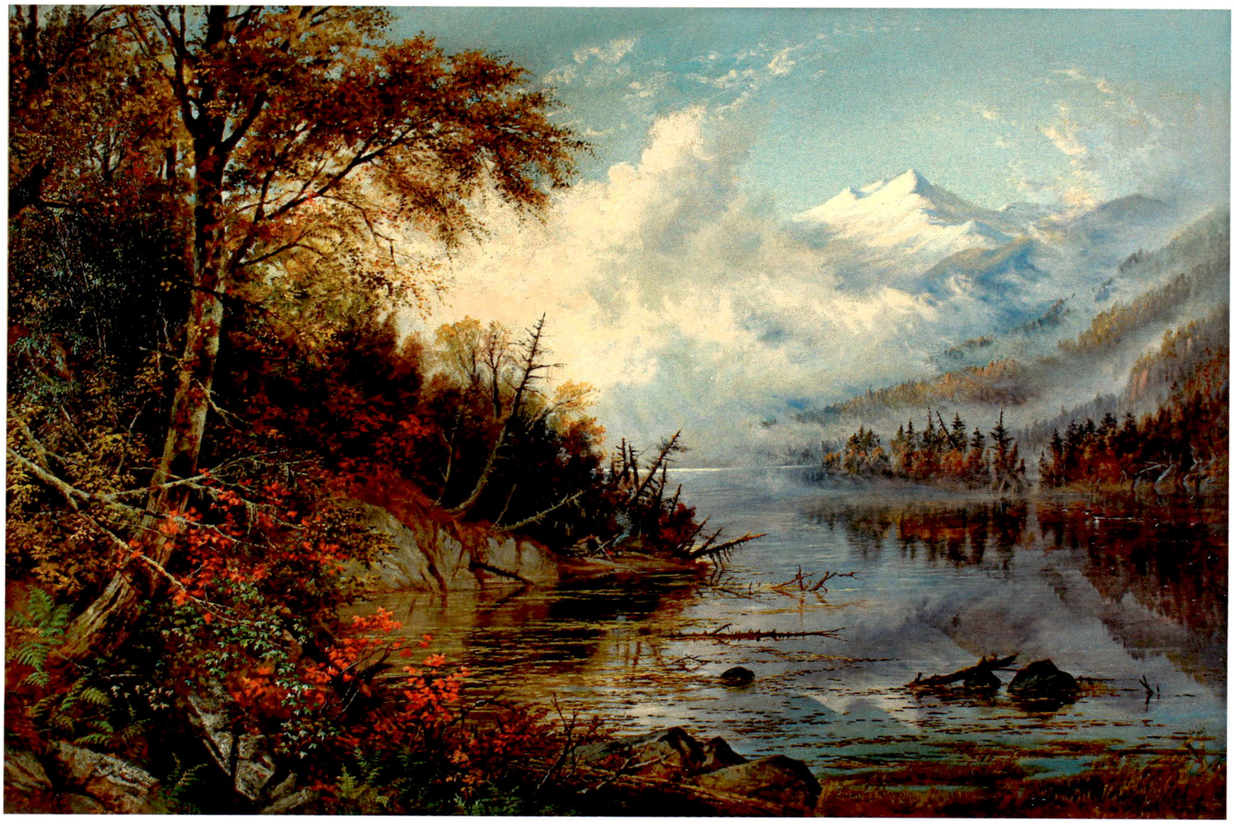

Fig. 18 Susie M. Barstow, *Mountain Lake in Autumn*, 1873, oil on canvas, 20 × 30 in., Private Collection, Photograph: Hawthorne Fine Art, New York, NY

Charles-François Daubigny, direct observation was complemented with sentiment, softer lines, and more diffuse forms. Exploring changes in atmospheric conditions, these French artists produced immersive landscapes, moody and romantic compositions that capitalized on a spiritual communing with nature (fig. 20). Barstow was enormously influenced by their work and by the paintings of Corot in particular. She kept newspaper clippings explaining his studio methods in her paint box, which was filled with supplies that included camel-hair brushes, porcelain palettes, watercolors, and heavily leaded white flake pigment (fig. 21).

Barstow witnessed the rise and decline of the American Art-Union and the financial distress of the National Academy of Design in the mid-1870s. She viewed the transcendent works of Martin Johnson Heade and Fitz Henry Lane and the veiled feminism of Lilly Martin Spencer. Post-Civil War, Susie would come to understand the tenets of Manifest Destiny and exhibited her work alongside western landscape scenes by Albert Bierstadt; she herself traveled to Yosemite (fig. 22) at the turn of the twentieth century. Born during the infancy of photography, Barstow saw its many technological advances that gave rise to a redefinition of realism—optical, social, and emotional. The photographic exposés of Jacob Riis, for example, were in line with her own commitment to social justice and charitable causes. Barstow's exhibition history took place on both sides of the

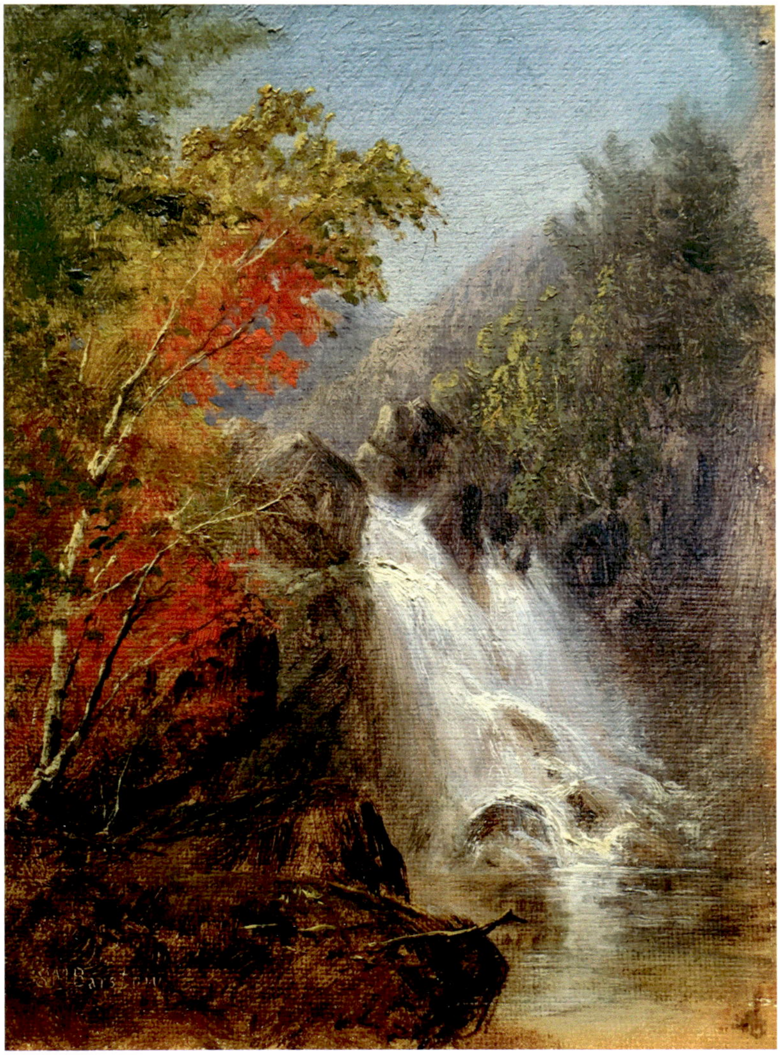

Fig. 19 Susie M. Barstow, *Autumn Waterfall*, ca. 1880, oil on canvas, 6 ⅛ × 5 in., Private Collection, Photograph: Hawthorne Fine Art, New York, NY

East River just as John A. Roebling was spanning the divide between Brooklyn and Manhattan with his Brooklyn Bridge (1869–83), making for easier travel between the two boroughs. Susie experienced the Age of the Skyscraper—an American architectural invention that rivaled the height of mountaintops, forever changing the skyline of urban landscapes. She knew the paintings of Thomas Eakins, Winslow Homer, George Inness, and John Singer Sargent—exhibiting with many of them—and attended lectures by William Merritt Chase, who clearly influenced her ever-evolving style. She was sketching in Germany as the Munich School replaced that of Düsseldorf. She understood the works of the French Impressionists and their influence on the American Impressionist movement, lecturing on the topic to members of the Brooklyn Art Club. She knew the early modernism of Robert

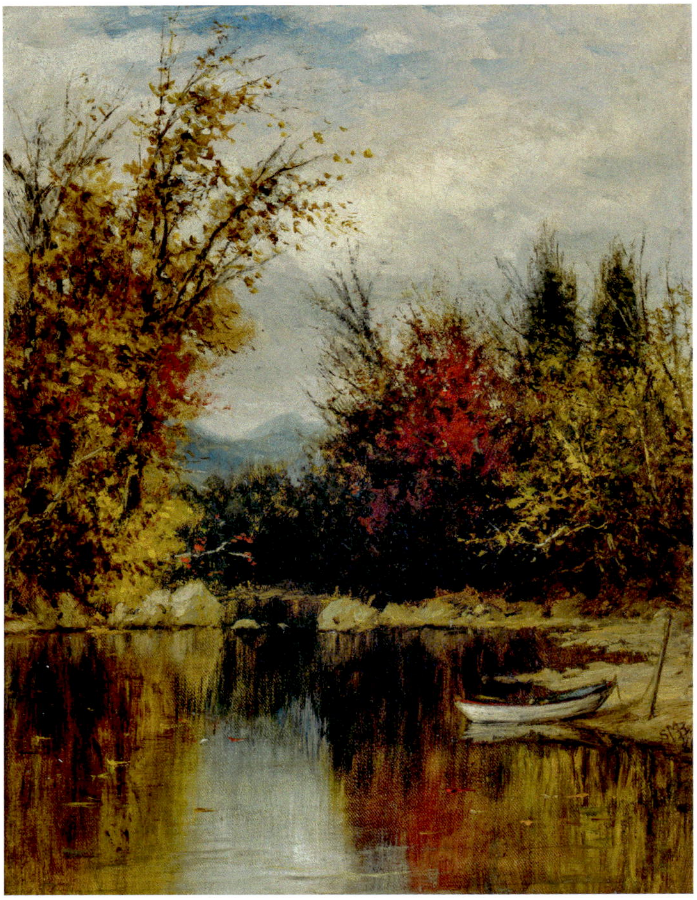

Fig. 20 Susie M. Barstow, *Early October near Lake Squam*, 1886, oil on canvas on board, 14½ × 12 in., Suzanne H. Arnold Gallery, Lebanon Valley College Fine Art Collection, Lebanon, PA, Gift of Hilary Peery Vesell, 2020.1.3, Photograph: Andrew Bale

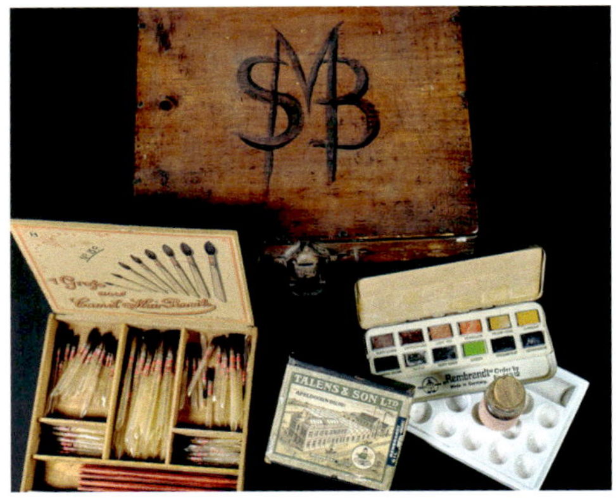

Fig. 21 Susie M. Barstow's paint box, ca. 1860, wood and assorted artist's supplies, 5¼ × 11 × 9¾ in., Private Collection, Photograph: Dennis DeHart

Henri's Ashcan paintings, the Stieglitz circle, Cubism, Futurism, and the revelatory Armory Show of 1913. To put the trajectory of her career into perspective, Barstow was painting the American landscape at the time of Édouard Manet's *Le Déjeuner sur l'herbe* (1863), Claude Monet's *Impression, Sunrise* (1872) and the First Impressionist Exhibition in 1874, James Whistler's *Nocturne in Black and Gold – The Falling Rocket* (ca.1875), Vincent van Gogh's *The Starry Night* (1889), Paul Cezanne's *Mont Sainte-Victoire* (ca. 1902–06), Pablo Picasso's *Les Demoiselles d'Avignon* (1907), Gustav Klimt's *The Kiss* (1908), Henri Matisse's *The Red Room* (1908–09), and Marcel Duchamp's *Nude Descending a Staircase (No.2)* (1912)—all the while continuously and successfully selling her work in the style of an evolving Hudson River School.

Having lived for 87 years, a lifetime spanning two centuries, Susie Barstow witnessed a vast array of political upheaval, scientific advances, cultural events, celebrations, and American progress defined broadly as part of a changing world. As a

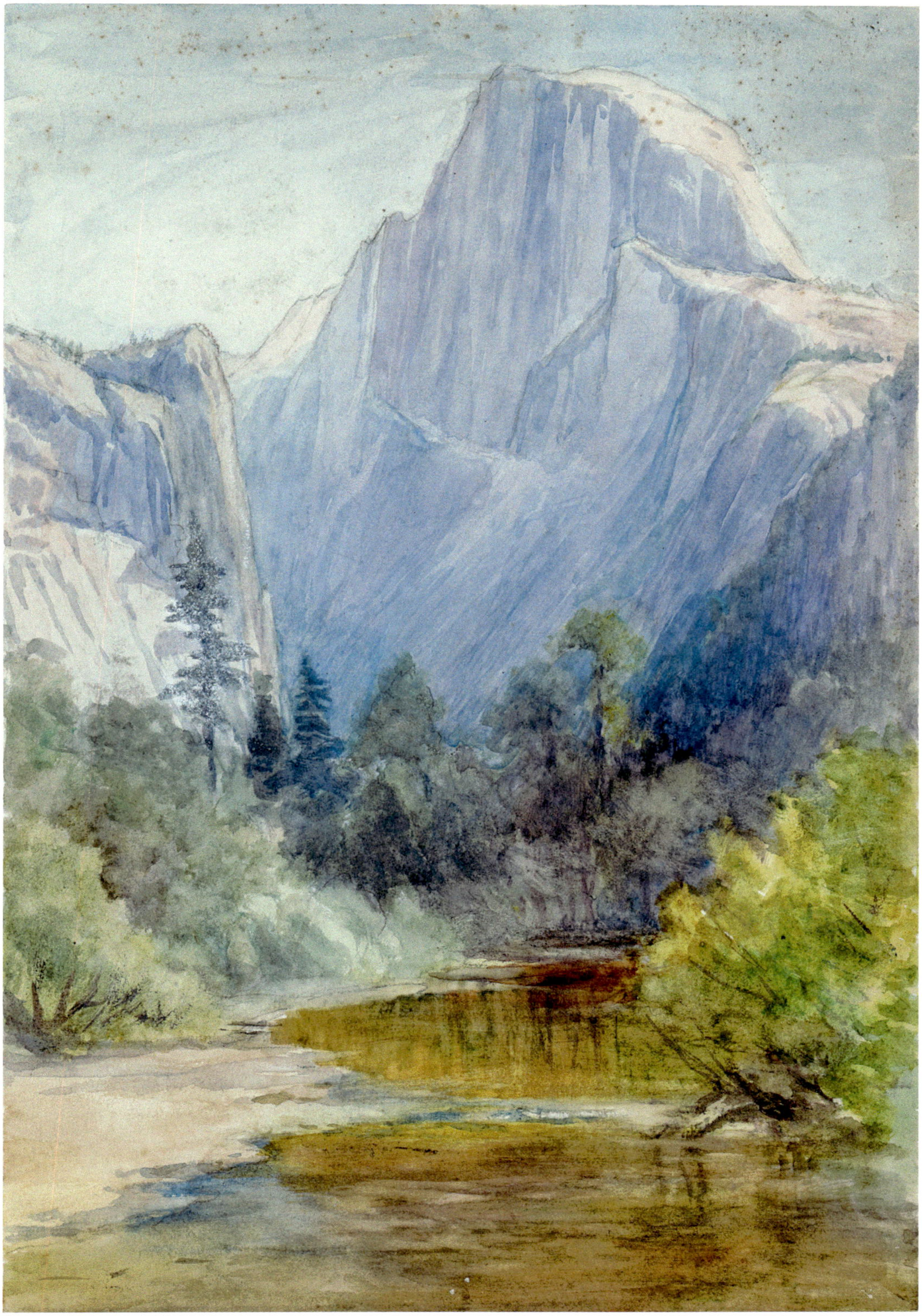

Fig. 22 Susie M. Barstow, *The Floor of Yosemite,* 1899, watercolor on paper, 14 × 10 in., Barstow Family Trust Collection, Photograph: Chrome Digital

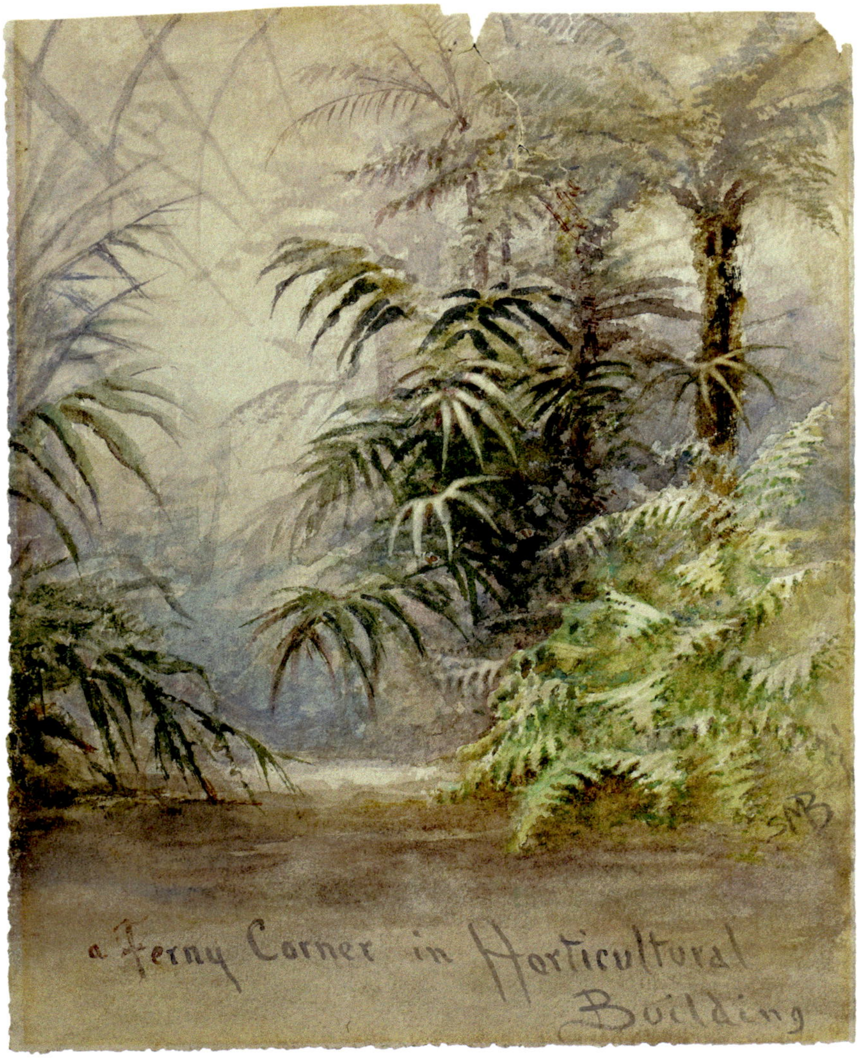

Fig. 23 Susie M. Barstow, *A Ferny Corner in Horticultural Building at the Columbian Exposition,* 1893, watercolor on paper, 10 × 8 ¼ in., Private Collection, Photograph: Dennis DeHart

young woman, she lived through the Civil War (1861–65) and later, the First World War (1914–18). She benefited from the development of pasteurization, the washing machine, and the sewing machine, and watched as New York streets converted from the horse and carriage to trolleys and then to the automobile. She experienced the shift from the telegraph to the telephone and Edison's invention of the phonograph and the electric lightbulb. Barstow attended Chicago's Columbian Exposition in 1893, making watercolor sketches and saving her entrance tickets as souvenirs (figs. 23, 24). She observed the myriad means by which motion and sound advanced in exciting ways: the roller coaster at Coney Island, the Wright Brothers' first flight at Kitty Hawk in North Carolina in 1903, the escalator, and talking motion pictures. The Museum of Natural History (1869), the Metropolitan Museum of Art (1870), the New York Public Library (1895), and the Brooklyn Museum of Art (1897) were all created during Susie's lifetime. And, of great importance, Barstow lived long enough to celebrate the ratification of the 19th Amendment on August 18, 1920, which

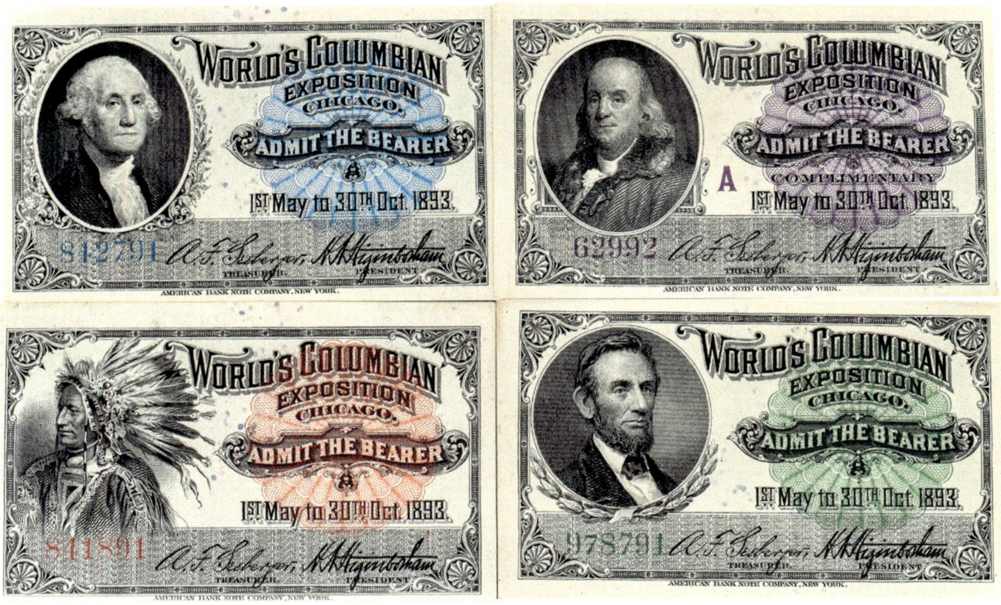

Fig. 24 Susie M. Barstow's tickets to the Columbian Exposition, 1893, 2¼ × 4 in. each, Private Collection, Photograph: Dennis DeHart

gave women the constitutional right to vote. What an incredible time in which to live and paint!

Barstow was ever curious to educate herself in both traditional and avant-garde artistic movements while always adhering to her passion for direct observation in nature (fig. 25). This outlook resulted in works that were praised, exhibited, and purchased throughout her extensive career, demonstrating her ability to commingle conservative and progressive styles popular with the American public. Her formal evolution is reflective of an artist who wished to remain relevant in the art world on both the east and west coasts, and her travels took her across the United States to capture the varied terrain (fig. 26). As an artist of determination and determined independence with a passion for exploration, Barstow often left her traveling companions to hike and sketch on her own. She enjoyed continuous bouts of wanderlust, using her Brooklyn home and studio as a place to unpack, paint, visit with family, entertain patrons in her characteristic witty manner, and then take off for new adventures. Whether traveling alone, with friends, or sometimes with her students to places of immense beauty to study, sketch, and commune, it was not uncommon for Susie to hike 8, 10, or 12 miles, only then to sit down and commence with the task at hand—to capture in detailed studies on paper or canvas the wondrous charm she encountered out of doors, inspired by the natural environment, especially the White Mountains (fig. 27).

So, too, was Barstow guided by her Christian faith. Her love of nature and love of deity fit hand in glove with the romantic sensibilities of landscape theories in the early to mid-nineteenth century. Like many of her female artistic colleagues, she was a supporter of numerous philanthropic causes, as was expected of a well-educated woman in New York. Henry Ward Beecher, the famed preacher, abolitionist, and ally of the women's suffrage movement, was an avid art collector and

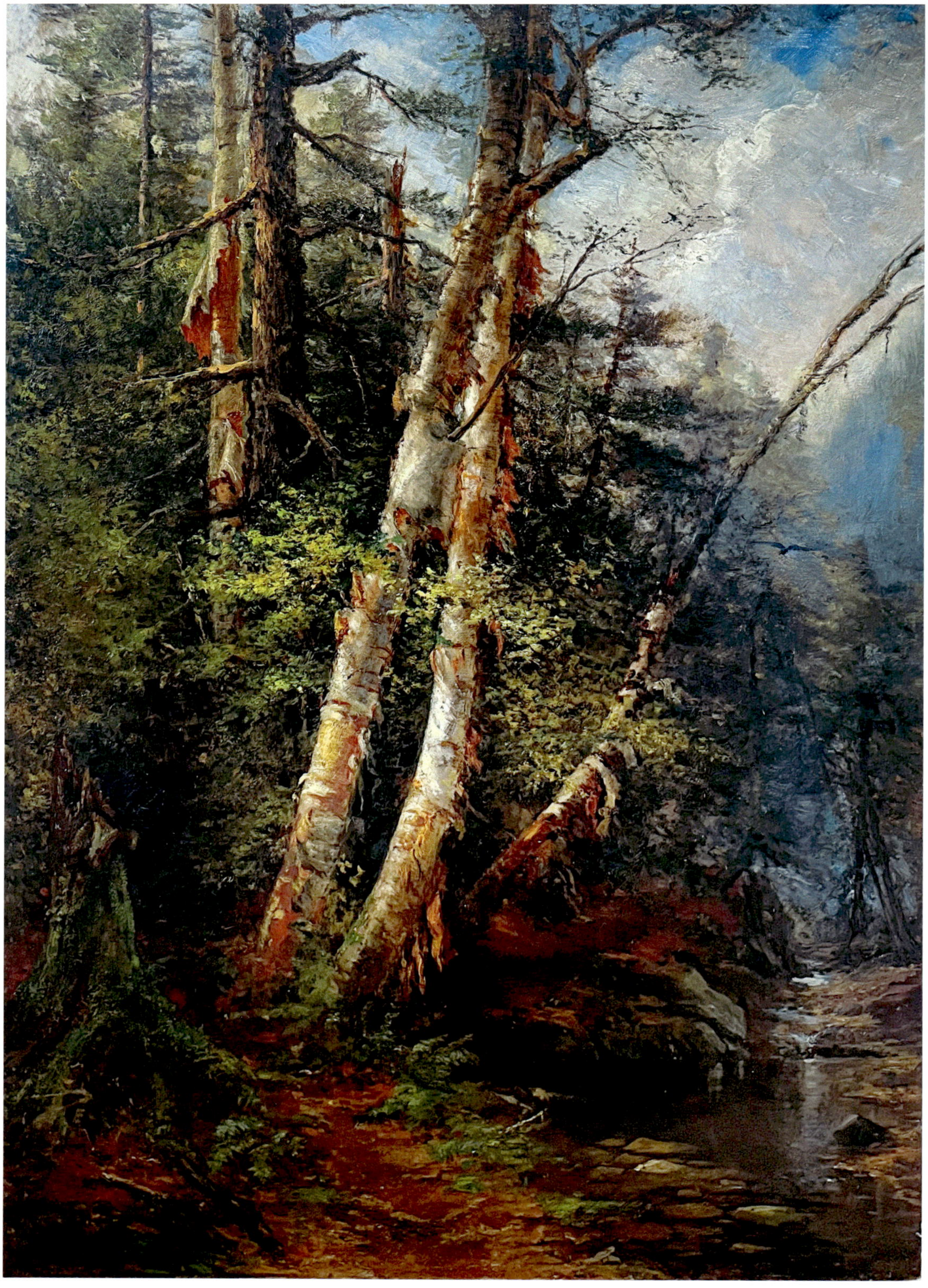

Fig. 25 Susie M. Barstow, *Wooded Interior*, ca. 1865, oil on canvas, 30 × 22 in., Thomas and Marilyn Tolska Collection in Memory of Jenni Tolska, Photograph: Chelsea Restoration Associates, New York, NY

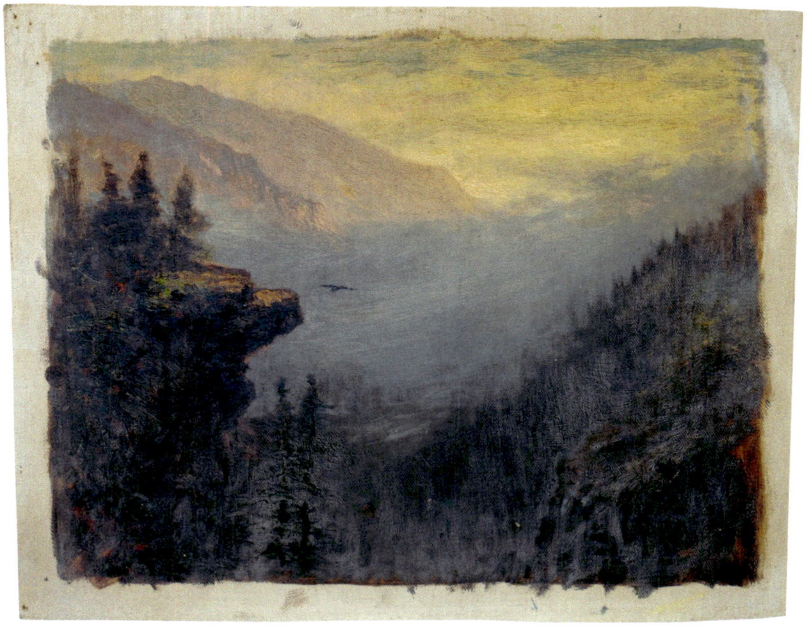

Fig. 26 Susie M. Barstow, *Untitled*, ca. 1870s, unstretched oil on canvas, 10½ × 13½ in., Private Collection, Photograph: Dennis DeHart

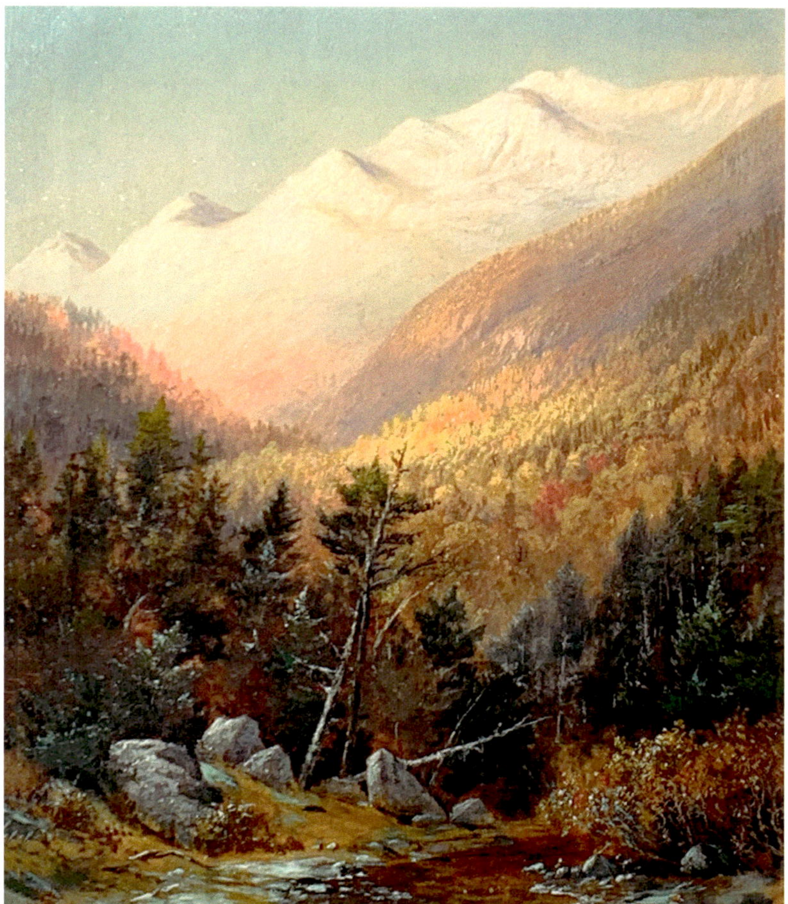

Fig. 27 Susie M. Barstow, *Fall, White Mountains,* ca. 1870s, oil on canvas, 13¼ × 11¼ in., Albany Institute of History & Art, Albany, NY, Photograph: Hawthorne Fine Art, New York, NY

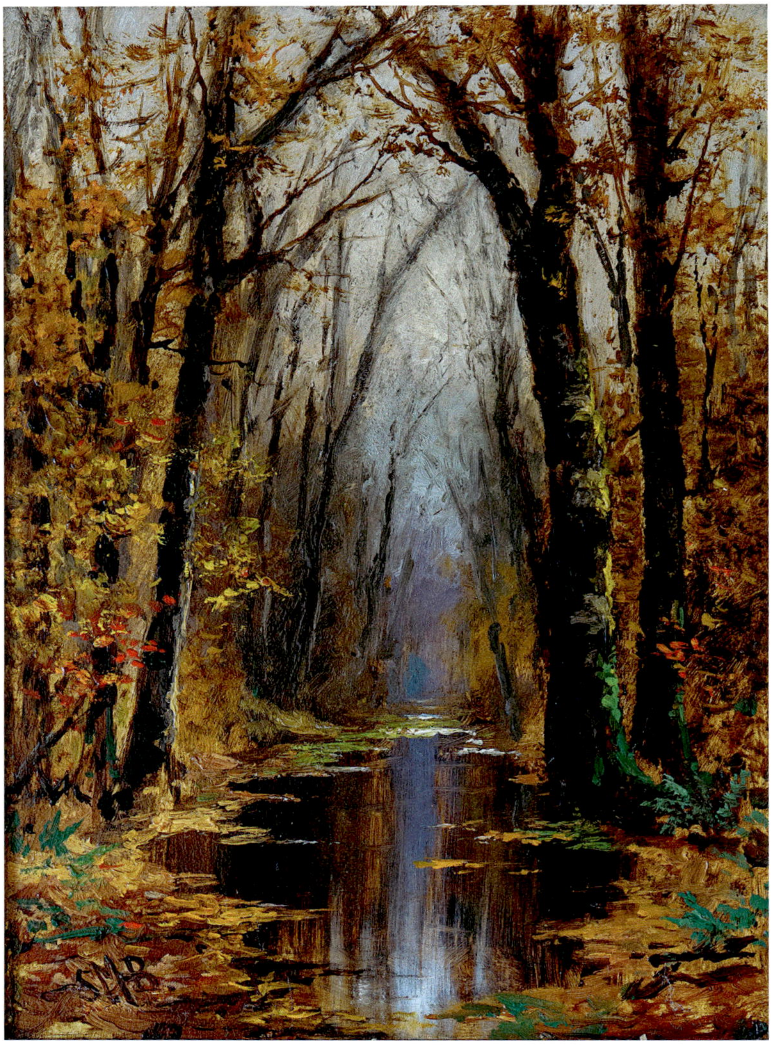

Fig. 28 Susie M. Barstow, *Pool in the Woods*, 1885, oil on canvas, 9½ × 7 in., Harriet Beecher Stowe Center, Hartford, CT, Photograph: John Groo

would come to purchase work by Barstow (fig. 28). With respect to her gender, she defied numerous social, educational, and professional expectations. But irrespective of her gender, Susie M. Barstow was a markedly successful artist whose acclaim and talent did not go unnoticed. In her day, she was recognized continuously in the press as an important artist, exhibiting with Asher Brown Durand, John Frederick Kensett, Sanford Gifford, Jervis McEntee, and Thomas Moran. Barstow's early works suggest the influence of "first-generation" artists such as Thomas Cole and Durand, while her mid-career style sparks comparisons to McEntee, with whom she hiked along the Hudson. Her studies of waterfalls and mountain views are breathtaking for their atmospheric accuracy, reflective of her interest in John Ruskin's philosophy regarding the truthful depiction of nature (fig. 29). Likewise, her later mature style reflects her knowledge and adaptation of European artists

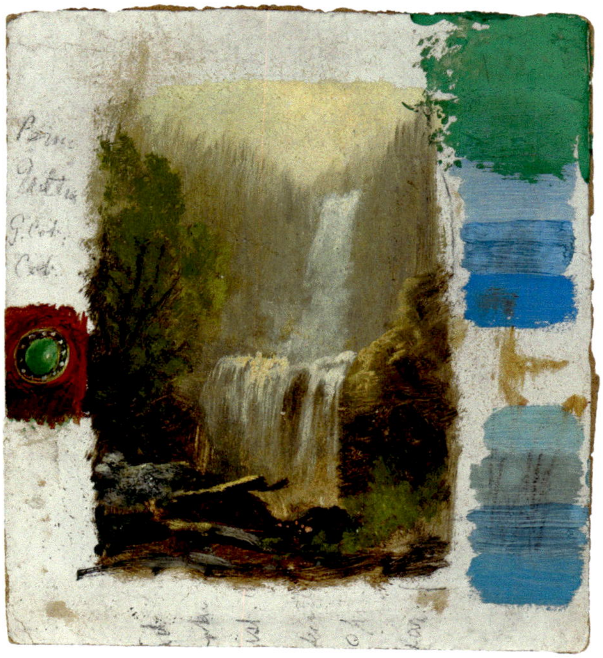

Fig. 29 Susie M. Barstow, *Haines Falls*, ca. 1870s, oil on board, 5 × 5 in., Barstow Family Trust Collection, Photograph: Chrome Digital

of the Hague School, such as Hendrik Willem Mesdag, with whom she studied (fig. 30), and those of the Barbizon School. However, there are problems with this analysis—comparing her work only to those male artists leaves out the stylistic comparisons to artists such as Julie Hart Beers, Fidelia Bridges, Sarah Cole, Charlotte Buell Coman, Edith Wilkinson Cook, Eliza Pratt Greatorex, Mary Nimmo Moran, Mary Josephine Walters, Laura Woodward...the list goes on and on. Beyond their supporting roles as wives, sisters, nieces, and daughters, these were talented and accomplished landscape painters who, until recently, have received little scholarly attention. Given the quality of their work and their reputations as professional artists who produced paintings, watercolors, and etchings of some of the most iconic imagery both at home and abroad, Barstow and these fellow women artists reframe and redefine the Hudson River School with greater inclusivity and broader accuracy.

Even today, the term "Hudson River School" remains problematic. Once described as "America's first true artistic fraternity,"[7] it has historically been associated almost exclusively with predominantly White male artists. Additionally, the term presents geographical limitations as it implies a specific locale. But artists, both male and female, painted truthful if somewhat romantic depictions of the American landscape in the abundant mountain ranges, glens, brooks, and wooded interiors all along the eastern seaboard and beyond. With regard to the historiography of the term, its earliest usage in the 1870s was meant to recognize modern European influences, casting the earlier style of landscape painting in America as out of date. What was considered an "American" school of art came under scrutiny as artists returned from Europe with fresh ideas and new means to express their experience in, and connection to, the landscape. Even the origin story of who first coined the term remains somewhat elusive. Was it the acerbic art critic Clarence Cook? Was it the artist Homer Dodge Martin? Unfamiliar to the likes of Cole, the term "Hudson River School" was used alternately as both a derogatory comparison to European art and a vehicle for praiseworthy nostalgia, replete with nationalistic overtones. Critics such as Cook found American art to be stagnant. He had little praise for women artists, whom he described as having "not as yet accomplished anything considerable in the field of art proper." He wrote of "the newly invented stigma, 'the Hudson River School,'" concluding that "in truth, it was time for the Hudson River School to at least begin to die. It had played its part and played it well."[8] Other critics concurred, finding the Hudson River School "depleted by senility and death."[9]

Certainly, by the late 1870s and 1880s, there were opinions on both sides of the aesthetic argument. While some critics vilified this traditional

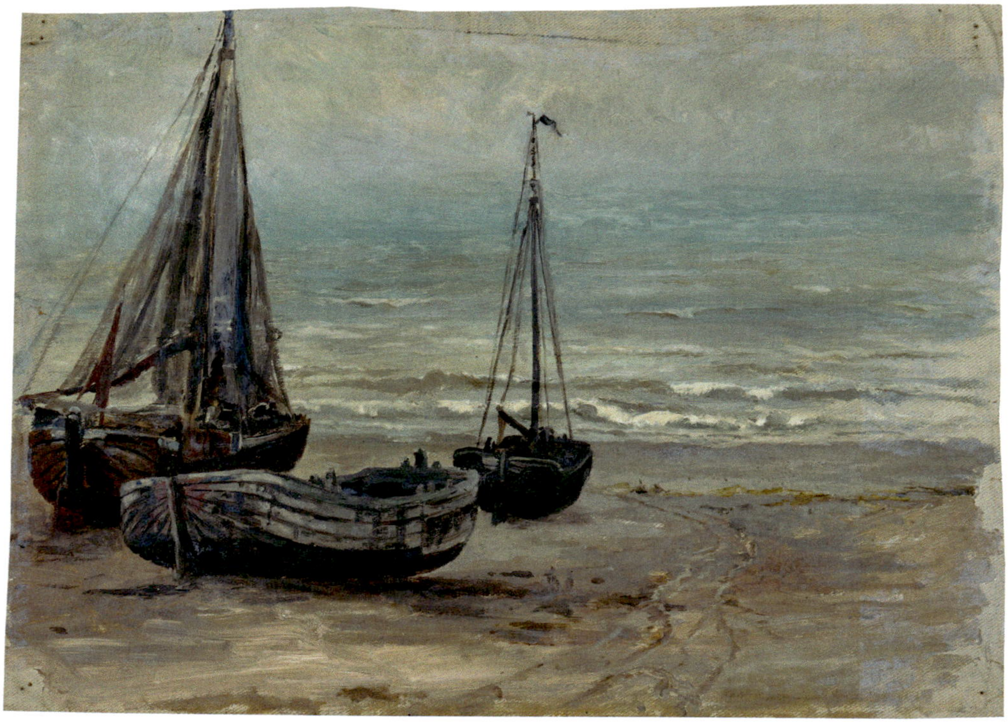

Fig. 30 Susie M. Barstow, *Fishing Boats, Scheveningen*, 1880, oil on canvas, 11 × 15 in., Barstow Family Trust Collection, Photograph: Chrome Digital

school of painting, there coexisted a complimentary cadre of writers who valued the enduring qualities of a style rooted in the identifiable American landscape, offering in its defense that though "the latter term has been applied almost in contempt, it need not be accepted in that spirit. There are no rivers worthier to create a school and few schools that have worked so sincerely,"[10] and "The old men of the Hudson river school, at least, dared to be original."[11] Scholars such as Kevin Avery have adeptly examined this struggle between the older, self-taught painters who dominated the walls and politics of the National Academy of Design and the younger American artists who sought training and influence from emerging European styles.[12] It also bears noting that the early 1870s were a time of great unrest in the conservative Academy. The valuation of American versus European styles was just one of a series of crises, including financial hardships and internal quarrels. Suffice it to say, those three words, Hudson River School, became a convenient and, at times, misogynistic catch-all that, until recently, went unchallenged well into the twentieth and twenty-first centuries.[13]

Regardless of categorization or terminology, Susie Barstow was committed to expressing the majesty she found in nature. In her "dainty little studio," she captured the larger American landscape experience as it evolved across the nineteenth century (fig. 31). While changing aesthetic tastes and cultural constructs were contributing factors to her creative process, the paintings themselves are front and center. This exhibition unpacks the life and art of Susie Barstow and positions her as the "prominent landscape artist, whose paintings won her wide renown," as her obituary would confirm, and explores the manner

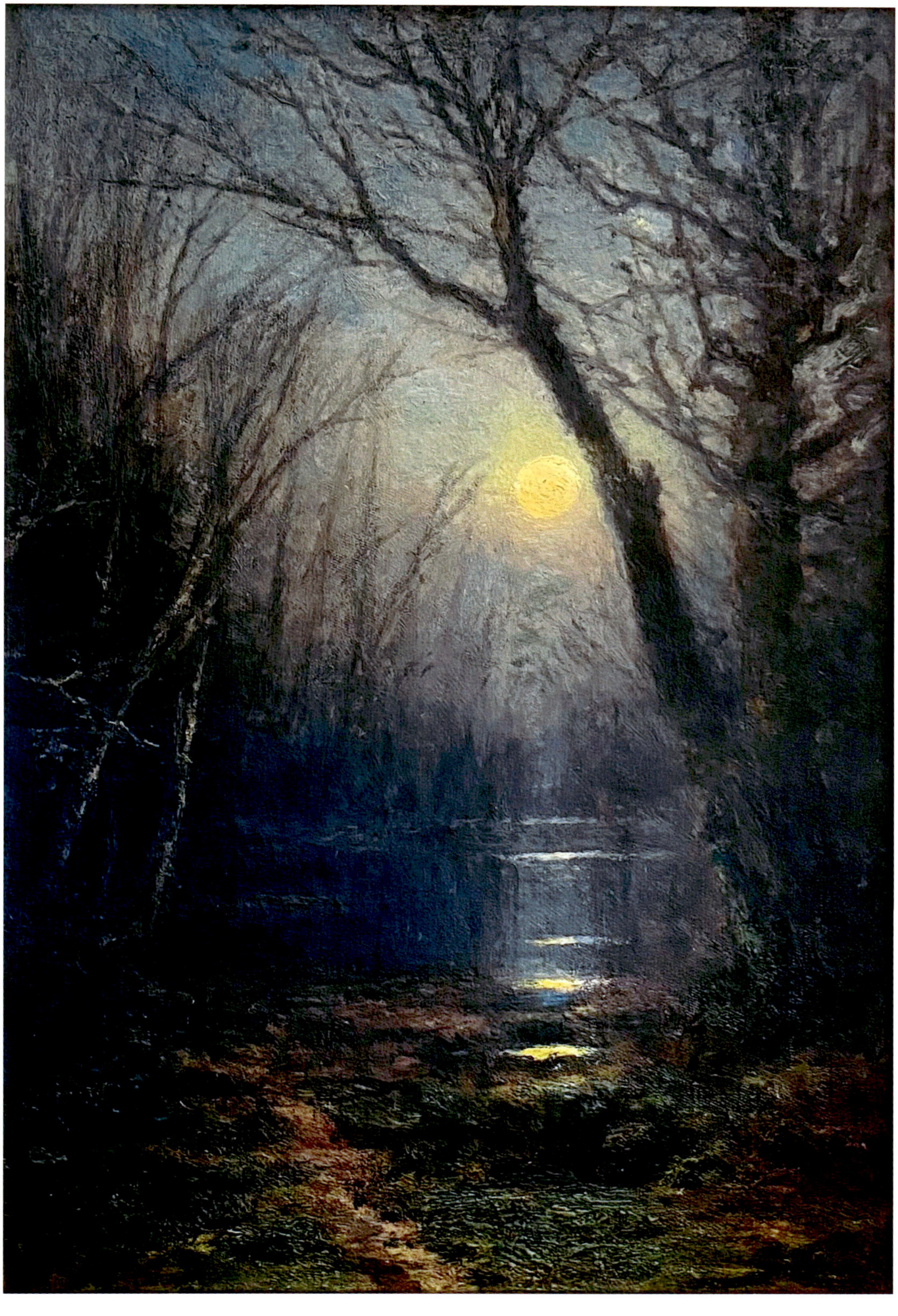

Fig. 31 Susie M. Barstow, *Night in the Woods*, 1890, oil on canvas, 20 × 14 in., Georgia B. Gosnell Collection, Photograph: Hawthorne Fine Art, New York, NY

in which she flourished and ultimately earned her living in the arts.[14] The time is long past due to bring forward this accomplished artist's story to illuminate an expanded history of the Hudson River School. This is her moment.

*A comprehensive biography and extended visual analyses of over one hundred works by the artist can be found in a companion publication, *Susie M. Barstow: Redefining the Hudson River School* (Lund Humphries, 2023).

Susie Barstow's Circle

By all accounts, Susie Barstow's artistic legacy was well established at the time of her death in 1923. Yet, within a mere few decades, her achievements and reputation, along with those of fellow women artists, were written out of history. Despite the abundance of evidence to support the professionalization of artistic training for women, the historical bias against their abilities found its way into scholarship well into the twentieth century. In an unexplainable moment of art-historical amnesia, the works by these artists failed to be included in exhibitions on American landscape and, with very few exceptions, were all but forgotten in catalogues, monographs, and collected essays. In a resurgence of interest at mid-century, after the century-long slumber that followed the Hudson River School's height of popularity, curators and scholars once again began to highlight the artists of the Hudson River School, but one was hard pressed to find any of the women included. The exhibition *Women Artists of America: 1707–1964* (The Newark Museum, 1965) attempted to explain the lack of women landscape painters as unsurprising "since the rigors of painting outdoors and the unseemliness of women engaging in this activity during the Victorian era acted as a deterrent."[15] Its curator, William H. Gerdts, wrote, "here too women painters are conspicuously absent." However, Sarah Cole was included: "the sister of the famous

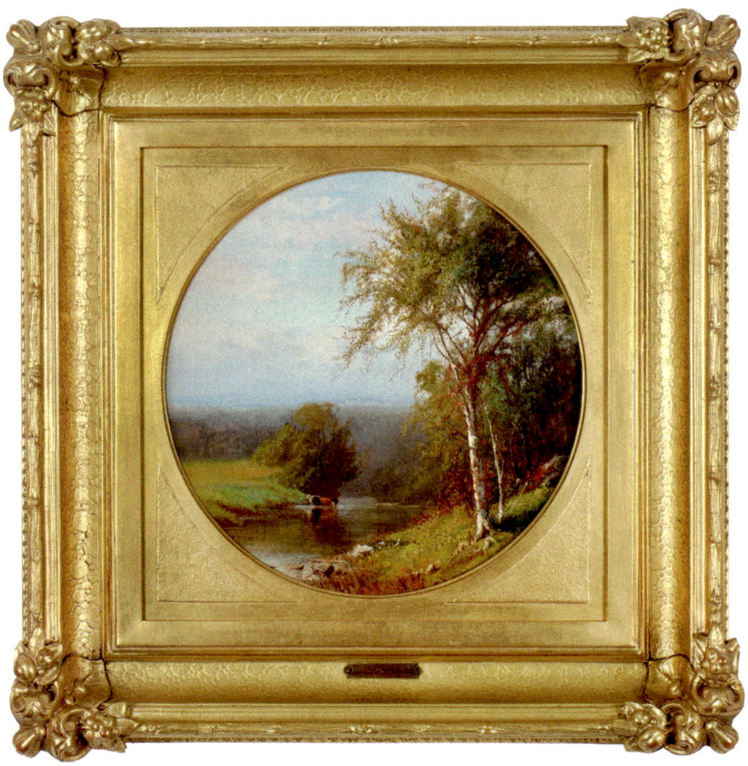

Fig. 32 Julie Hart Beers, *Scenic Landscape of the Catskills,* 1869, oil on canvas, 12⅔ in. diameter, Susan Livingston Collection, Photograph: Hawthorne Fine Art, New York, NY

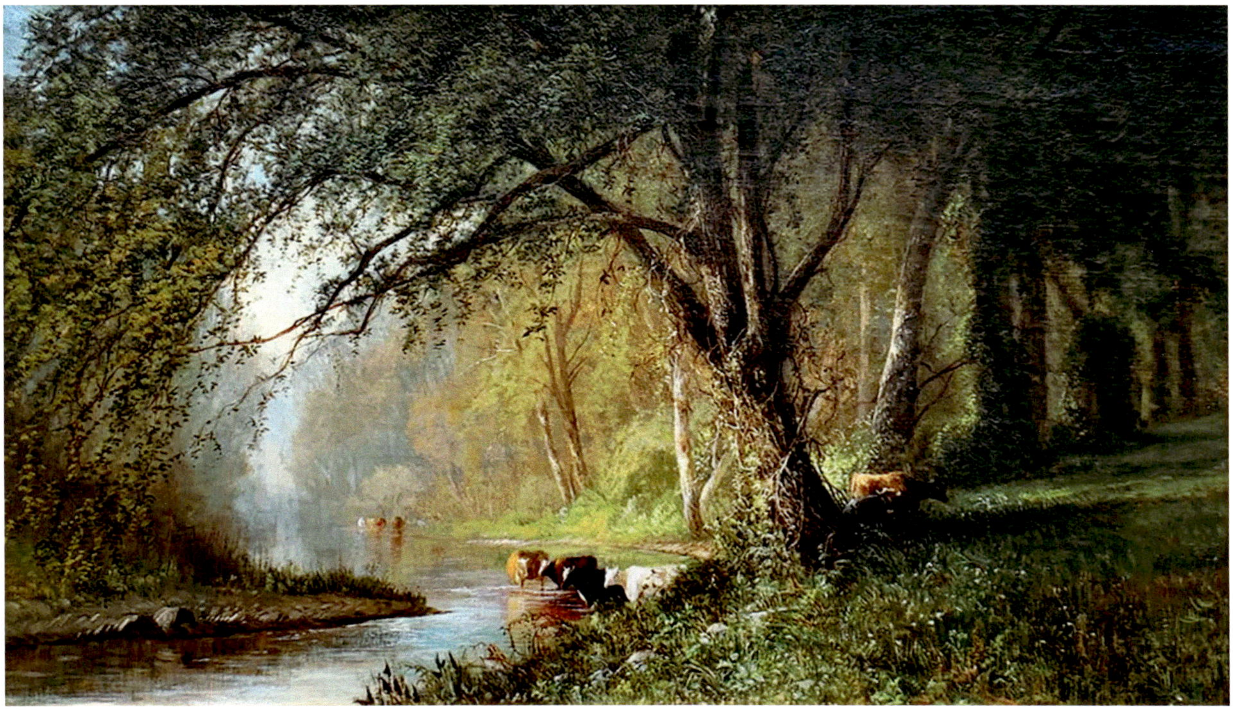

Fig. 33 Julie Hart Beers, *Woodland Stream*, 1877, oil on canvas, 12 × 20 in., Private Collection, CT, Photograph: Hawthorne Fine Art, New York, NY

landscapist, Thomas Cole, was almost the only woman to paint and exhibit landscapes professionally."[16] Although Gerdts' statement is clearly erroneous, how fitting that we include Cole within this revisioning of the Hudson River School: not Thomas, but Sarah (fig. 37). *Susie Barstow & Her Circle* seeks to reestablish a place for those "conspicuously absent" artists in a redefined canon. Indeed, each of the six women highlighted in this exhibition as part of Susie Barstow's circle deserves a retrospective of her own.

Julie Hart Beers (1835–1913) began her artistic career studying with her brothers—James McDougal Hart, who was formally trained in Munich and Düsseldorf, and William Hart, who was self-taught. Julie married in 1853 but was widowed young, at which time she moved with her two daughters into William's home in Brooklyn.[17] Beers shared a large studio with her brother at the Dodworth's Studio Building at 212 Fifth Avenue in Manhattan.[18] Throughout the 1860s to the 1880s, Beers spent a great deal of time hiking and sketching in the Catskill and Adirondack Mountains of New York as well as the White Mountains of New Hampshire. An accomplished painter, she took her students to sketch directly from nature, much as Barstow did. As part of an excursion to the Adirondacks in the summer of 1871, an unidentified artist in the group noted, "Mrs. Julie H. Beers, with six young lady pupils, are yet here, sketching along the Boquet River, which runs through the town...Some of the artists under the direction of Mrs. Beers, are working hard and have made fine progress."[19] Beers exhibited many of the paintings resulting from these trips together with works by Barstow, Fidelia Bridges, Eliza Greatorex, Mary Josephine Walters, and Laura Woodward at

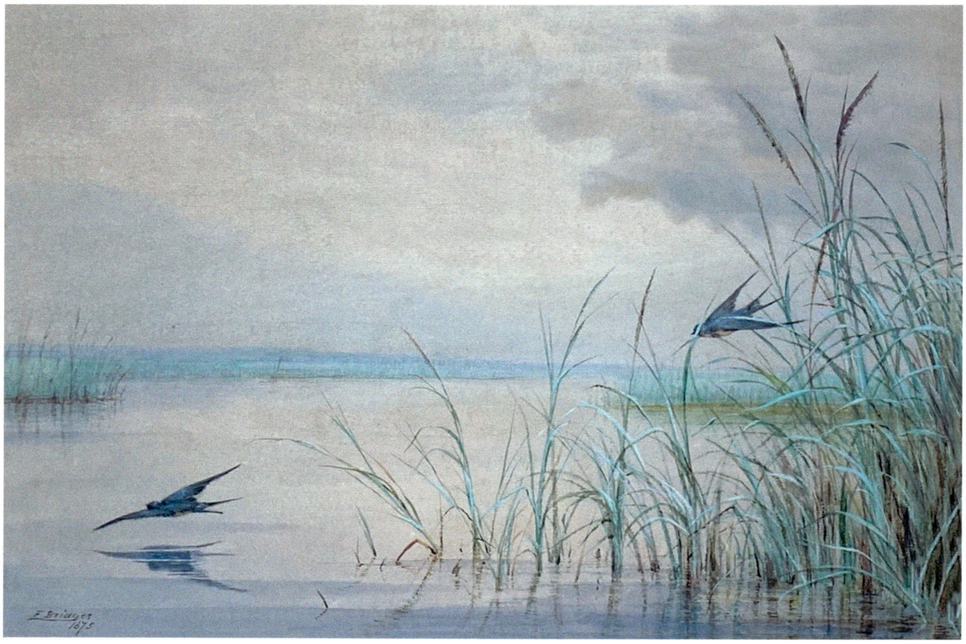

Fig. 34 Fidelia Bridges, *Barn Swallows*, 1875, watercolor on paper, 10 × 15 in., Mr. and Mrs. Max N. Berry Collection, Washington, DC, Photograph: Hawthorne Fine Art, New York, NY

the National Academy of Design, the Boston Athenaeum, and the Brooklyn Art Association. When Julie Beers married her second husband, Dr. Peter Kempson, at her brother James's home in Brooklyn on May 23, 1876, the quiet morning ceremony was attended by few friends, but Laura Woodward was among those supporting the nuptials. The bride, who had been widowed for 20 years, wore a soft, gray dress and was accompanied by her two children plus four of Kempson's children from a previous marriage.[20] She continued to use the Beers surname after her marriage, presumably as she had established a reputation under that name.

Beers painted not only on canvas but also on tin and composition board, including roundels to give the appearance of painted porcelain plates, thus blurring the separation between the fine and decorative arts.[21] *Scenic Landscape of the Catskills* of 1869 (fig. 32) replicates this tondo format but is a traditional oil on canvas. In this view of a bucolic summer's day, anchored on the right by a spreading birch tree and complemented with cattle cooling themselves in the river, Beers' loosening brushstrokes create a scene of languid beauty. Here, the American landscape is on full display. In the manner of fellow artists of this era, the linear crispness of the Hudson River School style blends effortlessly with the more diffuse tonality of Barbizon influences. Similarly, *Woodland Stream* of 1877 (fig. 33) invites the viewer into an intimate, secluded location of peaceful repose. Cattle wander in the meandering stream, which is framed by the bending boughs of trees above. The brushwork is tighter than that of the previous composition, but collectively, Beers' landscapes are breathtakingly beautiful and contemplative.

Fidelia Bridges (1834–1923) was born in Salem, Massachusetts, and orphaned at a young age. Having worked as a governess and teacher in her youth, Bridges turned her attention to the creative process, establishing and maintaining a prolific

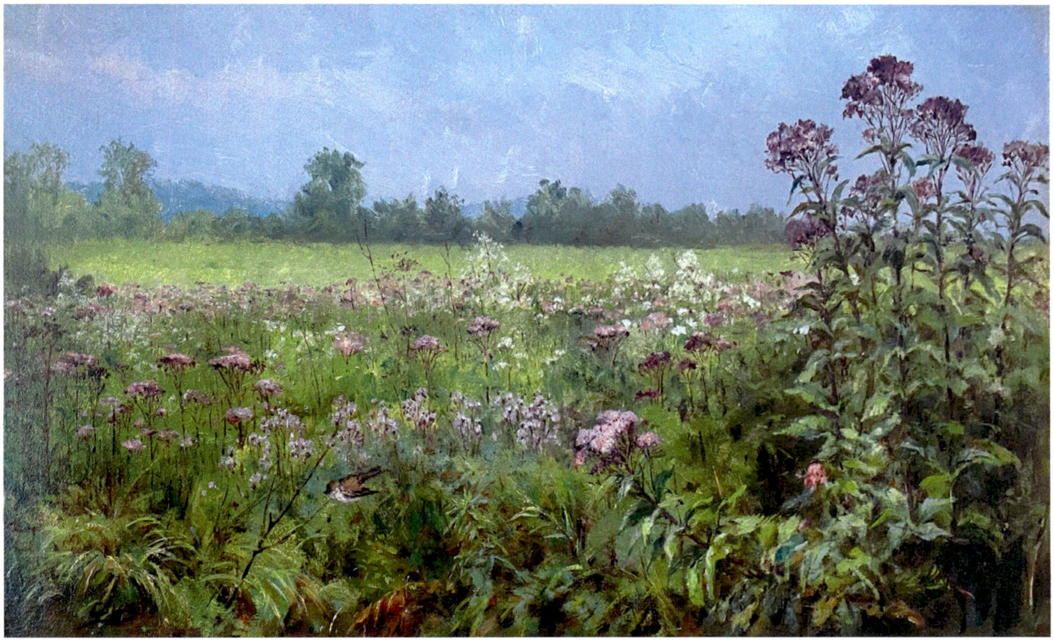

Fig. 35 Fidelia Bridges, *Small Bird with Flowering Ironwood*, ca. 1870, oil on canvas, 10 × 29 in., Midwestern Private Collection

career between the painterly and illustrative arts. Her engagement with the natural world often inspired her to produce watercolors of flowers and songbirds, which served as engravings and chromolithographs for numerous popular publications.[22] Bridges, like Barstow, never married, which afforded her greater freedom to travel within the United States and abroad. She spent extended periods in England, where her work was exhibited to much acclaim, and was lifelong friends with the artist Anne Whitney and her partner Adeline Manning, traveling with them to Rome in the late 1860s. She learned from William Trost Richards, admired the philosophies of John Ruskin, studied at the Pennsylvania Academy of the Fine Arts, and kept studios in Philadelphia and Brooklyn.[23] There, Bridges certainly knew Susie Barstow as Bridges often collaborated with Barstow's niece, Susie Barstow Skelding, providing beautiful botanical studies for Skelding's illustrated books of poetry.[24] Bridges' work was sought after by publishers of greeting cards and calendars, including the leader in the field of chromolithography, Louis Prang, whose business competed with and subsequently surpassed that of Currier & Ives by the late nineteenth century. Prang was well aware of the public's demand for inexpensive but beautifully crafted colored lithographs to frame and hang in one's home or to give as gifts. However, working with Prang was something of a double-edged sword. One critic noted that Bridges was unquestionably one of the most successful local artists but cautioned that her work would "continue to be popular with buyers until one or two fall into the hands of Prang or some other chromo publisher, [and] when reproduced in a cheap form they will become," the author noted, "a drug on the art market."[25]

While Bridges certainly supported herself through work that supplied a demand by middle-class consumers for inexpensive printed matter, like Barstow, she was also among those artists who were praised for their painterly acumen at the

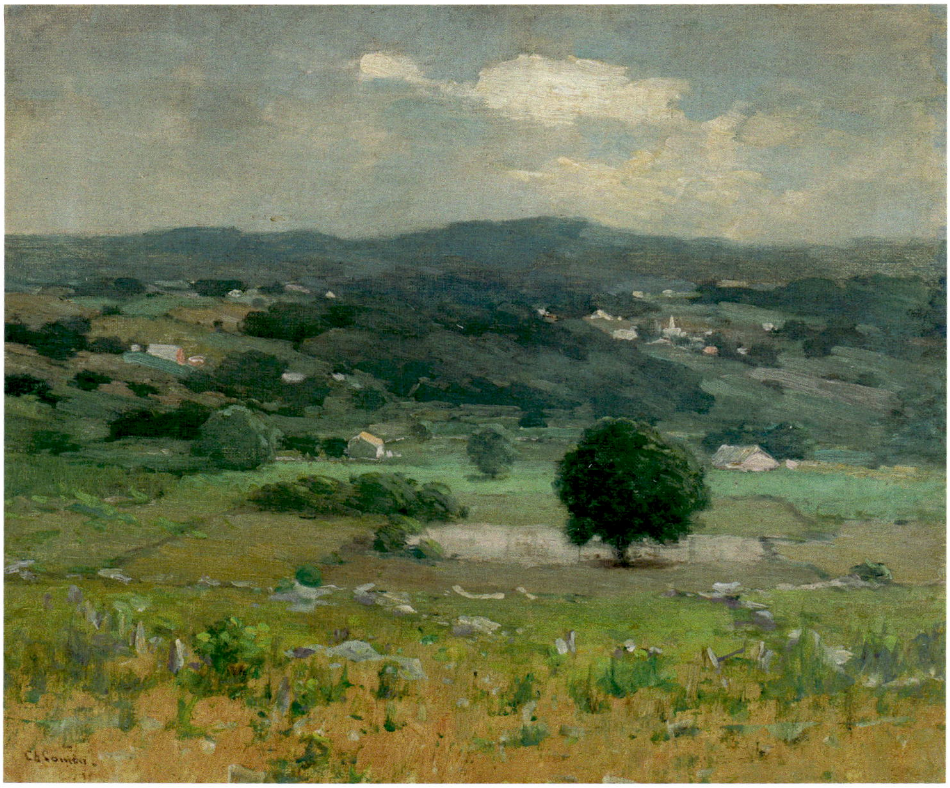

Fig. 36 Charlotte Buell Coman, *Landscape*, ca. 1900, oil on canvas, 13½ × 16½ in., Private Collection, Photograph: Andrew Bale

National Academy of Design and the Brooklyn Art Association. In 1873, members of the Academy "were so struck with the originality and beauty of the subjects that they elected her an associate of the institution."[26] Bridges honed her skills as a landscapist through numerous sketching trips into the Adirondacks, Catskills, and White Mountains, to Squam Lake in New Hampshire, along the rivers of Connecticut, and to the New Jersey shore. *Barn Swallows* (fig. 34) captures Bridge's characteristic command of atmospheric perspective, giving three-dimensionality to the tall grasses from which the swallows emerge, gliding with ease over the still, placid pond. By comparison, the visual prize in *Small Bird with Flowering Ironwood* (fig. 35) comes from finding the tiny creature still in flight, tucked among the dense foliage of the elegantly blossoming ironwood. Bridges' brushstrokes, at times likened to those of the Pre-Raphaelite painters, are readily apparent as the trees in the background and wispy cloud formations swirl with gentle energy across the canvas. Fidelia Bridges was once described as "shy and graceful as the Faun of Praxiteles."[27] She died at her home in Canaan, Connecticut, on May 14, 1923, a month before Susie Barstow. She was remembered as "the most gifted water painter in America...She possessed a fine natural talent that she developed to the highest artistic standard."[28]

Charlotte Buell Coman (1833–1924) was born in Waterville, New York, married Elijah Coman, and moved to Iowa City for a life as a "frontier wife." But Elijah died within a few years of their

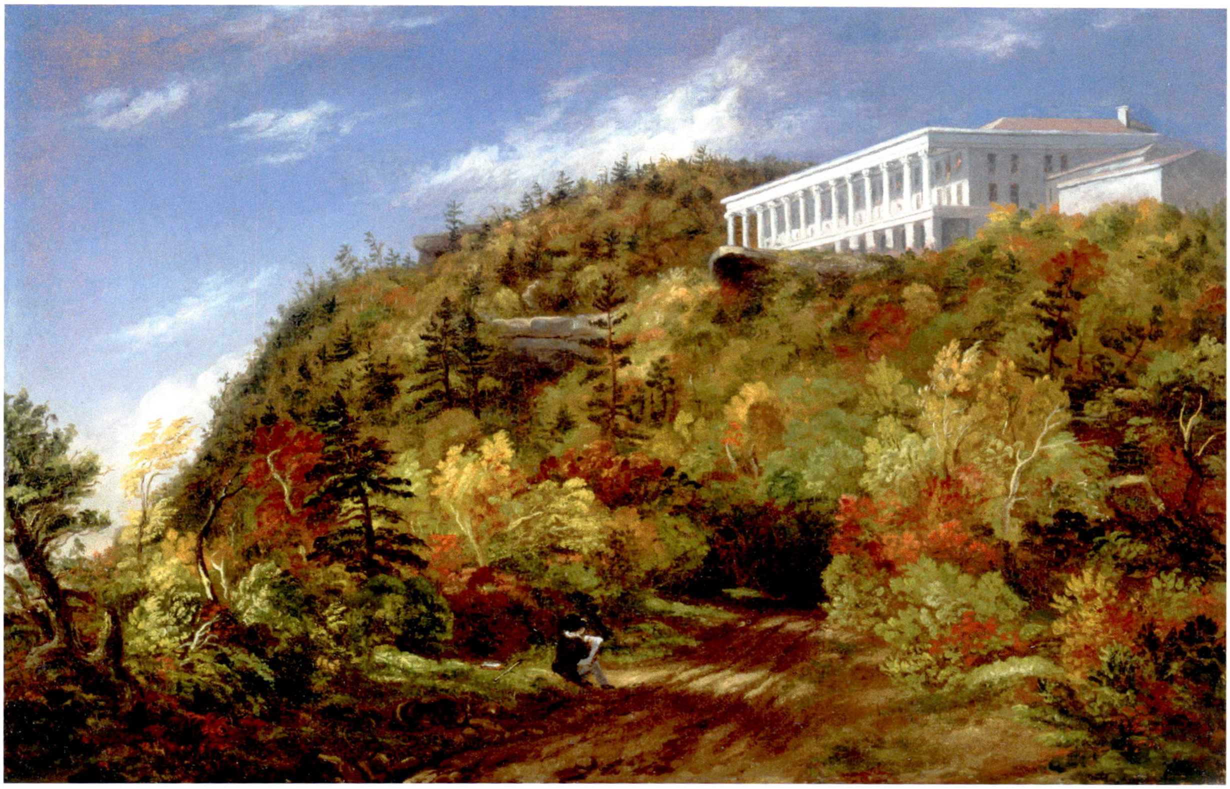

Fig. 37 Sarah Cole, *A View of the Catskill Mountain House*, 1848, oil on canvas, 15⅓ × 23⅜ in., Albany Institute of History and Art, Albany, NY, Albany Institute of History & Art Purchase, 1964.40

marriage, and Charlotte returned to Waterville, embarking on a career as a professional artist. Scholars have made note of her entrée into the field of landscape painters "late in life" (she was nearly 40 years of age at this time). Coman studied in New York with James Renwick Brevoort, from whom she learned the Hudson River School aesthetic, and then continued her studies abroad for nearly a decade, working with the French painter Émile Louis Vernier.[29] Like Barstow, her style was deeply influenced by the Barbizon artists, Corot and Daubigny. Coman began exhibiting her work almost annually from 1875 to 1899 at the National Academy of Design (where she was elected an Associate Member in 1910), among other national and international venues. She was a member of the National Association of Women Artists, the New York Watercolor Club, the New York Society of Painters, and an honorary member of the Pen and Brush Club.[30] Coman was praised for her work at the Philadelphia Centennial Exposition in 1876, exhibited at the Columbian Exposition in 1893, and was awarded a medal at the 1915 Pan-American Exposition in San Francisco. At the age of 72, she received the Julia A. Shaw Memorial Prize in 1905 from the Society of American Artists for her painting *September Afternoon*.[31] One critic proclaimed, "There is a brightness, a fresh color note and a happiness that bespeaks of eternal youth. This is a tribute to one of the most charming artists America has ever known."[32] Remarkably, Coman conducted her training, her travels, and her career as an artist almost entirely deaf, navigating mountain ranges and foreign countries, not

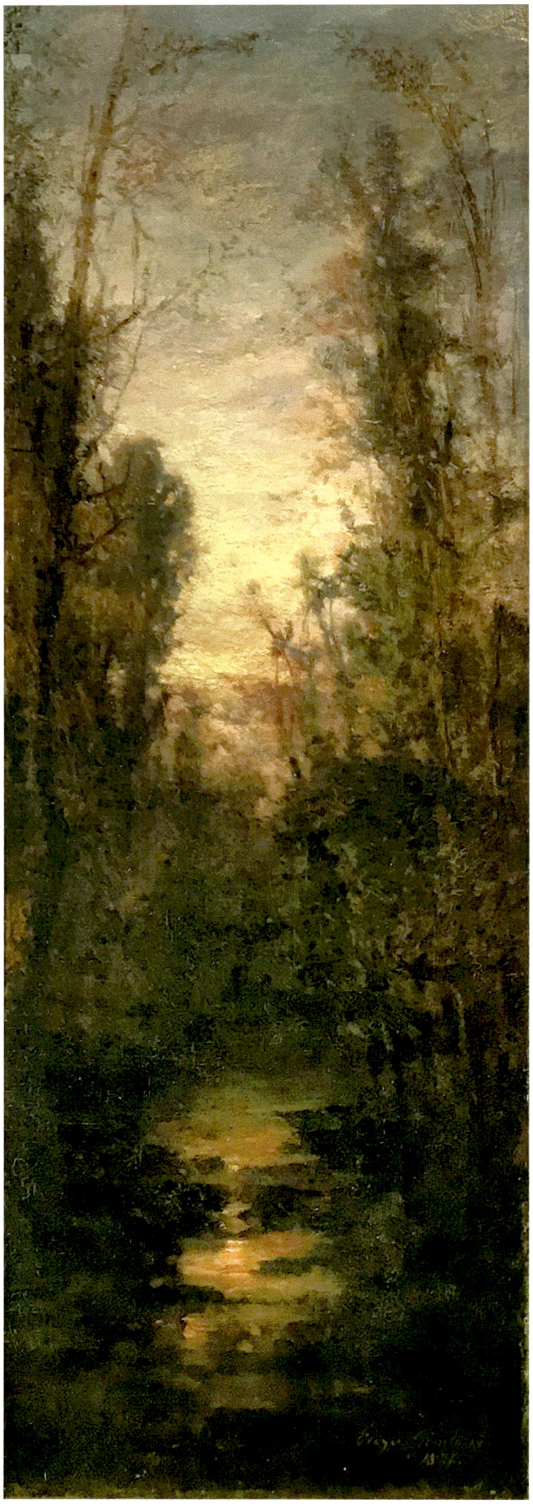

Fig. 38 Eliza Pratt Greatorex, *Rock Enon Springs from Sunset Hill*, ca. 1877, oil on board, 33½ × 12 in., Berg Family Collection

to mention the late nineteenth-century art world, "impaired" by both her gender and her hearing ability.

Landscape, ca. 1900 (fig. 36), with its prevailing tones of blues and greens, demonstrates the pervasive influence of the Barbizon School upon Coman's style. One can feel the warmth of the sun as if an ethereal veil of air were cast across the canvas. Likewise, the loose brushstrokes combined with a soft, tonal palette reflect Coman's interest in more sensory experiences. Coupled with a thick impasto application of paint, her association with the Tonalists and French Impressionist painters such as Mary Cassatt is clearly evidenced in this work. At the age of 80, Coman asserted that "age is no barrier to art" and opined, "I see no reason to keep women from working as successfully as men, except that, as you know, we women are always being called off to do things which no one expects men to do... I believe that home is the place for women except for painters and musicians. If one has a gift like that she should express herself."[33] Indeed she did; it was reported that over the course of her career, Coman painted 1,500 canvases.[34]

Eliza Pratt Greatorex (1819–1897) was one of only two women landscape painters singled out by Elizabeth Fries Ellet in her 1859 book, *Women Artists in All Ages and Countries*, the other being Sarah Cole. Ellet wrote of Eliza, "Mrs. Greatorex is a landscape-painter of merit, and is rapidly acquiring distinction. She has a deep love of wild mountain and lake scenery, dark woods, and rushing waters; and her productions are marked by the vigor of tone and dashing, impetuous freedom of touch especially adapted to that kind of subject."[35] Born in Ireland, where she had begun to paint, and brought to New York at the age of twenty-one, Eliza Pratt married the musician Henry Greatorex, with whom she had a son and two daughters, Kathleen (1851–1913) and Eleanor (1854–1897); both became accomplished artists and illustrators

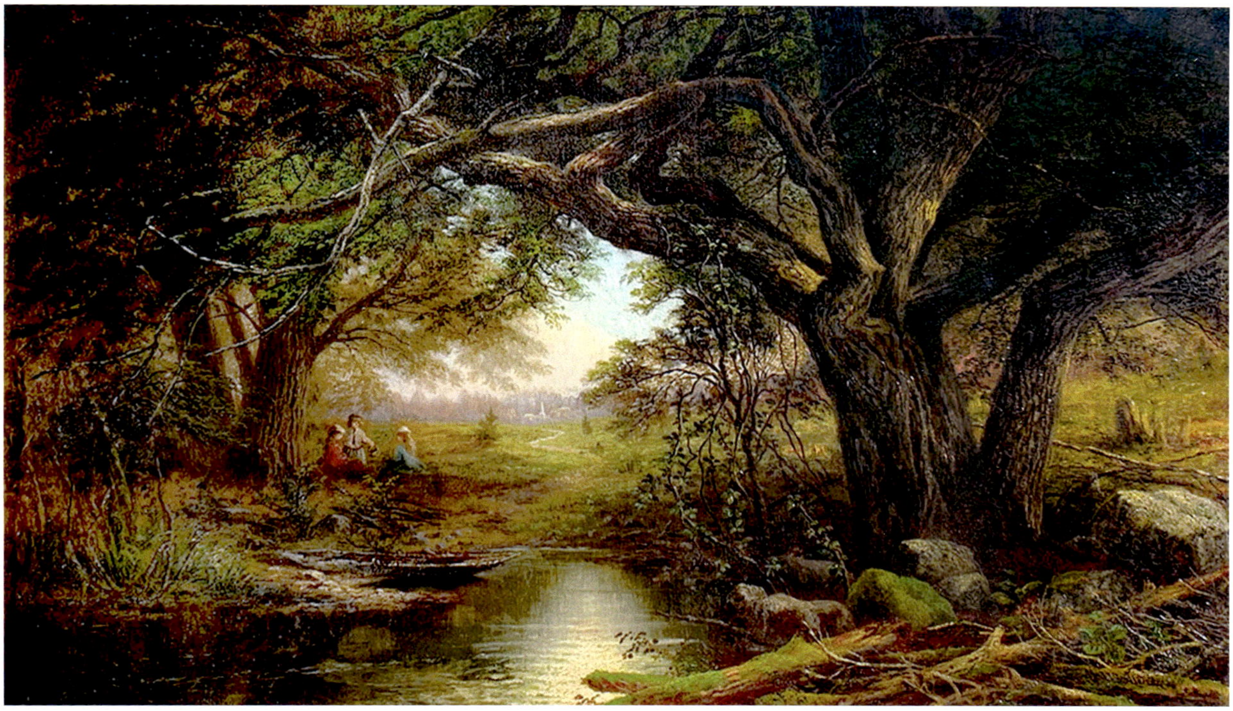

Fig. 39 Mary Josephine Walters, *Woodland Landscape*, ca. 1870s, oil on canvas, 14 × 24 in., Private Collection, PA, Photograph: Hawthorne Fine Art, New York, NY

in their own rights.[36] Henry died in 1858, leaving Eliza to provide for herself and her children. She took a studio in the Fifth Avenue Building, where she likely studied with James and William Hart—and undoubtedly began her friendship with Julie Hart Beers. Eliza was determined to provide her daughters (and herself) with the best education and access to as much art as possible. Multiple trips to Europe ensued from the 1860s to the 1880s. While in Germany, she witnessed the Passion Play in Oberammergau (as did Susie Barstow), and produced a series of twenty exquisite etchings after experiencing the famous pageant in 1871.[37] Greatorex's portfolio, *Old New York, from the Battery to Bloomingdale* (1875), with its collotype illustrations from her pen and ink sketches, provides an architectural tour of a city in transition, and her plates give evidence of buildings no longer in existence. In the summer of 1877, Eliza Greatorex traveled with her daughters to visit her brother Adam Pratt in Washington, D.C., then to Rock Enon Springs, Virginia, known after the Civil War for its healing mineral springs and baths. Eliza made numerous sketches, etchings, and two oil compositions of this southern vacation destination, including *Rock Enon Springs from Sunset Hill*, ca. 1877 (fig 38).[38] Taken by the scene's stunning verticality, the viewer's eye moves deep into the recesses of nature. The shimmering reflections of light coming from the springs carry one through the framing trees to the dramatic colors of dusk. Greatorex's painterly style clearly blends the tradition of the Hudson River School with that of the more European-inspired Barbizon style.

Greatorex was a prolific exhibitor of her paintings and etchings and was elected an Associate Member of the National Academy of Design in 1869.[39] Like Mary Nimmo Moran, Greatorex was

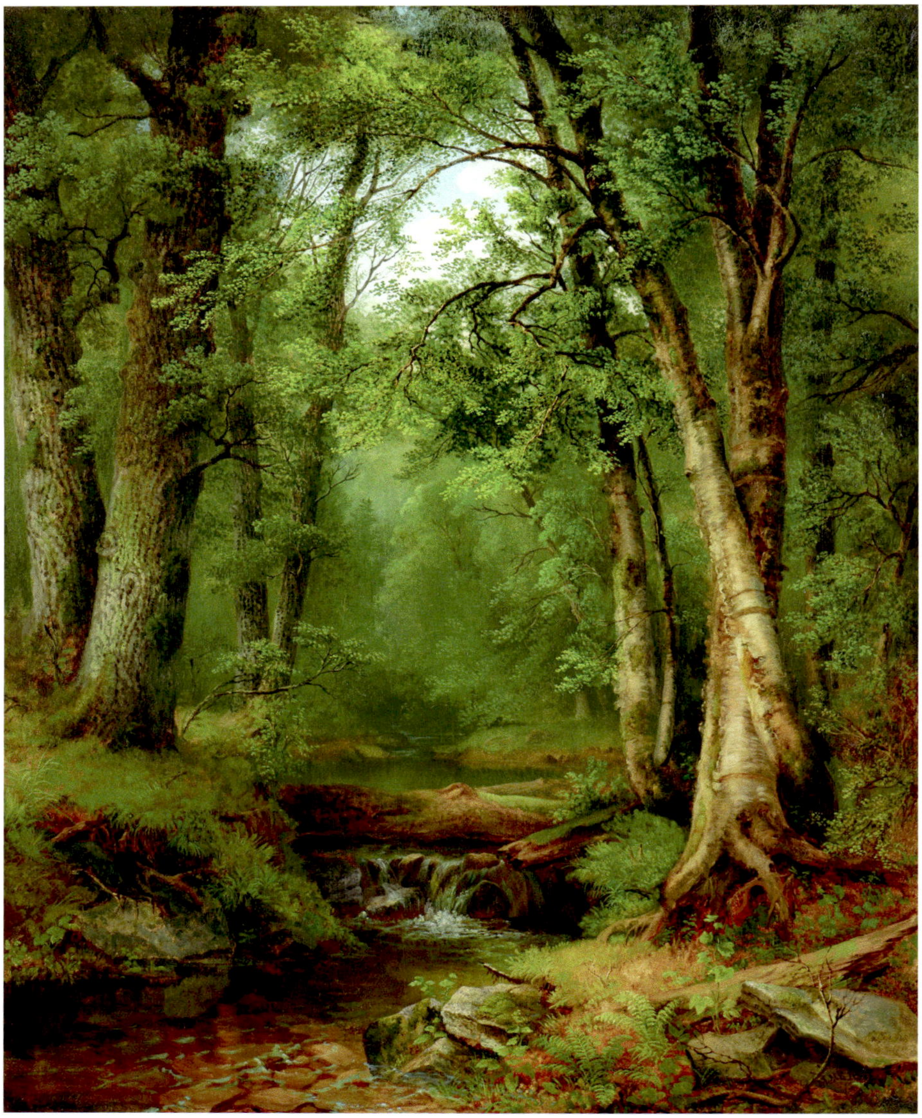

Fig. 40 Mary Josephine Walters, *In the Woods*, late 1860s, oil on canvas, 28 × 23⅛ in., Birmingham Museum of Art, Birmingham, AL, Museum Purchase with funds provided by the Harold and Regina Simon Fund, 2008.14

an important figure in the painter-etcher movement of the latter half of the nineteenth century. Their etched work was included in the influential 1881 *Exhibition of American Etchers* and the *Women Etchers of America* exhibition in 1887 ("the first comprehensive exhibition of the work of women artists by an American art institution"),[40] both curated by Sylvester Rosa Koehler at Boston's Museum of Fine Arts. The expanded version of this exhibition at New York's Union League Club had intended to include four "Proofs of plates etched in 1844" by Sarah Cole, added posthumously, but John Falconer, who owned the plates, failed to provide impressions.[41] Upon Eliza's death at the age of 78, one obituary noted that "Mrs. Greatorex was one of the best-known woman artists in this country."[42]

Mary Josephine Walters (1837–1883) was well regarded in the 1860s and 1870s as a landscape painter of great talent.[43] Like Barstow, and ostensibly with Barstow at times, Walters traversed the varied terrains of the Adirondacks, northern New Jersey, the White Mountains, and her beloved Catskill Mountains. Her paintings were selected annually from 1864 to 1883 for exhibition at the National Academy of Design, among other venues, where her work sold with great regularity. As for her artistic education, Walters consulted with Asher Durand. In his biography of his father, John Durand stated that of the pupils who worked with Durand Sr., it was "Miss Josephine Walters, whom he often advised in the pursuit of her studies."[44] In an "Art Gossip" column in *The Brooklyn Daily Eagle*, this association was duly noted: "Miss Walters has attained great excellence in landscape painting. Having been a student with Durand, Miss W. seems to have learned the manipulations of that master, and sketches and paints with delicacy and a good deal of elaboration."[45] Walters' work from the 1870s clearly suggests the influence of Durand. *Woodland Landscape*, ca. 1870s (fig. 39), is a secluded hideaway for the three children who find shade from the heat of summer under the spreading boughs of the trees. Their diminutive presence serves to make all the more apparent just how majestic a landscape they occupy. The light casting off the water's edge from this small lake where their punt—a flat-bottomed boat used to navigate shallow waters—has been stowed brings the viewer through the framing tree trunks and crisscrossing branches back to a winding path that ultimately leads to a church steeple, barely noticeable in the central distance. This literalizing of

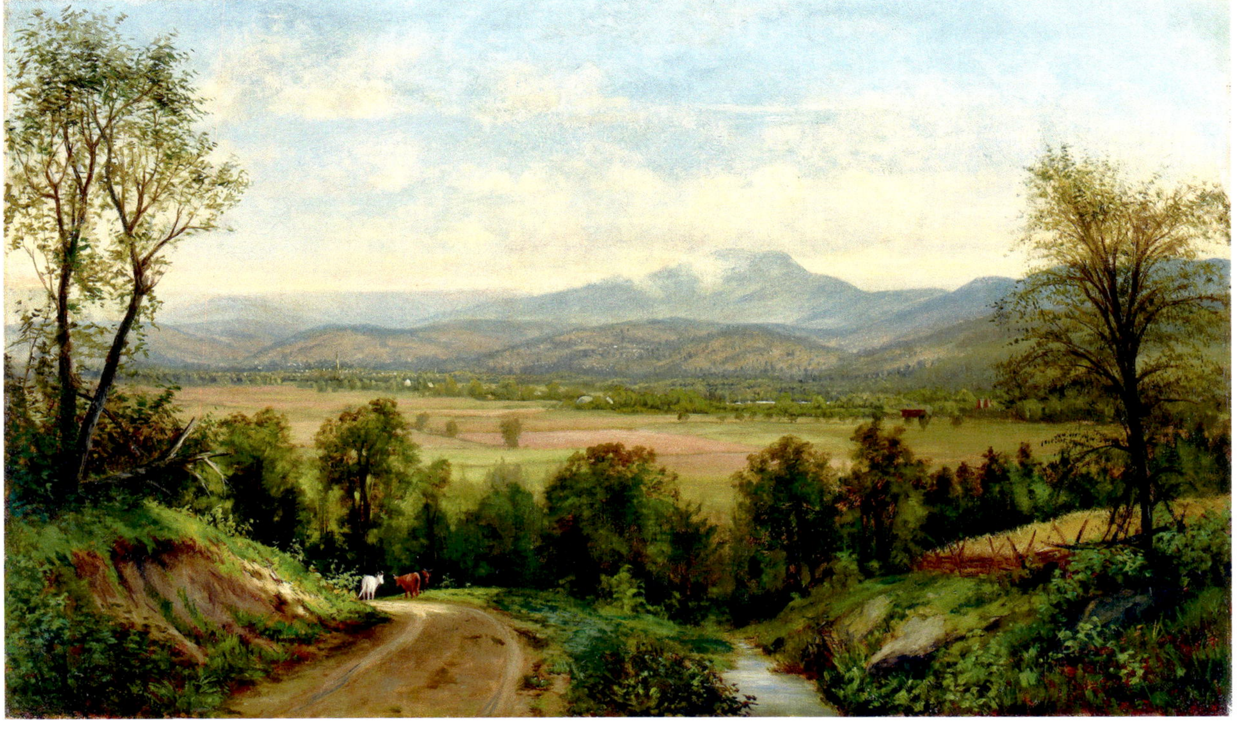

Fig. 41 Laura Woodward, *Looking Up Keene Valley, Adirondacks*, 1874, oil on canvas, 14 × 24 in., Edward and Deborah Pollack Fine Art, LLC

finding God within nature was part of the romantic Christianization of the American landscape so prevalent among first-generation Hudson River School artists. With soft forms and diffuse lighting, Walters instills this composition with an innate quietude. A painting by Walters, possibly *Wooded Landscape*, was exhibited at the Brooklyn Art Association in 1876 and described as follows by an art critic: "Miss Walters sends a view on a little cove with a boating party resting on its bank. The water is shaded by broad spreading trees and beyond a glimpse of quiet country landscape is given. The picture is of cabinet size and is carefully painted."[46] Breaking from her typical cabinet-size paintings, *In the Woods* (fig.40) is one of Walters' larger compositions. The viewer is invited to enter this scene along the banks of a cool, crisp stream. The gentle cascade below a fallen limb blocks the viewer's path, guiding us instead to the strong, towering trees of the verdant woods. This lush composition, with its framing boughs and hint of a blue summer sky in the distance, typifies Walters' commitment to Hudson River School aesthetics. Mary Josephine Walters died prematurely at the age of 46 after a long and severe illness, as reported by *The New York Times* on December 16, 1883.[47] One can only imagine how her style might have evolved and continued to entice viewers had she lived longer.

Laura Woodward (1834–1926) frequently exhibited her paintings alongside those of Susie Barstow, Julie Hart Beers, Eliza Greatorex, and Mary Josephine Walters. She began her career hiking and sketching in the Adirondacks, Catskills, and Green Mountains and reveled in summer and autumnal scenes of the American landscape throughout the 1870s and 1880s. Raised in Mount Hope, New York, Woodward moved to New York City, where she shared studio space at the Dodworth's Studio Building with the artists George and James Smillie, among others. Julie Hart Beers was there as well, while Charlotte Coman was another of Woodward's friends. Woodward neither married nor traveled to Europe.[48] She exhibited and sold her paintings at prestigious venues such as the Pennsylvania Academy of the Fine Arts, the Brooklyn Art Association, and the National Academy of Design, where her work could be found annually from 1872 to 1889.[49] With popular scenes of the Catskill Mountains, Lake George, and Clarendon, Vermont, as examples, Woodward's style was praised by members of the press for decades. "This artist is undoubtedly gifted with fine imagination and industry," wrote one reviewer, "a true feeling of Nature... fine drawing and happiness of composition," wrote another.[50] *Looking Up Keene Valley, Adirondacks* (1874), (fig. 41) has all the hallmarks of the Hudson River School at its apex in the 1870s. Partial to the Adirondacks before her move to Florida in the late 1880s, Woodward celebrates the open fields and vast mountain ranges of the East Coast; cattle on a winding path and a rustic fence on the right are all signs of benign domestication. In portraying a lovely summer day, foliage in bloom, Woodward often dotted her landscapes with hay bales, shafts of wheat, gentle cows, or deer. Such is the case in *By the Stream* of 1876 (fig. 42). Two deer make their way along the wood-lined stream. In a pastoral landscape filled with light in the middle ground, Woodward provides shade and depth to the foreground, thereby allowing for a somewhat soggy experience should the viewer venture forth beyond the rocks.

Throughout the 1880s, Woodward repeatedly traveled to Florida, a blossoming tourist destination and of interest to artists such as Mary Nimmo Moran and Martin Johnson Heade, with whom Woodward was friendly. Enamored with the exotic natural environment of the South, Woodward, as noted by Deborah Pollack, played an important role in the creation of Palm Springs as a new resort area for tourists and nature enthusiasts alike

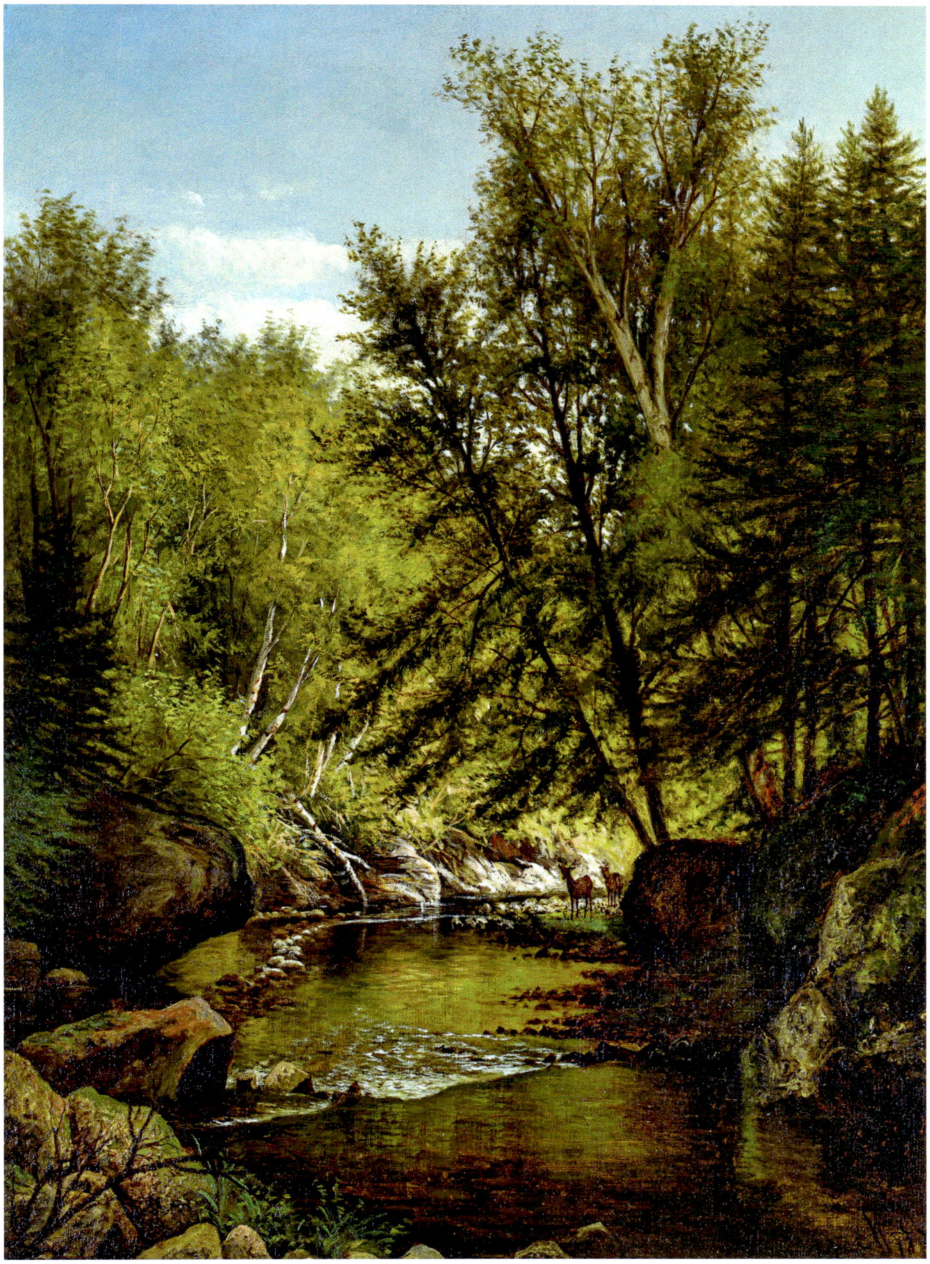

Fig. 42 Laura Woodward, *By the Stream,* 1876, oil on canvas, 24 × 18 in., Private Collection, Photograph: Andrew Bale

through her southern landscape views, trading elms and birches for palm trees.[51] First to St. Augustine and then to Palm Beach, Woodward was a popular artist and kept a studio-shop in the Royal Poinciana Hotel for as long as her health and eyesight permitted. At the age of 92, after many years of declining health, Laura Woodward died at the home of friends in St. Cloud, Florida.[52]

The lives and artistry of Susie Barstow and of the women in her circle clearly demonstrate that when Cole, Durand, and Church ventured into the Catskills, Adirondacks, and White Mountains, they most certainly were not alone. *Women Reframe American Landscape: Susie Barstow & Her Circle / Contemporary Practices* continues, and in some regards begins, a fresh evaluation of American landscape studies. Monographs and retrospective exhibitions related to additional women of the Hudson River School are already in progress. To quote Susie Barstow, "I will overcome every barrier to success and soon with the sun rising above every Earthly conflict make myself a name and position that will influence the whole world."[53] Indeed.

1 This scholarship includes April F. Masten, *Art Work: Women Artists and Democracy in Mid-Nineteenth-Century New York*, Philadelphia, University of Pennsylvania Press, 2008; Laura R. Prieto, *At Home in the Studio: The Professionalization of Women Artists in America,* Cambridge, Harvard University Press, 2001; and Kirsten Swinth, *Painting Professionals: Women Artists & the Development of Modern American Art, 1870–1930*, Chapel Hill, University of North Carolina Press, 2001.

2 A portion of the following narrative is adapted from the introduction to a companion publication to this exhibition, *Susie M. Barstow: Redefining the Hudson River School*, London, Lund Humphries, 2023.

3 *The Brooklyn Citizen*, Sunday, December 28, 1890, p. 13.

4 Emily A. Thackray, "Fair Mountaineers," *The White Mountain Echo and Tourist's Register*, 3 August 1889, p. 5.

5 *The Brooklyn Daily Eagle*, Sunday, September 26, 1915, p. 17; *The Brooklyn Daily Eagle*, Wednesday, June 13, 1923, p. 24.

6 Barstow's undated lecture notes, Private Collection.

7 Kevin Avery, "The Hudson River School," Heilbrun Timeline of Art History. Metmuseum.org/toah/hd/hurs/hd_hurs.htm, October 2004.

8 Clarence Cook, "Art in America in 1883," *Princeton Review*, vol. 11 (May 1883), pp. 312–13.

9 *The Brooklyn Daily Eagle*, Sunday, April 15, 1888, p. 10.

10 *The Brooklyn Daily Eagle*, Sunday, July 10, 1892, p. 17.

11 *The Brooklyn Daily Eagle*, Sunday, July 16, 1893, p. 9.

12 Kevin Avery, "A Historiography of the Hudson River School," in *American Paradise: The World of the Hudson River School*, Harry N. Abrams, New York, 1987, pp. 3–6. Avery attributes the first published use of the term "Hudson River School" to Earl Shinn in 1879.

13 Scholars such as Tim Barringer are actively refuting the outdated association with this terminology.

14 "Obituary Notes," *The New York Times*, June 13, 1923, p. 19.

15 William H. Gerdts, *Women Artists of America 1701–1964,* Newark, NJ: The Newark Museum, 1965, pp. 10–11.

16 Gerdts, *Women Artists of America: 1707–1964*, p. 10.

17 George Cuthbert Groce, *The New-York Historical Society's Dictionary of Artists of America, 1564–1860*, New Haven, Yale University Press, 1957, p. 365; Jennifer Krieger, "Painting Her Way: The Remarkable Lives of Female Hudson River School Artists," in *Remember the Ladies: Women of the Hudson River School*, Catskill, NY, Thomas Cole National Historic Site, 2010, p. 24; Paul E. Sternberg, *Art by American Women: Selections from the Collection of Louise and Alan Sellars*, Gainesville, GA, Brenau College, 1991, p. 20. Marion Beers is the name historically given to Julie's first husband. However, research by Jennifer Krieger through interviews with family descendants suggests that she married George Washington Beers. See Krieger, "Painting Her Way," p. 24.

18 *The New York Times*, Friday, August 15, 1913, p. 7; Pollack, *Laura Woodward*, pp. 17, 32.

19 *The Brooklyn Daily Eagle*, Thursday, August 24, 1871, p. 3.

20 *Daily Graphic*, May 26, 1876, no. 699. Thank you to Deborah Pollack for sharing this resource.

21 *The Brooklyn Daily Eagle*, Thursday, October 28, 1880, p. 2; the "plates" were included in the exhibition, *Remember the Ladies: Women of the Hudson River School*, Thomas Cole National Historic Site, Catskill, NY, 2010.

22 Katherine Manthorne's *Fidelia Bridges: Nature into Art*, London: Lund Humphries, 2023, is a monographic study devoted to the artist.

23 Sternberg, *Art by American Women*, p. 25; Katherine Manthorne, "'The Voice of Nature': The Art of Fidelia Bridges in the 1870s," *American Arts Quarterly* (Winter 2011/12), pp. 31–33.

24 *Boston Evening Transcript*, Saturday, November 5, 1887, p. 8.

25 *The Brooklyn Daily Eagle*, Thursday, July 30, 1874, p. 3.

26 *The Brooklyn Daily Eagle*, Friday, June 27, 1873, p. 2.

27 *Brooklyn Times Union*, Saturday, July 10, 1875, p. 2.

28 *Hartford Courant*, Thursday, May 31, 1923, p. 12.

29 Charlotte Streifer Rubinstein, *American Women Artists: From Early American Times to the Present*, Boston, G.K. Hall, 1982, pp. 58–59.

30 Groce, *The New-York Historical Society's Dictionary of Artists of America, 1564–1860*, p. 142; Peter Falk, *The Annual Exhibition Record of the Pennsylvania Academy of the Fine Arts, 1807–1870*, edited reprint of Anna Wells Rutledge's 1955 edition, vol.1, Sound View Press, Madison, CT, 1988, p. 140; "Mrs. Charlotte Coman, 91, Painter, is Dead," *Buffalo Evening News*, Friday, November 14, 1924, p. 22.

31 Peter Falk, *Who was Who in American Art 1564–1975*, Madison, CT, Sound View Press, 1999 edition of 1985 orig., p. 704, *The Brooklyn Daily Eagle*, Sunday, March 19, 1905, p. 6.

32 *The Standard Union* (Brooklyn), Saturday, April 1, 1905, p. 5.

33 *Macon* (Georgia) *Daily*, Wednesday, February 19, 1913, p. 6.

34 Charlotte Coman died in a rest home in Yonkers, New York, on November 11, 1924. *The Brooklyn Daily Eagle*, Monday, January 15, 1923, p. 3; *Los Angeles Evening Express*, Tuesday, March 27, 1923, p. 30; Groce, *The New-York Historical Society's Dictionary of Artists of America*, p. 142.

35 Elizabeth Fries Ellet, *Women Artists in All Ages and Countries*, NY, Harper & Bros, 1859, pp. 295, 234, 316.

36 Phyllis Peet, *American Women of the Etching Revival*, Atlanta: High Museum of Art, 1988, p. 57; *Buffalo Weekly Express*, Thursday, April 7, 1881, p. 4.

37 Katherine Manthorne's *Restless Enterprise: The Art and Life of Eliza Pratt Greatorex*, Oakland, University of California Press, 2020, one of few monographic studies dedicated to women landscape painters of the nineteenth century. See, in particular, pp. 133–134.

38 Guests could lodge at a hotel that was owned for a time by Adam Pratt. Manthorne, *Restless Enterprise*, p. 232.

39 Peet, *American Women of the Etching Revival*, pp. 57–58.

40 Ibid., p. 11.

41 Peet considered Sarah Cole to be the first woman etcher in America, ibid.

42 *New-York Tribune*, Thursday, February 11, 1897, p.12.

43 See Nancy Siegel, *The Cultured Canvas: New Perspectives on American Landscape Painting*, University Press of New England, Lebanon, NH, 2011, pp. 173–175; and biographical material provided by Stephanie Strass.

44 John Durand, *The Life and Times of A.B. Durand*, New York, Charles Scribner's Sons, 1894, p. 184. Walters has been described erroneously as Durand's favorite student. There is no evidence to suggest the validity of this statement.

45 *The Brooklyn Daily Eagle*, March 6, 1868, p. 2.

46 *The Brooklyn Daily Eagle*, Friday, January 7, 1876, p. 3.

47 *The New York Times*, December 16, 1883, p. 9.

48 A majority of our knowledge about Laura Woodward comes from Deborah Pollack, *Laura Woodward: The Artist Behind the Innovator who Developed Palm Beach*, Toronto, Blue Heron Press, 2009, pp. 15–24.

49 *National Academy of Design Exhibition Record, 1861–1900*, compiled and edited by Maria Naylor, 2 vols., Kennedy Galleries, New York, 1973, pp. 1059–1060; See also Falk, *The Annual Exhibition Record of the Pennsylvania Academy of the Fine Arts, 1807–1870*, vol. 1, p. 531.

50 *Courier Journal*, October 3, 1875, with thanks to Deborah Pollack for the reference; *The Brooklyn Daily Eagle*, Thursday, June 12, 1879, p. 1.

51 Pollack, *Laura Woodward*, chapter three: pp. 107–143.

52 *The Palm Beach Post*, Thursday, May 20, 1926, p. 2.

53 Susie Barstow's Journal of 1856/57. Private Collection.

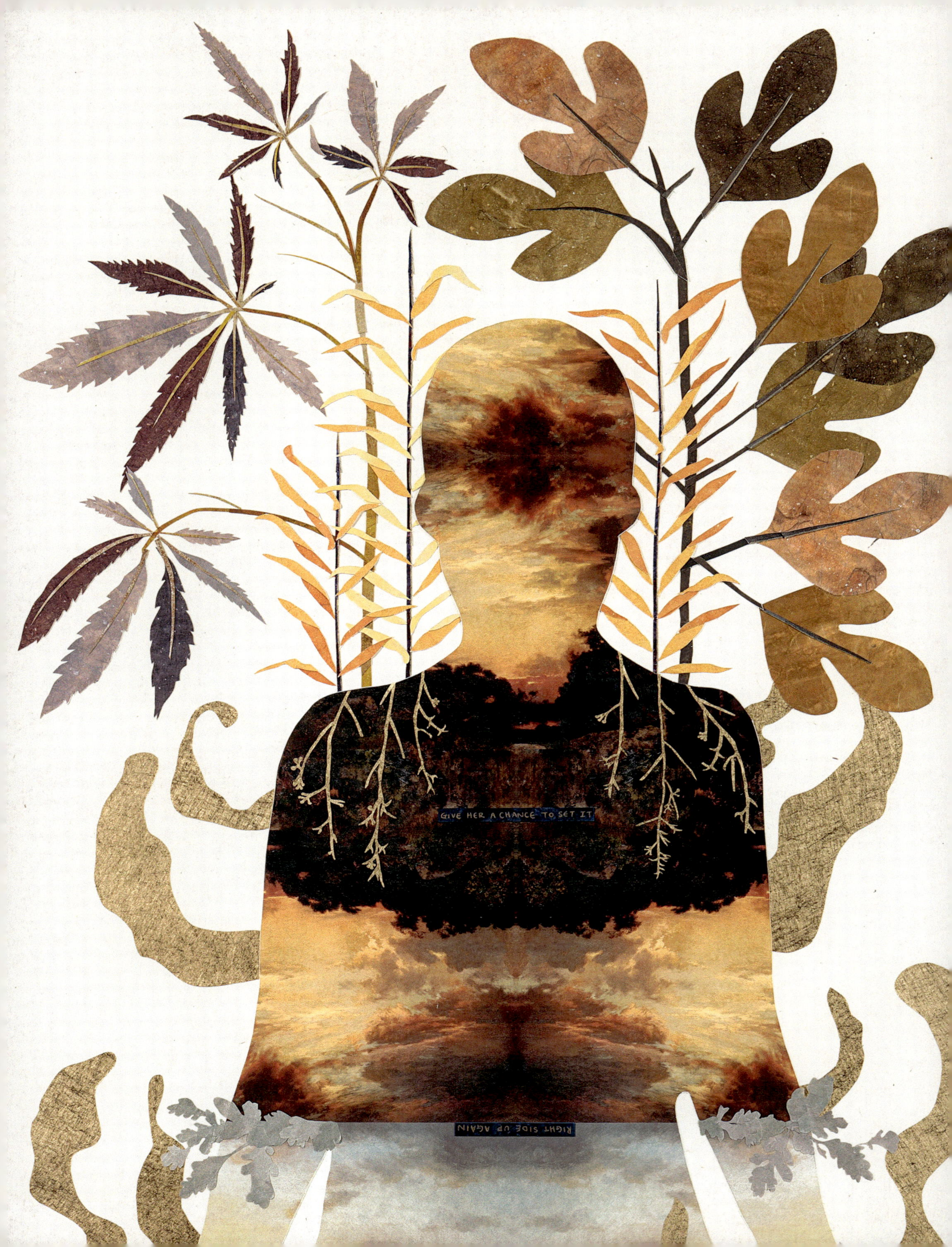
GIVE HER A CHANCE TO SET IT
RIGHT SIDE UP AGAIN

WOMEN REFRAME LAND: CONTEMPORARY PRACTICES

Amanda Malmstrom and Kate Menconeri

"All positions are political; there is not an outside, objective position from which to observe–the viewer...is part of the landscape." –Rebecca Solnit[1]

"There is no such thing as a static landscape. Every landscape is in a state of transition, undergoing a never-ending process of transformation brought about by forces of wind, water, and plate tectonics...landscapes shape human history." –Kate Morris[2]

"Before it can ever be a repose for the senses, landscape is the work of the mind. Its scenery is built up as much from strata of memory, as layers of rock..." –Simon Schama[3]

What is a landscape? What is it made of? What does it do? In the English language, landscape is a historic term that can be traced back to the sixteenth century,[4] and in a simple framework has been defined as a picture of natural scenery or "land 'captured' in the eye and depicted in paint through the use of single point perspective that positions the artist and viewer looking out to the horizon."[5] Today, artists no longer perceive landscape as Kenneth Clark wrote in 1949 as "unproblematic—a history of human spirit and its attempt to create harmony with its environment."[6] Instead, contemporary artists and thinkers are redefining and reframing what landscape can be, and meaningfully expanding how we understand our inextricable relationship to land. As Rebecca Solnit notes, artists have transformed landscape into "the principal battlefield of our time," recognizing "landscape not as scenery, but as the spaces and systems we inhabit, a system our own lives depend on."[7] Within this context, landscape art can be understood not just as an aesthetic depiction of land as perceived through the human eye, but as a description of land tied to historic, political, economic, cultural, ecological, spiritual, social, gendered, and personal realities.

It is critical and generative to realize, as Simon Schama states, that "[e]ven the landscapes that we supposed to be most free of culture may turn out, on close inspection, to be its product."[8] Landscape is always subjective, a product of culture and the artist's specific perspective. Yet, art historians have extensively focused their study and scholarship on landscapes as seen, defined, and pictured by European-American men, including the "fraternity" celebrated as the Hudson River School painters.[9] In the field of American Art, landscape has thus come to be largely seen over time—in museums, in literature, and culture—through representations created by a White male canon.

Even the names used to identify certain places and geographical features of the United States employ masculine geological adjectives and coding. As Martin A. Berger has noted, in the unceded lands of Yosemite Valley, for instance, "frequently the most valued rocks were associated with male actors—sentinels, brothers, and captains—whose forms evoked stereotypical masculine adjectives like 'massive,' 'solid,' and 'powerful.'"[10] In contrast, nature has often been gendered as feminine; consider the term "Mother Earth." Ecofeminists, emerging in the 1970s and 80s concurrent with the rise of the Women's Movement, were some of the first to point to the ways in which the manipulation of land mirrored the subjugation of women.[11] Catherine Nash and Gillian Rose have examined the ways that male geographers, and artists in turn, can "'gaze' at the landscape with its assumed feminine qualities in a manner that is reminiscent of and gives the same kind of pleasurable experience as that felt by the male spectator of the female nude."[12] To assume that the male-dominated canon of American landscape art represents an unproblematic "universal" is to ignore the masculine history of geography, land relations, and landscape art.[13]

Despite very real restrictions and harmful stereotypes, women have always been making and exhibiting landscapes alongside their male counterparts. The full names of over fifty women associated with the Hudson River School have been identified to date, and that number will only continue to grow with increased scholarship.[14] However, in a study of twenty iconic, public Hudson River School collections, only 15 out of a total of 1,175 paintings were by women, or 1.3%.[15] It was only in 2021 that the Metropolitan Museum of Art, which holds what is considered one of the world's definitive American Art collections, purchased its first nineteenth-century Hudson River School landscape painted by a woman (*Summer Woodlands* by Julie Hart Beers). According to a major 2019 study, a data analysis of 18 major US art museums found their collections are 87% male and 85% White.[16] At the time of writing, until now, with Susie Barstow's debut in 2023 at the Thomas Cole National Historic Site, there has never been a solo exhibition given to a 19th-century woman painting landscape in the United States.

Celebrating its fiftieth anniversary in 2021, Linda Nochlin's seminal essay, "Why have there been no great women artists?", asks its readers to question and scrutinize the systems that discouraged women from pursuing careers in art, but also the systems that encouraged the neglect of women's work in scholarship. Working in a field that has given more opportunities to men, women creating art have historically encountered impediments with regard to equal access to educational training, facilities, institutional support, and mentorship.[17] Many women who did achieve visibility were privileged with familial or personal connections to successful male artists. And what about painting the landscape? In addition to structural barriers, women in the Hudson River School experienced different and unequal treatment. Painter Worthington Whittredge went so far as to claim that women were physically incapable of producing landscape painting because they "do not know how to stick an umbrella into the ground."[18] Whittredge obviously did not know about the outings of Susie Barstow, who scaled the Catskills, Adirondacks, White Mountains, Alps, and Black Forest Mountains and is known to have hiked twenty-five miles a day.[19]

Embracing that there are myriad ways to artistically interpret land, this project engages diverse, multigenerational perspectives and practices to launch an expanded narrative that strongly recenters women in the canon of American landscape art. We challenge the historic gap, in part by amplifying and bringing attention to specific, outstanding artists and thinkers who are women and whose work expands not only the confines of medium and material, but who have radically influenced, complicated, and transformed the way we see and understand land and landscape today. *Women Reframe American Landscape* includes the first solo show of Susie Barstow, a contemporary exhibition (featuring the work of the Guerrilla Girls, Anna Plesset, Tanya Marcuse, Teresita Fernández, Saya Woolfalk, Ebony G. Patterson, Wendy Red Star, Jaune Quick-to-See Smith, Kay WalkingStick, Cecilia Vicuña, Jean Shin, Mary Mattingly, and Marie Lorenz), and this book which

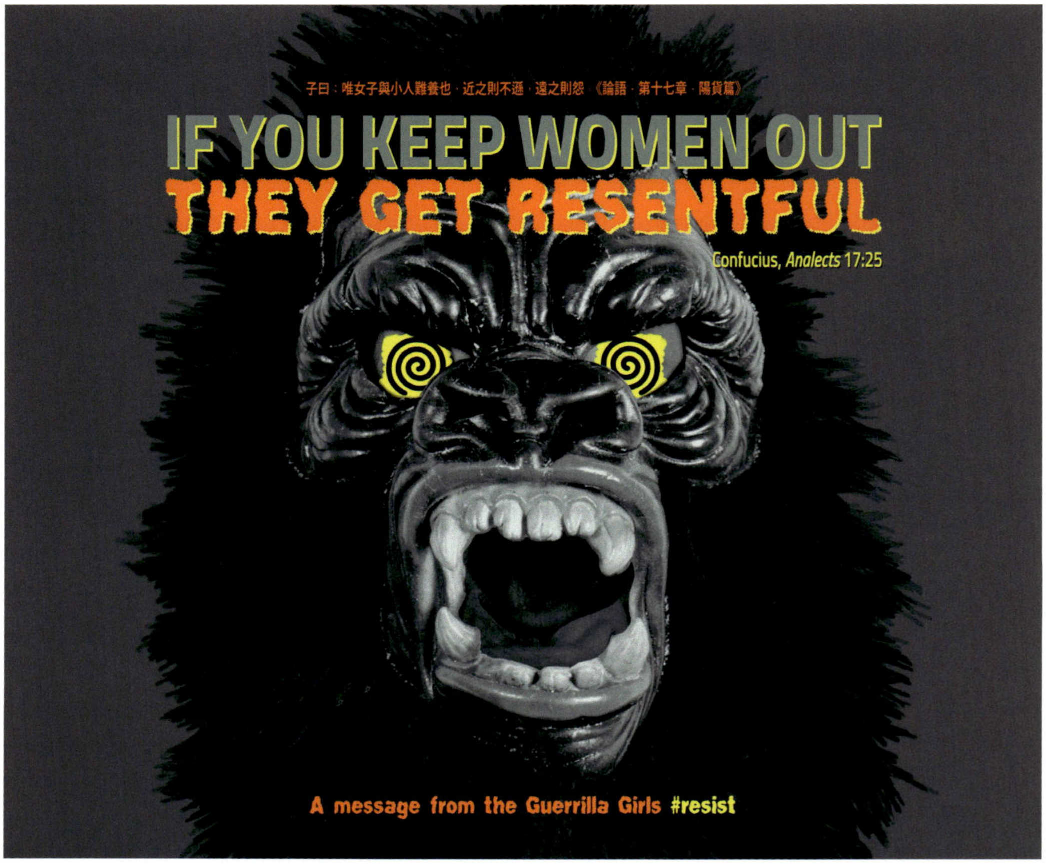

Fig. 1 Guerrilla Girls, *If You Keep Women Out They Get Resentful*, 2018, digital poster, Copyright © Guerrilla Girls, Courtesy guerrillagirls.com

includes original writing by the curators, artists, and Candice Hopkins and Jolene Rickard.

We are deeply indebted to and influenced by the work of artists, scholars, and activists who have traced and challenged the history of the gendered landscape.[20] We come to this discourse with openness to possibility in a moment when the very terms in use—“landscape,” “American,” and “women artists”—feel inadequate, if not problematic, to fully represent the complexities of gender and our relationship with land and place. This project does not attempt to propose a single definition of “landscape” or “America,” nor to draw lines between a male or female perspective. Instead, this is one initiative among many at the Thomas Cole Site and the museum field to continually rethink landscape art in the United States as dynamic, multifaceted, and evolving, and as also created and interpreted by women.

As asked by Nochlin, how can we “as a community together change the discourse and the production of our field...in this intersectional, evolving, varied, ongoing project?”[21] While there has been a major shift in the art world to better balance opportunities across genders in the fifty years since Nochlin’s essay, there is still a long way to go, specifically in considering landscape art in the United States. Nochlin’s words feel as urgent and as galvanizing today: “Feminist art history is there to make trouble, to call into question, to

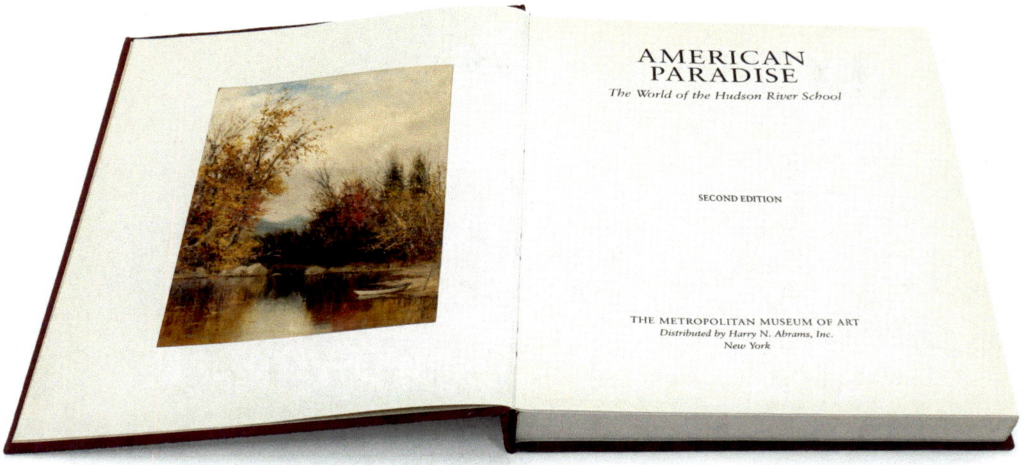

Fig. 2 Anna Plesset, Rendering for *American Paradise (Second Edition)*, 2022, Courtesy the artist

ruffle feathers in the patriarchal dovecotes...We will need all our wit and courage to make sure that women's voices are heard, their work seen and written about. That is our task for the future."[22] *Women Reframe American Landscape* takes up this call and consciously participates in this ongoing feminist work.

Shifting Art Histories

Of inspiration to us in this project, the **Guerrilla Girls**—the anonymous collective of feminist artists and activists—have been consistently fighting sexism and racism in the art world, politics, and pop culture since 1985. Calling themselves the "conscience of the art world," members of the Guerrilla Girls wear gorilla masks, use pseudonyms of deceased female artists, and engage in "guerrilla tactics" and interventions, realized through street posters, billboard art, videos, books, and direct action and protest. In their popular 1989 poster, *Do women have to be naked to get into the Met. Museum?* the Guerrilla Girls note that "Less than 5% of the artists in the Modern Art sections are women, but 85% of the nudes are female" (cat. 92). In 2018, the Guerrilla Girls created a poster with an angry gorilla mask and text emblazoned across it: "IF YOU KEEP WOMEN OUT / THEY GET RESENTFUL" (fig. 1). Made over 30 years since the Guerrilla Girls coalesced, this poster serves as a proclamation and warning: feminists will stay angry and active until sexism is ousted from our cultural institutions. This poster serves as a siren to us to continue studying, exhibiting, and publishing work by women. On the occasion of *Women Reframe American Landscape*, the Guerrilla Girls will be making a new work in dialogue with the exhibition's critical conversations around land and art.

Joining this work, the artist **Anna Plesset** reframes and directly challenges the male-dominated history of the Hudson River School. Drawing on a research-based practice that spans painting, print, and sculpture, Plesset illuminates women's contributions to nineteenth-century American landscape painting and explores the

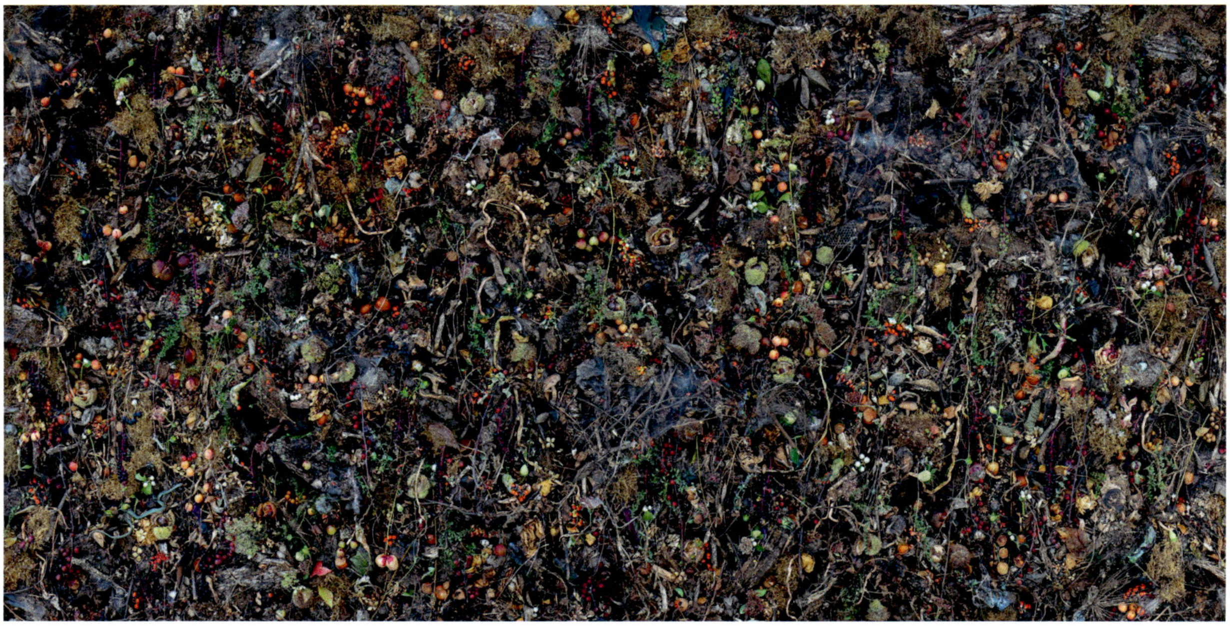

Fig. 3 Tanya Marcuse, *Woven № 9*, 2015, pigment print, 62 × 124 in., Courtesy the artist

processes that create, preserve, and share historical narratives. Plesset was galvanized by *American Paradise*, the seminal Hudson River School exhibition and publication organized by the Metropolitan Museum of Art in 1987, which included 84 works by 25 male artists and not a single work by a woman. In this iconic, canon-defining narrative of American art history, women artists are completely omitted and systematically erased. As an act of revision, Plesset inserts the work of women landscapists back into Hudson River School history by creating a new edition of the original *American Paradise* catalogue. The first of Plesset's "new editions" will feature the book open to the interior cover page with an illustration of a painting by Susie Barstow as the frontispiece (fig. 2).

Plesset's painting *A View of the Catskill Mountain House / Copied from a picture by S. Cole copied from a picture by T. Cole / 1848*, references the 1848 painting by Sarah Cole, a Hudson River School painter in the earliest years of the movement alongside her brother Thomas Cole (cat. 95). Plesset uses traditional painting techniques in a to-scale reproduction of Sarah Cole's depiction of the Catskill Mountain House, which itself is a copy of Thomas Cole's 1835 painting. Plesset's version of the scene, however, is a work in progress and intentionally unfinished, alluding to history as an ongoing narrative. Alongside this is a small painted trompe-l'oeil painting of results from a Google search of Sarah Cole's painting. Rendered in stunning accuracy, this smaller painting is, according to the artist, "the actual true copy."[23] Replicating other artists' artworks was common among nineteenth-century painters, sculptors, and printmakers, who used the process as a learning tool or as an earnest reproduction to honor a fellow artist. However, art historians are guilty of heightened criticality of copies made by women. Sarah Cole, for example, is often called a "copyist after Thomas Cole" instead of "artist of the Hudson River School." Plesset flips the table, and reclaims this act as valuable, stating, "By copying the works of these women and intentionally leaving my paintings in progress, I hope to make visible the act of historical recovery, and acknowledge it as never finished."[24] With both works, Plesset reminds us that history is a subjective construction and asks her viewer to envision more accurate histories of landscape art in the United States. What might fill an updated *American Paradise* publication if it paid heed to and showed interest in the work and perspectives of women?

Reimagining the single-point perspective and horizon line that has historically defined "landscape" in many Hudson River School canvases, **Tanya Marcuse** literally turns the view to the ground on which she stands, to the earth and all that it is made of. In her *Woven* series, Marcuse composes landscapes that are made of carefully arranged flora, fauna, and materials found and foraged along walks in and around her Hudson Valley home (fig. 3 and cat. 96). Once a composition is assembled, the artist photographs multiple exposures that are stitched together, creating a portrait of the natural elements that is also a document of time. The work, like the flora and fauna featured within and like land itself, is not fixed but in a constant state of evolution, decay, and change. The artist uses the remains and ruins of the elements from the previous work to create her next work, mimicking the cycles of decay and regeneration of the natural world. As in an ever-changing ecosystem, birth and death are inextricably linked, constant, and simultaneous in Marcuse's work.

Informed by the mythic Garden of Eden, botany, history, medieval tapestries, Hieronymus Bosch, Thomas Cole, and natural cycles, Marcuse's *Woven* works are at once intimate and epic. They call for close inspection, and offer deeply detailed encounters with vast, tangled, interconnected elements of life that are carefully described on their own. Together, they become an extreme horizontal plane, like a garden bed or forest floor, exploding with the dynamic and biodiverse matter of land and life itself. These landscapes speak to the relationship between the part and the whole, the macro and the micro, echoing the fact that we do not live in a landscape, but within a living ecosystem that is made of interdependent and interconnected life forces, all of which play a vital role. This is further expressed in the way that, unlike horizon-based landscapes, there is a democracy of description in Marcuse's works—everything is in equal focus. This too mimics the symbiotic relationships of living things within a biome; here, the birds and flowers are as important as the mountain. All elements within this work, as in land, are interwoven.

Reframing American Landscape

Who gets to define the American Landscape? What is "American Art"? What happens when we shift from "landscape" to "land"? These questions posed by artist **Teresita Fernández** in her essay "Artist as Arsonist: Burning Down The Myth of the American Landscape" reflect her ongoing work to rethink how we understand landscape in the United States. Drawing inspiration from the natural world, the artist poetically challenges conventional representations by acknowledging land not just as a physical geographic site, but also as a place where we live, a place that carries historic, cultural, social, and political stakes. She states:

> "I am trying to radically redefine and reframe how we think about place and about landscape. It is less about this framed vista in front of your eyes, and more about understanding what happened there, who lived there. The less visible aspect of the landscape that is residing right underneath the surface of what we look at and what we think we see when we describe a place."[25]

Fernández densely layers charred charcoal to create *Fire (United States of the Americas) 2* (cat. 89), a map of the continental United States that as she states "reinserts the shape of Mexico, newly configured and reimagined as so immense that its redemptive, ghostlike presence starts to dissolve into the cosmos, looming large over the United States."[26] Leaving space between each state, this work brings attention to the messy borders of this country, drawn not by nature but through relations of power, conquest, and ownership. It is intentional that the artist made the map using charcoal, pieces of land itself, burned trees, and scorched earth forged through fire. For the artist and in ecological systems, fire represents destruction but also creation. Fire here poetically signals the ongoing violence of climate crisis, as well as the colonial legacy of displacement, genocide, and enslavement. Yet fire also illuminates a generative history of sophisticated, deliberate slash-and-burn agricultural practices used by Indigenous people across the Americas for thousands of years to foster sustainable land relationships.

With this work and *Small American Fires 3,* (fig. 4), a series of twelve drawings made with colored ink and pencil, the artist brings to light how Indigenous land management practices across the hemisphere kept land sustainable and healthy in ways that were obliterated by colonization, even as the land was later romanticized as "beautiful landscapes" by nineteenth-century Hudson River School painters including Thomas Cole. While lamenting the destruction of landscape in the United States by commercial industrial exploitation and advocating for its protection, Cole longed for a "wilderness" that he incorrectly believed was untouched by human hands. He was naïve with regard to the ongoing generative interactions of Indigenous people with the land. Fernández

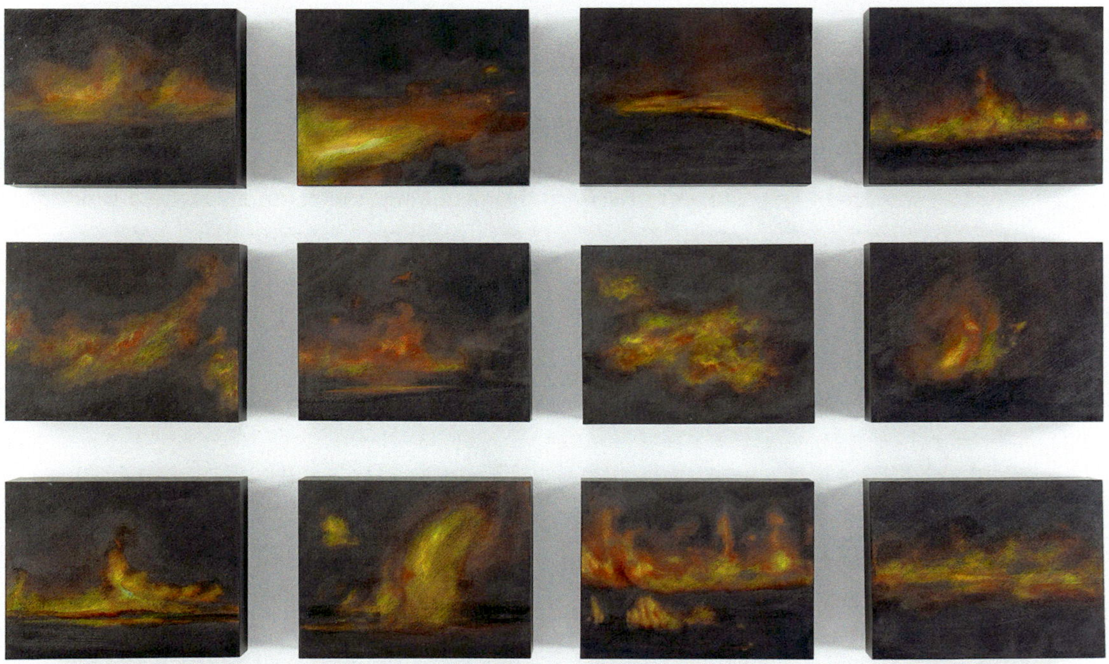

Fig. 4 Teresita Fernández, *Small American Fires 3*, 2016, colored ink and pencil on wood, 12 panels, each 6 × 8 × 2 in., 22 × 28 × 2 in. (overall), Courtesy the artist and Lehmann Maupin, New York, Hong Kong, and Seoul

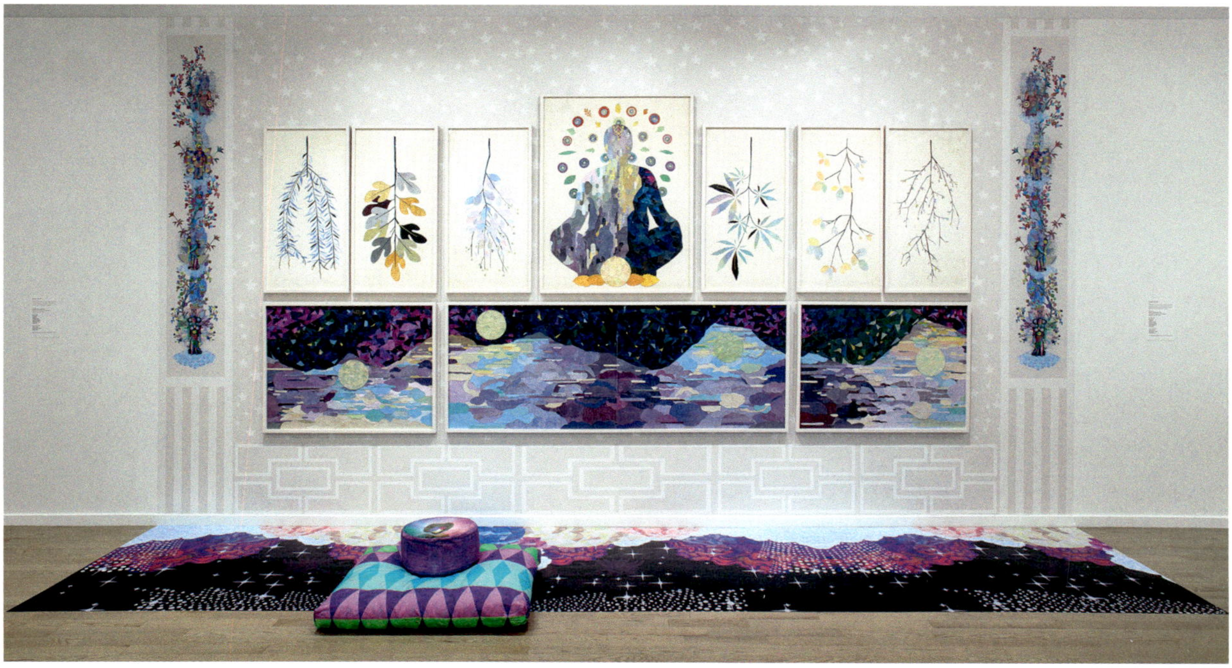

Fig. 5 Saya Woolfalk, *Birthing a New Sky*, 2021, installation view from *Saya Woolfalk: Field Notes from the Empathic Universe* (2021–22), digitally-designed vinyl and mixed-media collage: watercolor and gouache on hand-painted and stained rice paper, Bristol paper, and Japanese gold foil paper, with Nepalese Lhakpa paper chine-colléed onto Arches and Strathmore drawing paper, 120 × 218 ¾ × 2 ¾ in., Courtesy the artist and The Newark Museum of Art, Newark, NJ, Photograph: Richard Goodbody

challenges this, and states, "When there is only one narrative attached to what American Landscape is, there is simultaneously an erasure of another narrative."[27] Her work, in contrast to Cole's, adamantly rejects this myth of "untouched, virgin wilderness,"[28] still prevalent today, and makes visible the complex layers of land and human connection. The artist states:

> "My work aims to be both poetic and political; beautiful, but also very fierce and confrontational in terms of prompting viewers to imagine a country that could have a different kind of future based on understanding its past."[29]

One portal to imagine and build generative relationships with land can be found in the multimedia works of **Saya Woolfalk**, whose practice spans painting, collage, sculpture, video, and performance. Drawing upon African American, European American, and Japanese influences, the artist activates new cosmologies and hybrid worlds informed by science fiction, feminist theory, mythology, and ecology. In 2021, during a residency at the Newark Museum, Woolfalk created *Tumbling Into Landscape* (cat. 99), a new installation and intervention within the American Art galleries at the museum. Like a time-traveler, Woolfalk brings together past and present in this work that features six nineteenth-century Hudson River School paintings assembled around a central life-size self-portrait of the artist. The silhouetted body of the artist in the center is made of remixed fragments of the historic paintings that surround it. The figure is adorned by swirling medicinal plants found in the museum's herbaria

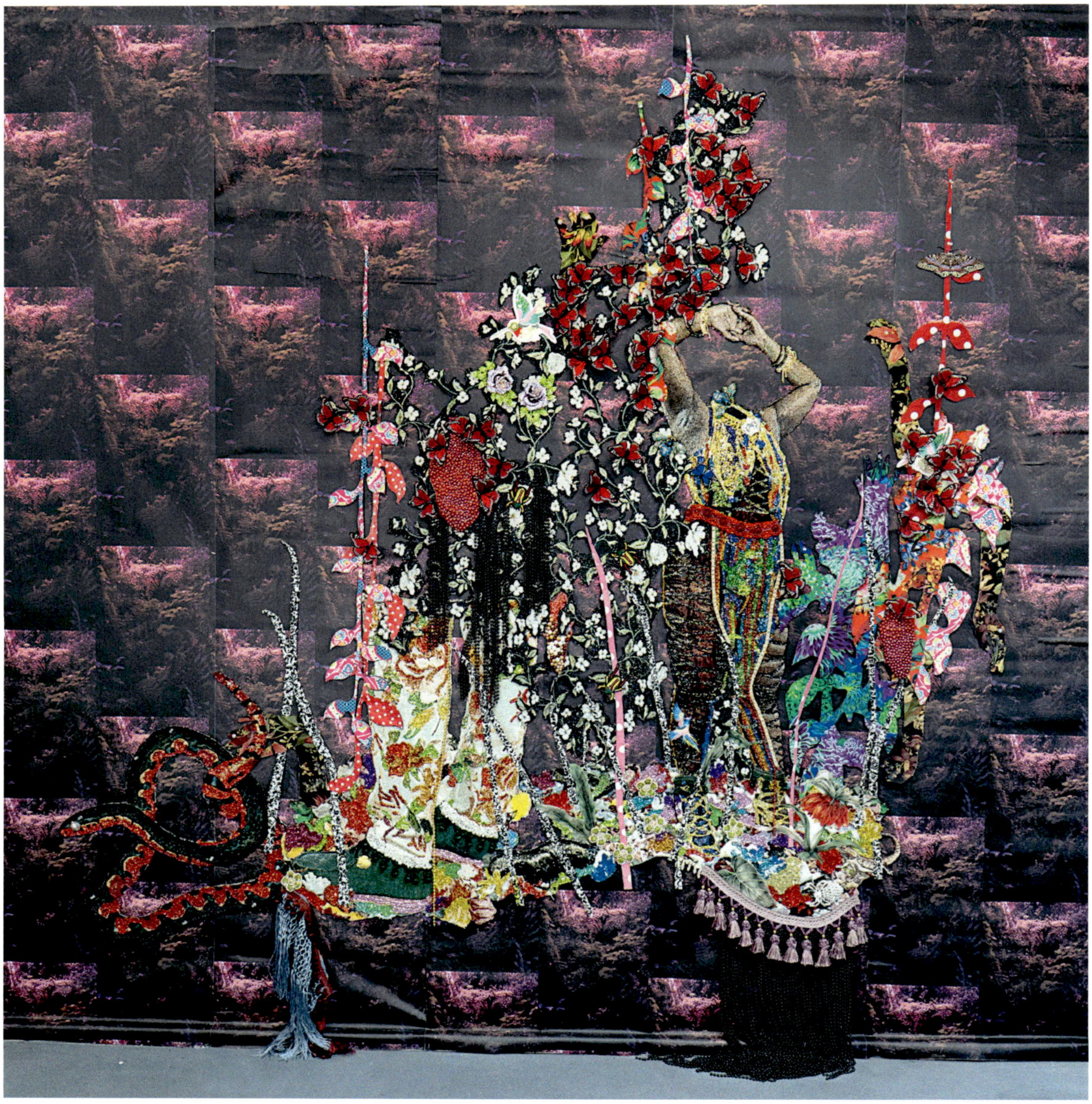

Fig. 6 Ebony G. Patterson, *...the wailing...ushers us home...and there is a bellying on the land...*, 2021, mixed media on jacquard woven photo tapestry and custom vinyl wallpaper, approximately 96 × 104 in., Courtesy the artist and Monique Meloche Gallery, Chicago, IL

collection. In the center of the body are words from abolitionist and women's rights activist Sojourner Truth, specifically a line from her famous 1851 speech: "Well if woman upset the world, do give her a chance to set it right side up again."[30] In her self-portrait, Woolfalk includes "Give her a chance to set it" near her throat and heart, and "right side up again" upside down, above the belly.

In this reframed landscape, Woolfalk co-exists with, embodies, and becomes the land, spinning a multi-layered narrative that exposes the historic paintings as constructions, while recentering the extraordinary capacity of nature and the people who are a part it. Seen in museums across the country, the Hudson River School landscapes are speculative fictional constructions that circulate as American creation myths that often leave out the people, like Sojourner Truth, and the history of rupture and violence that took place across the lands of what is now called the United States, a "democratic nation that was founded on liberty and slavery."[31] Woolfalk deconstructs and turns Hudson River School paintings inside out and upside down, disrupting how we read them and shaping them into her own physical form. In doing so, the artist challenges Thomas Cole's "We are still in Eden" myth, activating a deeper story about landscape and American history.[32]

Woolfalk is aware that each day, through storytelling, we are always making history as the world changes around us, and we keep transforming and evolving in response. *Tumbling Into Landscape* is meaningfully in conversation with Woolfalk's created multi-verse centered around the *Empathics*, as well as her fictional future race of "Woods Women" who can travel across time and space, and her "No Placeans" who share genetic material with plants. In works like *Birthing a New Sky* (fig. 5), Woolfalk's Goddess, adorned by healing plants including goldenrod, sassafras, meadowsweet, and wild strawberry, gives life to a new landscape and a world centered on connection, healing, and symbiotic relationships. In this landscape, things are turned upside down, opening a realm where sky becomes water and water, sky. The real space and the fantastical space come together as a space of possibility where "life expands, forcing its way out as new light, new land—a new sky."[33]

What does the land hold? Like Fernández Marcuse, and Woolfalk, Jamaican-born artist **Ebony G. Patterson** asks us to look below the surface, using the garden as a metaphor. Her ornate, multimedia works and textured tapestries are composed with glitter, jewelry, wallpaper, collaged images, and found objects. Their beguiling beauty draws the eye and mind into densely-layered landscapes. Patterson has explained, "In many ways, I think of the work as the flower and the audience as the bees. The bee is first attracted to the flower because of its color, but it's not until you start peeling back the layers that you understand what's happening with the nectar."[34] In Patterson's *when the land is in plumage...*, a peacock sculpted of jewels is looking back at its own tail, unfurled into a burst of color and ornament onto the wall behind it (cat. 101). Upon closer inspection, the bird is molting and behind this shedding of plumage, something darker begins to emerge—fragmented human body parts. In a manner that suggests death or defeat, human hands dangle downwards within the bedazzled tail, while other hands appear, palms up, underfoot. Patterson stated that when she made this work, she was "thinking about the idea that somehow the land holds secrets. That the land also holds the truth."[35] Patterson's peacock, "witnessing its own molting, its own collapsing, its own growing, its own oozing," reads like an allegory for the violent histories of human loss, control, death, and injustice that have occurred on American soil. Simultaneously it suggests the possibility of reparation and transformation.[36]

Patterson, like many of the artists in this project, is interested in the history of erasure as well as current climate and social injustices, including rampant wild fires, racial violence, and working class struggles. Patterson's work, titled *...the wailing...ushers us home...and there is a bellying on the land...* weaves together another intricate garden (fig. 6). Within paper cut-outs of flora, a swarm of three-dimensional butterflies, and a glittered snake, an extravagantly-dressed female figure stands tall. Patterson, who often adorns human figures in her work with beautiful clothing and jewelry, has noted: "I'm interested in the way we use dress, and its relationship to pageantry and beauty, particularly with working-class people—how that becomes an act of gardening, but gardening that's happening on the body."[37] Patterson connects beauty with class, land, and labor, noticing that "a number of working class spaces often have names that reference land, and that references the beauty and possibility of land, but somehow socially and socioeconomically, these spaces are the least attended to."[38] Indeed, in this work, the female figure stands without a head, signifying harm inflicted upon her. In the words of the artist, the layering of violence with beauty prompts us to ask: "What happens when these bodies that live in neglected gardens decide to use these tools of beauty, these tools of embellishment on their own bodies?"[39] For Patterson, layered ornamentation on her figures become a statement of presence, resilience, and protest for the working class that mirrors the labor required to care for a garden. Patterson's presentation of land as a garden serves as, in the artist's words, "a metaphor for death, burial, renewal, but also a space for love and care. The garden is a site of possibility, a chance to shift."[40]

Challenging Stereotypes

In addition to projecting myths, some traditional landscape depictions have also perpetuated stereotypes. Multimedia artist **Wendy Red Star**, a member of the Apsáalooke (Crow) tribe, uses humor, surrealism, primary source imagery, and a research-based practice to confront stereotypes of Indigenous peoples prevalent in historic settler-colonial landscapes. In her watershed work *Four Seasons*, Red Star breaks down inaccurate and harmful ideas about American landscape and depictions of the Indigenous peoples who inhabit it (fig. 7 and cat. 103). *Four Seasons* is a series of photographs that feature Red Star herself within a constructed, artificial landscape diorama that progresses through spring, summer, fall, and winter. The settings are made from Astroturf, inflatable and cardboard animals, plastic flowers, wrinkled fabric backdrops printed with landscape imagery à la *National Geographic*, and other kitsch props. The artist sits wearing authentic Crow regalia, an elk tooth dress, and maintains composure and seriousness. By poking "fun at the boundaries between conceived authenticity and stereotypical portrayals of Native American subjects," *Four Seasons* prompts questioning and criticality of stereotypes of Indigenous people and their connection to the land.[41] What is more, "the scenes lampoon Westernized notions of the 'noble savage' coexisting in harmony with nature, once again wryly thrusting the colonial gaze back on itself."[42] Red Star states: "The conqueror has set up an image of what Native people are...We've lost our individuality as different nations. We were stereotyped into one thing."[43] By letting dominant styles of landscape art and depictions go unquestioned and uncriticized, we reinforce certain false narratives, ones that leave out, stereotype, and mischaracterize Indigenous peoples. Red Star's work celebrates Crow culture and sends "the message that her community's landscape is best documented by someone from the inside."[44]

An enrolled Salish member of the Confederated Salish and Kootenai Nation, **Jaune Quick-to-See Smith** has been a practicing artist for over sixty years. Working across painting, printmaking, and mixed media, she creates narrative landscapes that pay homage to Indigenous history, culture, and activism while confronting settler-colonial violence committed against Native communities and the environment. Included in this project are maps made by Smith that bring a critical framework to question and overturn their power as "objective" descriptions of land. In *Unhinged (Map)*, Smith rotates the map of the United States on its head, surrounding the landmass in energetic swirls of line and color, with Canada at the bottom and Mexico at the top (fig. 11). This reoriented perspective takes away the objectivity, universality, and accuracy associated with the American map

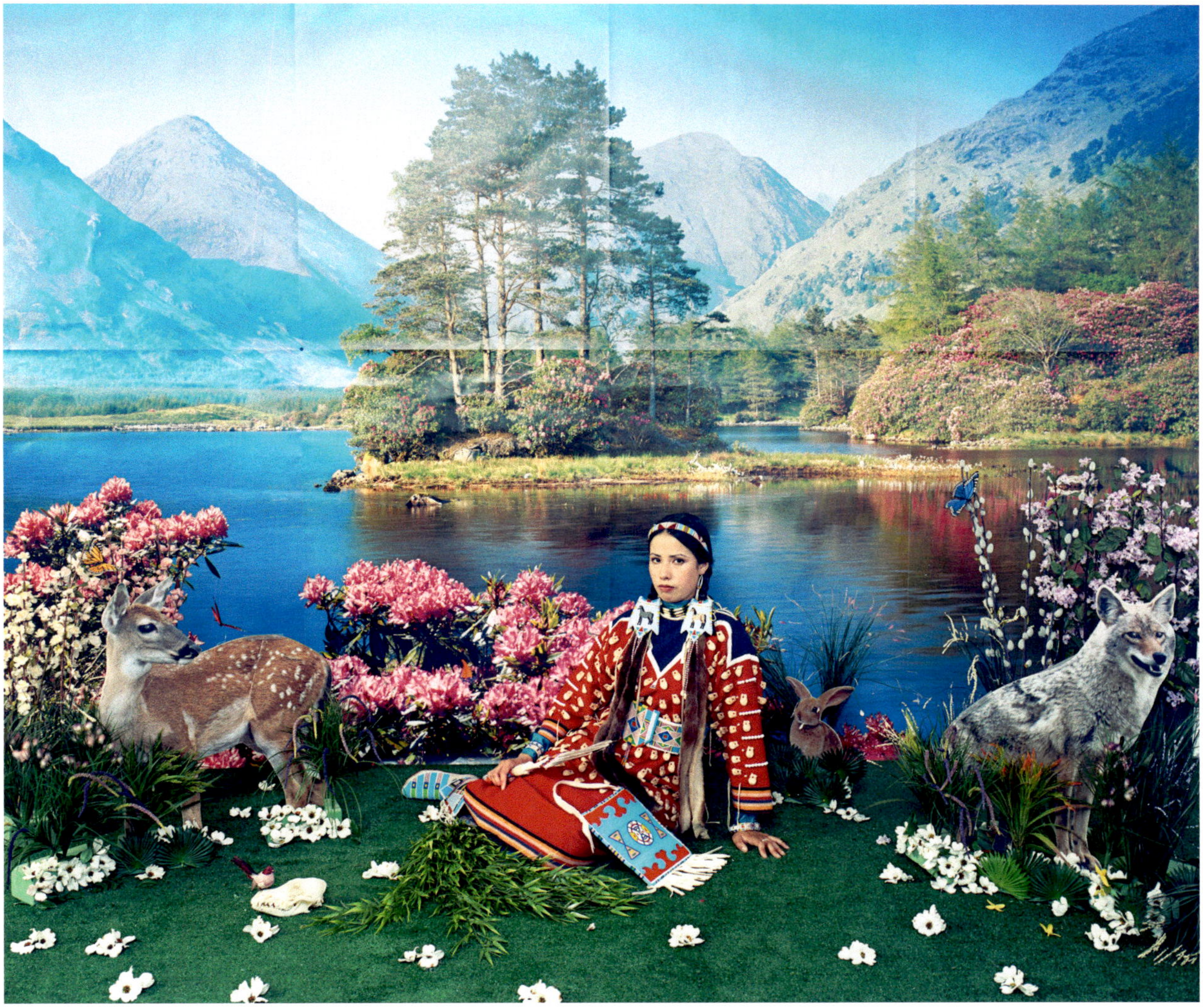

Fig. 7 Wendy Red Star, *Spring*, from the *Four Seasons* series, 2006, archival pigment print on Sunset Fiber rag, 21 × 24 in., Art Museum of West Virginia University, Morgantown, WV, Courtesy the artist and Sargent's Daughters, New York, NY

form that we are accustomed to seeing. Through the simple rotation, which also calls attention to Christopher Columbus's navigational errors in sailing to India that resulted in his landing in the Caribbean, Smith notes that the map becomes a "thing of Indian power."[45] These works remind us that maps have been used as tools to assert power and to justify stolen land and territorial expansion on Turtle Island, the Indigenous name for the land now called the United States.

In a group of smaller map works made of colored beads, the artist includes terms and symbols emblazoned across the United States map (figs. 12–15), including "SHE / HER / HERS," "AMERIKA," "STOLEN," and "$." Through these terms, Smith sparks conversation and connection amongst land, maps, ecofeminism, womanhood, racism, Indigenous land, the commodification of land, and the prioritization of money over ecosystem health. In *Smoke Signals Map*, Smith also

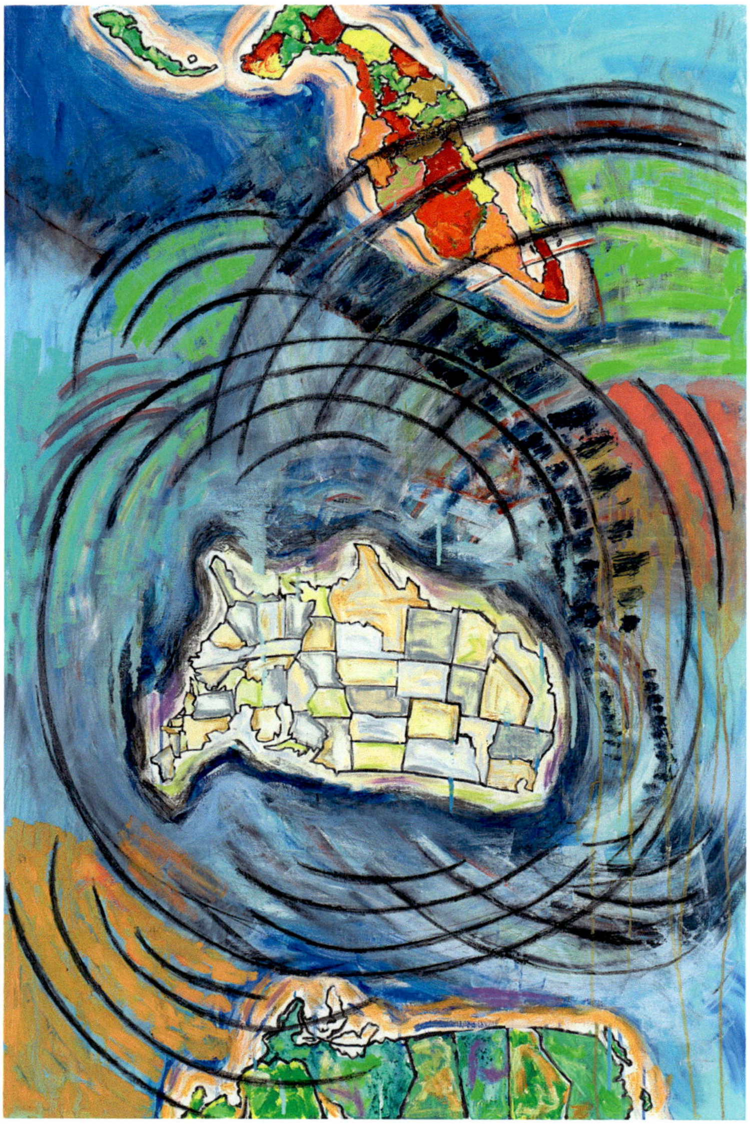

Fig. 11 Jaune Quick-to-See Smith, *Unhinged (Map)*, 2018, mixed media on canvas, 60 × 40 in., Courtesy the artist and Garth Greenan Gallery, New York, NY

pastes appropriated text and images atop a colorfully painted, rotated map of the United States (cat. 105). The center text, "Climate Change is Giving Smoke Signals," is accompanied by a quote from feminist poet Alice Walker and images of ancient fertility symbols. Thus, Smith reclaims the idea of Mother Earth and connects the destruction of land with violence against women.[46] The use of beads and terms such as "Smoke Signals" reinserts Indigenous history and culture into the land that the maps describe.

Land, Climate, and Connection Now

> "Nature and landscape...are not just where we picnic but also where we live and die. It is where our food, water, fuel, and minerals come from, where our nuclear waste and shit and garbage go to, it is the territory of dreams, somebody's homeland and somebody's gold mine."—Rebecca Solnit[47]

Artists in this project have critically reimagined how we consider the history of landscape art,

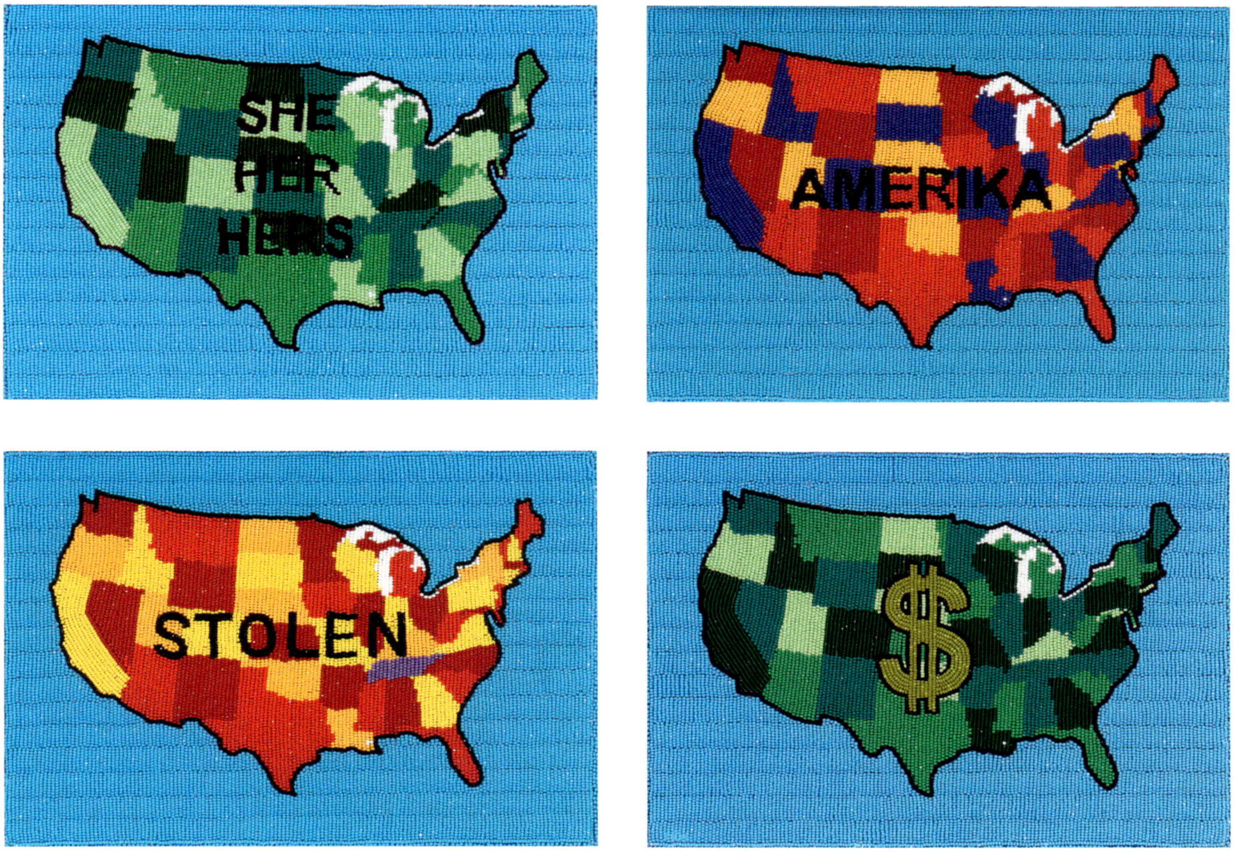

Fig. 12–15 Jaune Quick-to-See Smith, from top left to bottom right: *She, Her, Hers Map* / *Amerika Map* / *Stolen Map* / *$ Map*, 2021, beads, 8¼ × 12 in. each, Courtesy the artist and Garth Greenan Gallery, New York, NY

asked us to look below the surface, and challenged territorial borders. Additionally, they engage land in a moment when climate and social justice are critically and inextricably linked. In a career spanning over sixty years, **Kay WalkingStick**, a citizen of the Cherokee Nation of Oklahoma, has worked across abstraction and representation, painting American landscapes with reverence and knowledge of the physical, spiritual, political, and cultural dimensions of land. The artist celebrates Earth in her recent paintings, which feature epic landscapes like those made in the nineteenth century by artists now associated with the Hudson River School. WalkingStick has noted, "our beautiful planet deserves to be described beautifully."[48] But in contrast to and deeply expanding on some nineteenth-century interpretations, WalkingStick overlays onto her painted landscapes patterns created by the Indigenous people who have inhabited the land or who live there now.

The artist spends time drawing and photographing each place represented in her work before returning to her studio to paint and to conduct research on the Indigenous people connected to each location. Selecting designs from their baskets, beadwork, and pottery, WalkingStick stencils and paints each chosen pattern onto the painted land. *Wampanoag Coast, Variation II* (fig. 16), for instance, is a landscape that pictures the Northeastern coast with an overlay of a pattern designed by the

Wampanoag tribe who live there. *Winter Passage* (cat. 107), painted across two joined wooden panels, features a view of the Sierra Nevadas near Mono Lake, Mono County, California with a basket design created by the Mono Lake Paiute people, who live there and who are well known for their basketry.

Drawing upon craft and expressive verve, WalkingStick's landscapes embody an experience of land that is literally and conceptually layered; it is at once geological, cultural, spiritual, personal, and peopled. Through the bands of patterning that float on top and hover between the viewer and the land, the artist effectively disrupts and shifts how one has been trained to see landscape. Here one cannot see the land without also seeing the culture and people who live within it. The artist expands, "The fact is that we're living on Indian land. There are Indian people everywhere in this country, all over the country...This beautiful land is Indian land."[49] With this work, WalkingStick activates space for joy and reverence. In combining specific Native American designs with specific places, the artist reclaims and asserts the sovereignty of Native land, offers a band of protection, and makes visible the presence of the people who belong to the particular place. This is not a land to conquer or exploit, but a place of beauty to honor, protect, and sustain; as the artist notes, "I want people to remember what we have."[50]

Artist, poet, and activist, **Cecilia Vicuña** created her "documentary poem" *Kon Kon* on the beaches of Concón, which Vicuña describes as "one of the most sacred places in Chile, at the foot of the Aconcagua mountain, a place where people have been doing art for ten thousand years."[51] Concón's nature preserves were chosen as the site of the Aconcagua oil refinery, built in the 1970s. Constructed atop an ancient burial ground, the refinery altered the landscape and ravaged the ecosystem of this culturally and spiritually important place. *Kon Kon,* the film, which the artist notes was made in collaboration with the ocean, addresses the artist's

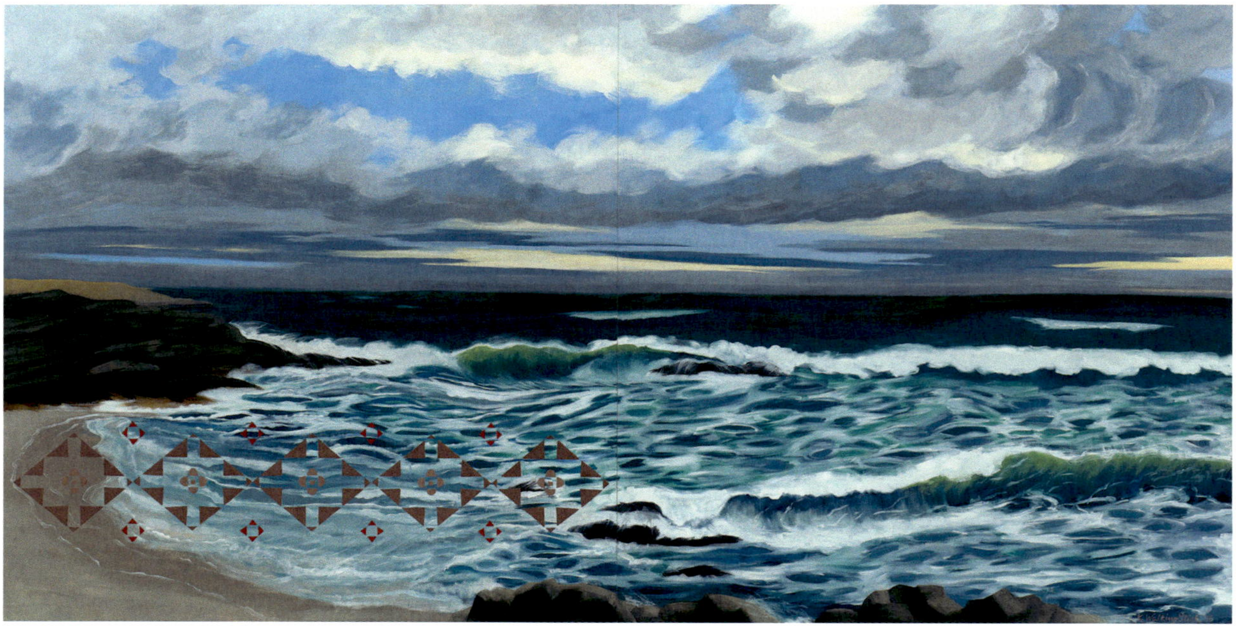

Fig. 16 Kay WalkingStick, *Wampanoag Coast, Variation II*, 2018, oil on panel in two parts, 40 × 80 × 2 in., Courtesy the artist and Hales Gallery, London and New York, NY

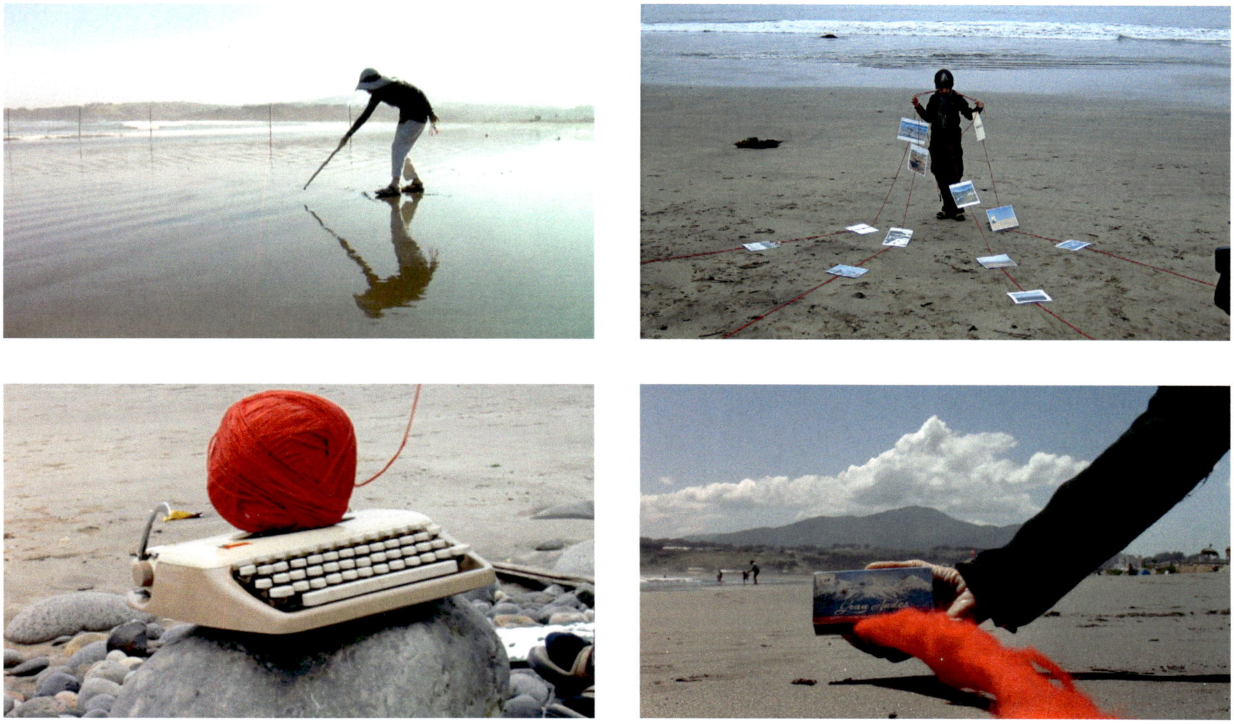

Fig. 17 Cecilia Vicuña, *Kon Kon,* 2010, film stills, color, sound, HD video, Spanish with English subtitles, 53:55 min., Courtesy the artist, Lehmann Maupin, and Electronic Arts Intermix, New York, NY

deep connection to this place as well as the ecological and cultural losses and disappearances that are tied to overfishing, pollution, corporate development, economic greed, and political corruption.

In the 54-minute film, Vicuña traverses the beaches, dunes, hills, and rocks of Concón, drawing, singing, and placing found objects and debris into the sand and attaching images of landscapes lost to the oil refinery to a *quipu* (the ancient Inca process of record-keeping using knotted string) (fig. 17 and cat. 109). The artist explains this process in an interview:

> "I was still a teenager, and I was on the beach in Chile. And suddenly, I felt the wind was alive, and it was sort of caressing me, moving around my body like a snake. I turned around, and I could see I was being sensed as much as I was sensing the world around me. And so, in awe, it was like I melted. And I bent down and I picked up one of these *precios*, a piece of debris right there on the beach. I touched it, I brought it up, and I planted it in the sand. And that was the beginning of my precarious art. So what is it for me? It is the acknowledgment of the precariousness of life, the precariousness of the beauty of being. It is an act of acknowledgment of that fact that we will die. That we are dying as we live. For someone like me, the words nature and environment separate us from who we truly are. We are nature. We are the environment. Especially us as a group, as a human group. We are not individuals. We are simultaneously an individual, different from everyone else, and at the same time, we are one."[52]

Working with reverence and in communion with the sea, the wind, and earth in *Kon Kon*, Vicuña weaves together deeply spiritual interconnections between land and life. Through her work, words, and enactment of rituals, she brings to life an offering of energy and healing. The artist's practice illustrates how land is a living force, alive and holding memory and culture, as well as the source of all life and death. *Kon Kon* serves as an ode to Concón amidst its destruction and a reminder that if we are one with each other and one with the land, the destruction of nature is violence committed against all of us.

New York City and Hudson Valley-based artist **Jean Shin** collects discarded objects and materials to create sculptures and artworks that encourage thoughtful reflection on consumption and human impact within ecosystems. Shin's materials are often ubiquitous parts of our consumerist, capitalist culture and our personal, everyday lives within them—cast-off electronics, cell phones, clothing, plastic bottles, lottery tickets, umbrellas, and more. Shin's work addresses landscape in an expanded field of the Anthropocene that acknowledges the impact of global economies and industry in a moment of climate crisis across the land.

Freshwater, Shin's 2022 installation at Philadelphia Contemporary, is a looped water system that runs through glass orbs, the homes of live mussels born at a nearby mussel conservatory (fig. 18 and cat. 111). Pumped in from and returned to the Delaware river, the water that flows through this system is filtered by the ecologically-valuable but endangered mussels, magnified for view by the orbs when the water is clear. The pool below is made up of pearl buttons, made from shellfish and leftover from overproduction during a nineteenth-century fashion craze. Shin sees this excess as an ecological "tragedy"—mussels were "extracted from all over the world and made into incredible, beautiful buttons that were never used...I feel like this extinction was for absolutely no reason, just that we thought we wanted them."[53] It is undeniable that our landscapes today are rife with tragedies just like the one Shin highlights in *Freshwater*. Many scientists refer to our Anthropocene era as the "Sixth Extinction," since species and organisms are dying at a rate thousands of times greater than considered normal. Shin's work asks its viewer to see human action as deeply connected to the health of our land, landscapes, and ecosystems. Through unchecked consumerism and industrial production, our way of life

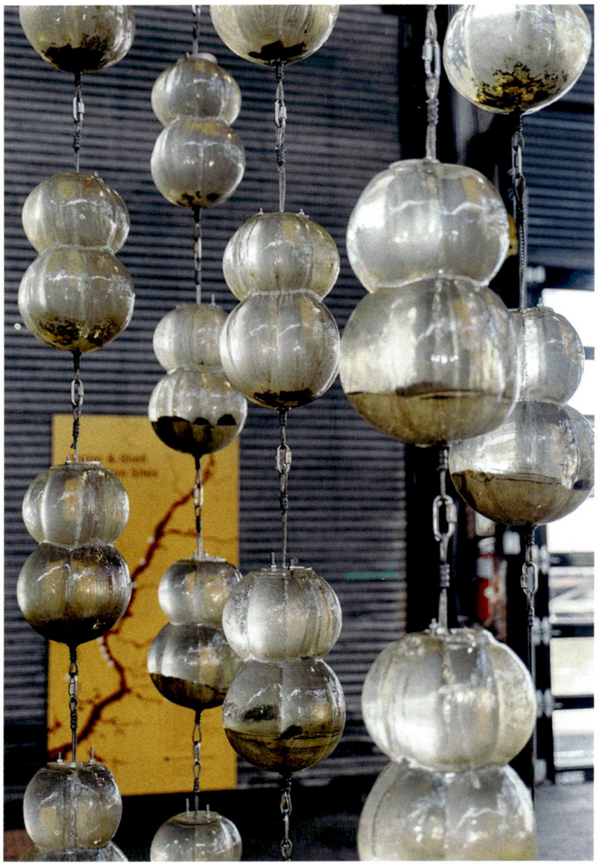

Fig. 18 Jean Shin, *Freshwater* (detail), 2022, Freshwater mussels, glass vessels, sand, water pumped from the Delaware River, vintage mother-of-pearl shell buttons, metal basins, Perspex mirror and cables, various dimensions, Installation at Cherry Street Pier, Philadelphia, PA, Commissioned by Philadelphia Contemporary, Courtesy the artist and Philadelphia Contemporary, Photograph: David McDowell

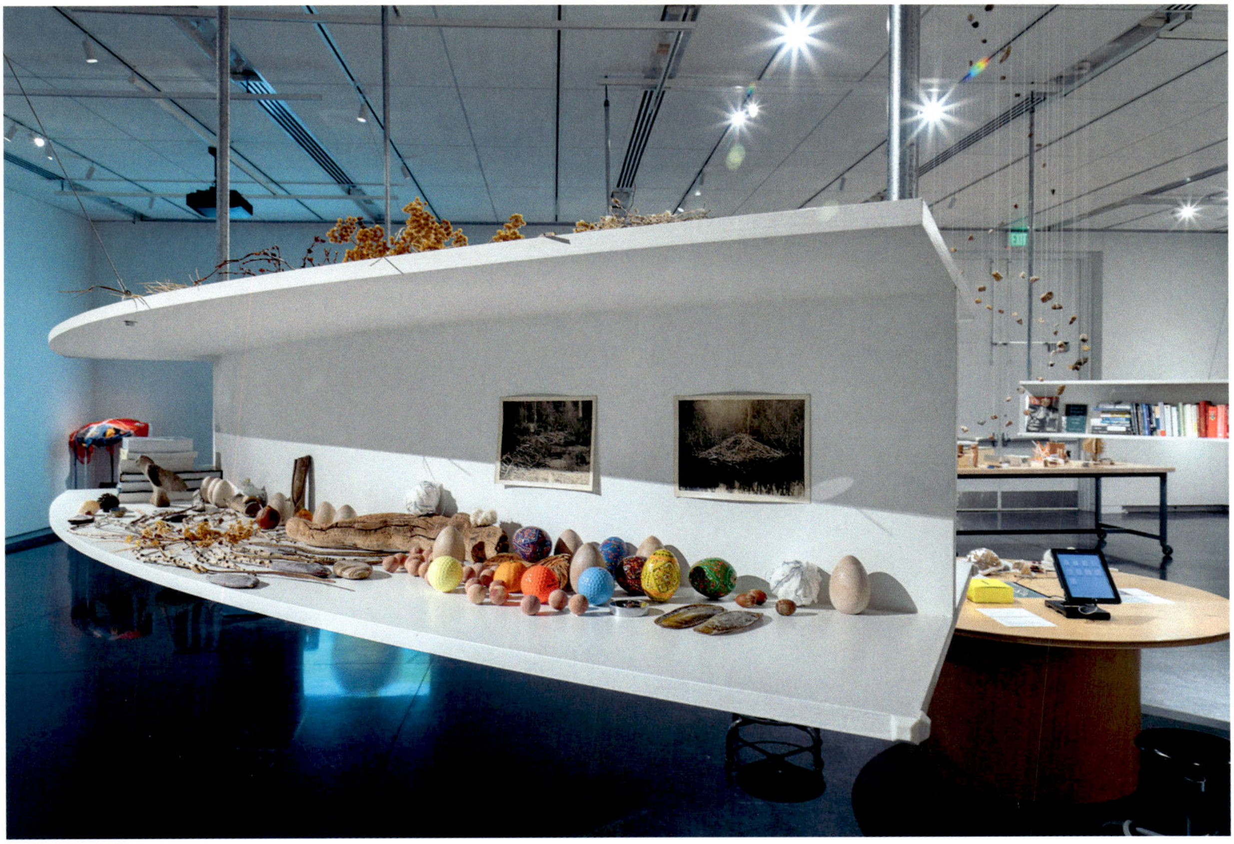

Fig. 19 Mary Mattingly, *Ecotopian Library*, 2020–ongoing, rotating collection of books, natural and cultural objects that have been donated to share, various dimensions, www.ecotopianlibrary.com, Courtesy the artist and Robert Mann Gallery, New York, NY, Photograph: Jeff Wells

becomes "incredibly inequitable for the planet and for others who don't get to choose how they live."[54]

Shin's practice reminds us that a greener, healthier landscape requires intentional labor. On the occasion of this exhibition, the artist is creating *Displaced*, a "time capsule" on the grounds at the Thomas Cole Site. The capsule will consist of a previously-used art shipping crate, filled with displaced earth as well as waste and scraps from the artist's past projects. This installation makes visible the way our earth and soil have become forever polluted by microplastics and human waste. For the artist, this work "brings a self-critical lens to the struggle to maintain a zero-waste art practice." Furthermore, it encourages critical self-reflection on the environmental impact of the art and museum world, largely characterized by traveling exhibitions that require cross-country shipping and robust wooden art crates, which are often destroyed and disposed of afterwards. This new project, and Shin's body of work as a whole, uses excessive and defunct materials from our consumerist society to create systems and connections that bring acute attention to the labor required, on a personal and systemic level, to achieve sustainability and ecologically-healthy landscapes.

Mary Mattingly is an interdisciplinary artist who engages land and landscape, not through pictorial or symbolic representation, but through the creation of community spaces and environments that imagine and encourage new futures based in reciprocity. Recognizing that we live in a complex living ecological system, the artist works like an activist, responding to the current and future climate crisis. She cultivates a practice that rises to the urgency of this moment, noting, "Art for me is about new possibilities, it's about life and survival. Art is urgent, and its thoughtful. I believe I have a duty to imagine food as a public service, to reinforce water as a human right, and work with people to cocreate common spaces."[55] Mattingly's work often takes the form of an offering, one that may provide sustenance or one that provides space for community engagement and environmental education. In *Swale*, the artist created a floating edible landscape to provide free food to the people of the South Bronx, one of the biggest food deserts in the United States (cat. 113). Planting a garden on a barge, and using recycled water from the vessel's hull to water the garden, *Swale* helps us envision a society where land and its gifts are not commodified under capitalism, but food, shelter, and water are accessed and shared freely in community. The artist reflects: "There is sadly something that is utopian about this. And it's utopian because we are in a time where it feels like it's such a stretch to consider food a right, or a service, or public."[56]

Additionally, Mattingly has created several community spaces across the country that she calls *Ecotopian Libraries.* With the goal of sparking meaningful and lasting social changes, these libraries bring together writing, ideas, and installations on the topics of forestry, botany, ecology, art, literature, and the sciences that allow community members of all backgrounds to share knowledge and together brainstorm generative ways forward through climate change (fig. 19).[57] For *Women Reframe American Landscape*, the artist is creating an *Ecotopian Library* that draws upon the land at the Thomas Cole Site, as well as artists Thomas Cole and Emily Cole, who also directly engaged with nature, environmental preservation, and local flora and fauna. Mattingly has stated, "I think we are in this really unique time right now where it's like kind of before the storm. We are probably doomed as humans if we do not start thinking in a posthumanist way. If we don't start taking everything into account, our surroundings or environment, we are doomed to fail as a human race because we won't be able to live on this earth."[58] Mattingly's work asks us, if we are indeed to envision a future where land is valued for its ability to sustain us and our communities, instead of exploited for its capitalistic value, what actions must follow?

On the history of landscape, Rebecca Solnit writes: "...much of the landscape tradition comes out of the classical pastoral mode which celebrates purity of the rural in contrast to the corruption of the urban...and does so in a mood of deep nostalgia and longing. For the ideal world of the pastoral is always in the past and has its parallels in Eden, the lost Golden Age, the landscape yet undiscovered."[59] In contrast to the imaginary pristine and idealized landscapes often found in historic paintings, artist **Marie Lorenz** creates interactive work that engages and embraces the urban, industrial landscape in and around her New York studio. Through projects like *Tide and Current Taxi*, Lorenz does not attempt to picture the landscape, but rather reclaims it—with all its wonder and destruction, life and toxicity—as an everyday space for observation, work, play, and movement (fig. 20). Beginning in 2005, the artist began welcoming people onto her rowboat and out into the waterways of New York. Passengers can choose a departure point and destination, and Lorenz uses a chart of the tides and currents to plan the voyage. This participatory, socially-engaged practice is dependent on reading the natural cycles of the land and water, and brings people directly into unconventional parts of the New York City landscape. The voyage allows them to see the landscape of the city from a new orientation, and places them in close contact with plants, birds, industrial urban

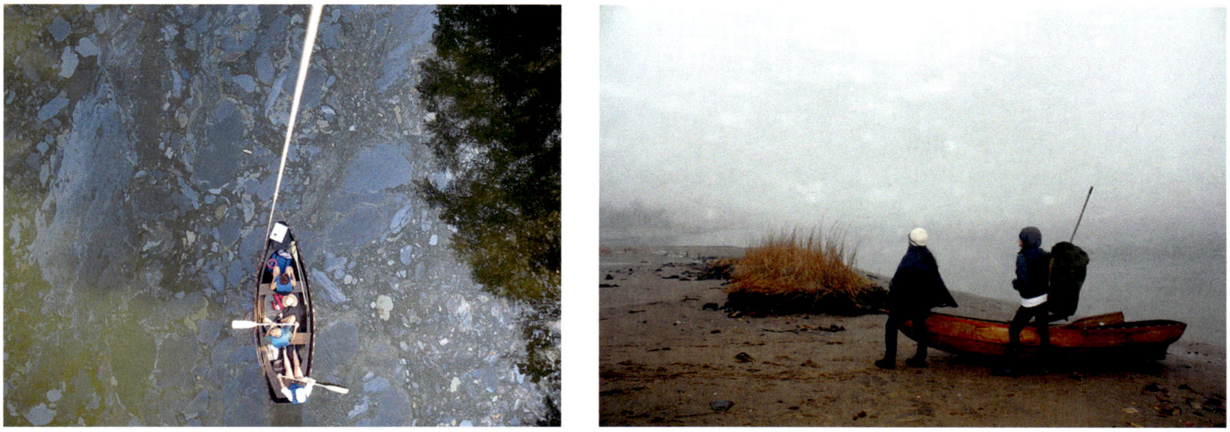

Fig. 20 Marie Lorenz, Views of *Tide* and *Current Taxi*, 2012–2013, Photographs: Nicholas Weist and Marie Lorenz

formations, and islands. Travelling along the creeks, bays, rivers, canals, and harbors, *Tide and Current Taxi* brings people not into the aesthetic space of landscape, but rather the places where the intersections and collaborations between nature and urban development are evident and remarkable.

In her sculpted works too, Lorenz combines and conflates natural elements with synthetic debris found on and within the land. These hybrid works of discarded and forgotten objects and the opportunity to experience land afforded through Lorenz's practice reflect the real elements of our landscapes today—places full of plastics and toxins, as well as minerals, life, and dirt. This is not the wild, untouched, Arcadian state, but a real, viable, messy and active space in which we live, where the synthetic and natural coexist in the urban industrial landscape. For Lorenz, despite the transformation of time and pollution, the land continues to be a space of possibility. Most recently, the artist has been experimenting with sound and theater, including works that bring full operatic performances into the waterways, and her sounds boats, like *Wave Chime*, which she launched on Catskill Creek (cat. 115), Thomas Cole's favorite spot to walk and paint. In these experiential works, passengers are transported physically into the space of land and wonder, engaging our senses through sounds, sight, touch, and smell, centering and grounding the human body into the landscape. In *Wave Chime* Lorenz references the mythology of the Underworld and River Styx, suggesting our own mortality and connection with a land that is dynamic, marred, and ever-evolving.

Conclusion

Land is the material of our home and the sustainer of life, and landscape art reflects our myriad, diverse understandings of this at-once complex, elemental, beautiful, and formidable place. Multifaceted and different perspectives on land, the ecosystems we inhabit, and our connection to place strengthen us as a human community as we aim to forge healthier, more reciprocal relationships within and across natural environments, especially in a moment of climate change and catastrophe. This brings to mind the work of author and scientist Robin Wall Kimmerer, who acknowledges that while many are aware of the negative impacts of humans on the environment, what about the possibility of positive interactions? In her book *Braiding Sweetgrass*, Kimmerer writes: "Wild meadow sweetgrass grows long and fragrant when it is looked after by humans. Weeding and care for the habitat and neighboring plants strengthens its growth...The problem is not humans, but the relationship between humans and the environment. While some people have mined, consumed, drained natural resources, others have interacted with the land in sustainable, and generative ways."[60] Through this project, we aim to recenter the important critical and generative perspectives of women artists who reframe land, in all of its complexity and possibility. As the featured artists have made clear, landscape cannot be understood through a single perspective, lens, or medium. Landscape can only be understood in relation to land, in our current moment, and as something that is not "other" or outside of us, but something we are interdependent upon and a part of. We are all made of the same elements as stars, connected always to the earth, sky, and water. Just as land is always shifting, evolving, changing, so too is the writing of our histories and the urgency of our moment. Our critical, cultural, political, and ecological work is dynamic, interconnected, and ongoing. In this study of landscape that collides with feminist efforts, we echo the motto of the Guerrilla Girls: "Do one thing. If it works, do another. If it doesn't, do another anyway. Keep chipping away!"[61]

1 Rebecca Solnit, *As Eve Said to the Serpent: On Landscape Gender and Art*, 2001, (Athens, GA: University of Georgia Press), p. 56.

2 Kate Morris, *Shifting Grounds: Landscape in Native American Art* (Seattle: University of Washington Press, 2019), p. 27.

3 Simon Schama, *Landscape and Memory* (New York: Vintage Random House, 1996), p. 7.

4 Schama (see note 3), p. 13.

5 Morris (see note 2), p. 5.

6 Steven Adams and Anna Gruetzner Robins, *Gendering Landscape Art* (New Brunswick, NJ: Rutgers University Press, 2001), p. 5.

7 Solnit, (see note 1), p. 47.

8 Schama (see note 4), p. 12.

9 Kevin Avery, "The Hudson River School," Heilbrun Timeline of Art History, metmuseum.org/toah/hd/hurs/hd_hurs.htm, October 2004. For more, See Monk, Janice, "Approaches to the Study of Women and Landscape," *Environmental Review* (1984): pp. 23–33.

10 Martin A. Berger, *A Sight Unseen: Whiteness and Visual Culture*, (University of California Press, 2005), p. 57.

11 Adams and Gruetzner (see note 6), p. 2.

12 Ibid., p. 4.

13 Monk (see note 9), p. 26.

14 We are indebted to many scholars and researchers, including Dr. Nancy Siegel, who have conducted this critical research.

15 Research conducted in 2022 by Sofia D'Amico, 2022–2023 Cole Fellow.

16 Chad M. Topaz, et al., "Diversity of artists in major U.S. museums," *Plos One* 14, no. 3 (2019): https://doi.org/10.1371/journal.pone.0212852.

17 Linda Nochlin, *Why Have There Been No Great Women Artists*, 50th Anniversary Edition, (London: Thames and Hudson, 2020), p. 42.

18 See Nancy Siegel and Jennifer C Krieger, *Remember the Ladies: Women of the Hudson River School,* (Catskill, NY: Thomas Cole National Historic Site, 2010).

19 Siegel (see note 18).

20 Our research and thinking across this project are indebted to and drawn from the important work of each the featured artists, as well as Nancy Siegel and the work and writings of Steven Adams, Josephine Curbia, Lorraine Dowler, Teresita Fernández, Candice Hopkins, Robin Wall Kimmerer, Lucy Lippard, Caroline Merchant, Janice Monk, Kate Morris, Catherine Nash, Linda Nochlin, Sherri Ortner, Jolene Rickard, Anna Gruetzner Robins, Gillian Rose, Simon Schama, Rebecca Solnit, Bonj Szczygiel, and Alan Wallach.

21 Nochlin (see note 17), p. 100.

22 Ibid., pp. 102–104.

23 Anna Plesset, "Conversation with Lisa Panzera for *ID: Formations of the Self*," https://www.annaplesset.com/portfolio/american-paradise [accessed on 28 Oct.,2022].

24 Plesset (see note 23).

25 Teresita Fernández, "Teresita Fernández's Stacked Landscapes," *National Gallery of Art*, June 18, 2022, https://www.youtube.com/watch?v=ClbI7M6XGGI [accessed on 28 Oct., 2022].

26 Teresita Fernández, "The Year 2019, as Seen by Five Artists," *The New York Times,* December 3, 2019, https://www.nytimes.com/2019/12/03/opinion/the-year-2019-as-seen-by-five-artists.html [accessed on 28 Oct.,2022].

27 Fernández (see note 25).

28 Conversation with Teresita Fernández, November 15, 2022.

29 Teresita Fernández, Video, *Philadelphia Museum of Art,* https://philamuseum.org/calendar/exhibition/teresita-fernandez-fire-united-states-americas [accessed 10.28.2022].

30 Sojourner Truth, "Ain't I A Woman?," Speech delivered in 1851 at the Women's Rights Convention in Akron, Ohio, *Women's Rights National Historical Park, National Park Service*, https://www.nps.gov/wori/learn/historyculture/sojourner-truth.htm [accessed 28 Oct.,2022].

31 Berger (see note 10), p. 72.

32 Thomas Cole, "Essay on American Scenery," *American Monthly Magazine* 1 (January 1836).

33 Saya Woolfalk, "From the Archives of Earth, The Woods Woman Mythology, Creation Myth, no. 2754, the Use of North American Medicinal Plants," in *Saya Woolfalk: Field Notes From The Empathic Universe*, ed. Tricia Laughlin Bloom, (Newark Museum of Art, 2021).

34 Grace Ebert, "Elaborately Layered Gardens by Ebony G. Patterson Hide Haunting Messages Within Dazzling Displays," *Colossal*, March 10, 2022, https://www.thisiscolossal.com/2022/03/ebony-g-patterson-gardens/ [accessed on 28 Oct.,2022].

35 Ebony G. Patterson, "when the land is in plumage...a peacock is in molting...," Contemporary Art Museum St. Louis, September 7, 2020, https://soundcloud.com/user-469652853/3-ebony-g-patterson-pt-2?in=user-469652853/sets/ebony-g-patterson-when-the-cuts-eruptthe-garden-ringsand-the-warning-is-a-wailing [accessed on 28 Oct.,2022].

36 Patterson (see note 35).

37 Ebony G. Patterson, in Victoria Stapley-Brown, "Ebony G. Patterson: new garden-inspired installations reveal an original thinker in full bloom," *The Art Newspaper*, December 7, 2018, https://www.theartnewspaper.com/2018/12/08/ebony-g-patterson-new-garden-inspired-installations-reveal-an-original-thinker-in-full-bloom [accessed on 28 Oct.,2022].

38 Ebony G. Patterson, " ....when the cuts erupt...the garden rings...and the warning is a wailing...," Contemporary Art Museum St. Louis, September 9, 2020, https://soundcloud.com/user-469652853/sets/ebony-g-patterson-when-the-cuts-eruptthe-garden-ringsand-the-warning-is-a-wailing [accessed on 28 Oct.,2022].

39 Patterson (see note 38).

40 Ibid.

41 Nadiah Rivera Fellah, "Wendy Red Star: A Scratch on the Earth," in exh. cat., ed. Nadiah Rivera Fellah and Tricia Laughlin Bloom (Newark Museum of Art, 2019), https://www.wendyredstar.com/four-seasons [accessed on 28 Oct.,2022].

42 Tiffany Midge, "Wendy Red Star's Indigenous Gaze," *The New York Times*, July 18, 2022, https://www.newyorker.com/culture/photo-booth/wendy-red-stars-indigenous-gaze [accessed on 28 Oct.,2022].

43 Wendy Red Star, in Abaki Beck, "Decolonizing Photography: A Conversation With Wendy Red Star," *Aperture*, December 14, 2016, https://aperture.org/editorial/wendy-red-star/ [accessed on 28 Oct.,2022].

44 Lauren Moya Ford, "Wendy Red Star's Empowered Vision of Crow History," *Hyperallergic,* April 21, 2022, https://hyperallergic.com/717699/wendy-red-star-empowered-vision-of-crow-history/ [accessed on 28 Oct.,2022].

45 "Jaune Quick-to-See Smith: Woman in Landscape," *Garth Greenan Gallery,* https://garthgreenan.com/exhibitions/jaune-quick-to-see-smith-woman-in-landscape/press-release [accessed on 28 Oct.,2022].

46 Ibid.

47 Solnit, (see note 1) p. 11.

48 Conversation with the artist, October 3, 2022.

49 Ibid.

50 Ibid.

51 Tatiana Flores, "In Conversation with Cecilia Vicuna," *Water Writing: Anthological Exhibit 1966–2009* (2009-–10) Virtual Catalog, https://www.academia.edu/8354713/In_Conversation_with_Cecilia_Vicu%C3%B1a_for_Water_Writing_An_Anthological_Exhibition, pp. 21–42 [accessed on 28 Oct.,2022].

52 Cecilia Vicuña, "Meet the artists: Cecilia Vicuña," video for Art Basel, posted on June 3, 2022,, https://www.youtube.com/watch?v=gAqzigyfFtA [accessed on 28 Oct.,2022].

53 Isabella Segalovich, "Jean Shin Wants to Change the Tide of Pollution and Extinction," *Hyperallergic,* September 18. 2022, https://hyperallergic.com/759052/jean-shin-philadelphia-contemporary/ [accessed on 28 Oct.,2022].

54 Sarah Cascone, "Sculptor Jean Shin on Using Live Mussels, Old Clothes, and Mountains of Dead Cell Phones to Force the Question of Sustainability in Art," *Artnet*, March 7, 2022, https://news.artnet.com/art-world/jean-shin-sustainability-2078314 [accessed on 28 Oct.,2022].

55 Mary Mattingly, "Swale," video, posted on May 1, 2016, https://www.youtube.com/watch?v=Bzs3XpkXTS0 [accessed on 28 Oct.,2022].

56 Mary Mattingly, "Floating a Public Food Forest," video for A Blade of Grass, https://abladeofgrass.org/fieldworks/fieldworks-mary-mattingly/ [accessed 28 Oct.,2022].

57 "Ecotopian Library," Anchorage Museum, https://www.anchoragemuseum.org/exhibits/ecotopian-library/ [accessed on 28 Oct.,2022].

58 Mary Mattingly, "Mary Mattingly Owns Up," Art21, video, posted on July 19, 2023, https://art21.org/watch/new-york-close-up/mary-mattingly-owns-up/ [accessed on 28 Oct.,2022].

59 Solnit (see note 1), p. 48.

60 Robin Wall Kimmerer, *Braiding Sweetgrass: Indigenous Wisdom Scientific Knowledge and the Teachings of Plants* (Minneapolis, Minnesota: Milkweed Editions, 2020), pp. 61, 86.

61 Guerrilla Girls, "Reinventing the 'F' Word: Feminism," https://www.guerrillagirls.com/our-story [accessed on 28 Oct., 2022].

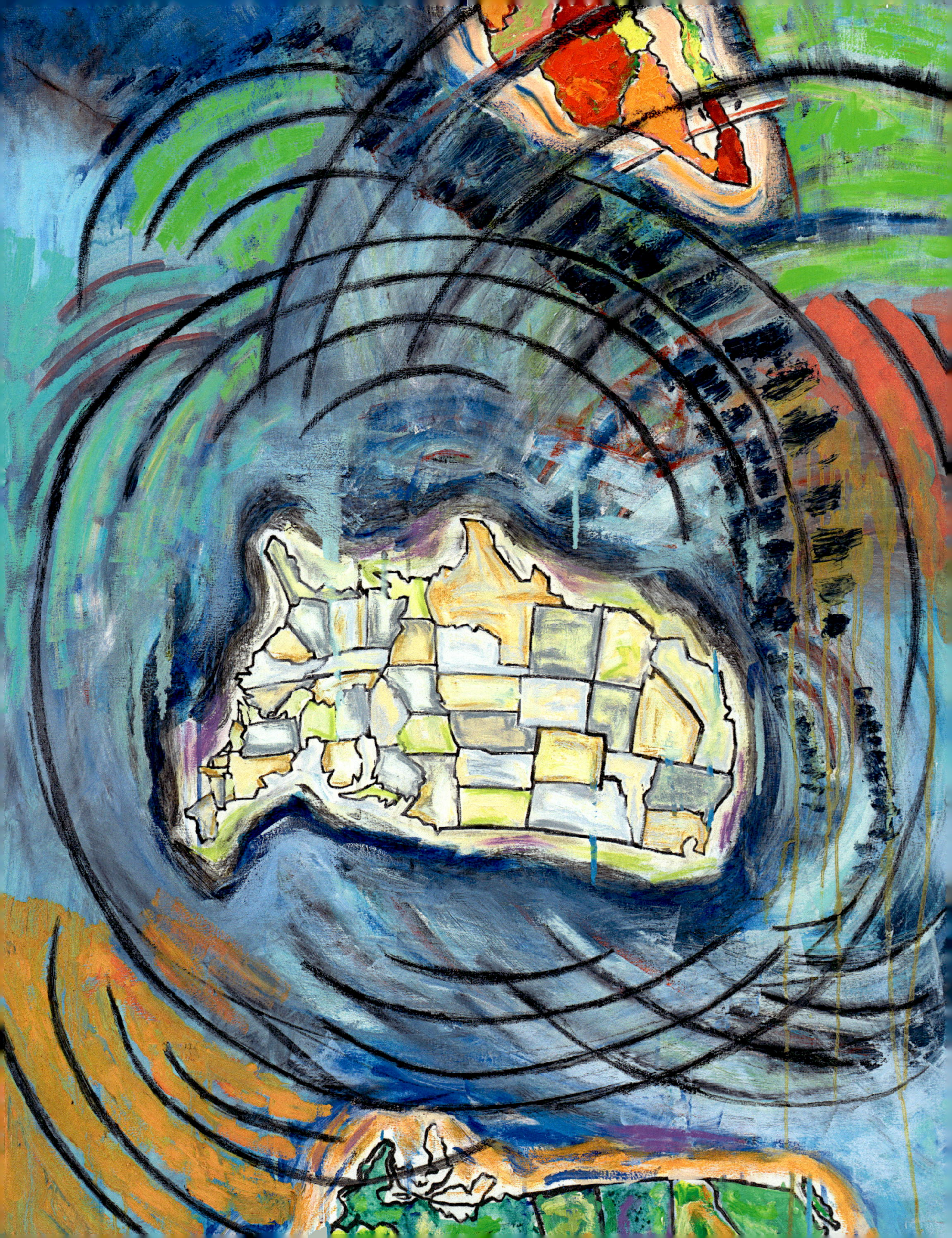

UPTURNING THE MAP: NATIVE WOMEN AND REPRESENTATIONS OF LAND AND LANDSCAPE

A Conversation with
Candice Hopkins and Jolene Rickard

This is an edited excerpt of a conversation that took place on September 21, 2022. **Candice Hopkins** is a citizen of the Carcoss/Tagish First Nation and the Executive Director and Chief Curator of Forge Project, Taghkanic, NY. **Jolene Rickard** is from the Tuscarora Nation (Turtle Clan), Hodinöhsö:ni Confederacy, and is an Artist, Curator, and Associate Professor of History of Art & Visual Studies, Cornell University, Ithaca, NY.

Candice Hopkins:
The first question is, how can we better understand and inform ourselves about the intersectionality and cultural complexities of land and art in what is now called the United States? What does it mean to talk about land in the United States, where so much land has been stolen or developed through the unpaid work of enslaved people?

Jolene Rickard:
That's a big one, isn't it? I guess I have a couple of questions right now. There's the question of how thoroughly this discussion has been vetted within Indigenous art-making practices and certainly in the fields. Land is at the center of the field of Native American and Indigenous studies. There's [also] the question of answering it in relationship to where knowledge keepers, holders, people in Indigenous communities are; and then there's the question of how to think about this in terms of allied and settler awareness. There are different threads. There's Canada, there's the United States, there's Central America, Mexico, the Caribbean, and then there's the Global South. There's Latin America. People situated in these environments, as Indigenous people, would all answer this with slight variance. But based on the experience that I've had at Cornell, it's that there is an unwillingness, it would appear, to acknowledge the fact that the United States exists because of the unlawful dispossession of Indigenous people. There's an interesting conversation or a compelling realization that the discussion of enslavement is working its way through the academy, working its way through governance. But I've yet to see anything that really begins to acknowledge how we account for the formation of the United States as based on the dispossession of Indigenous land. What do we do with that?

One of the most ongoing misunderstandings about this, in relationship to art and land, is that moment of Land Art, that is from what I would call the last throes of the modernist, high modernist Western Theory—the *Spiral Jetty*, for instance, which is the confirmation of the difference between the relationship that people in our communities or Indigenous communities assert, and the way in which land is a site to express one's personal aesthetic.

CH: Right, or even the very idea that land itself can be material for art. Some of the early Land artists who were making this work tended to be male, aside from a few folks like Nancy Holt. They saw it as their domain to transform and reshape [land] in their own vision, which is, looking with the lens that we have now, not so dissimilar from the way that the land has been pictured, as a place of settler desire.

Jolene, I don't know if you agree, but I was thinking that a lot of Native artists didn't always picture the land because that seems like not always the most complex way to understand our relationships to land. One thing I was thinking of while preparing for this conversation was, for example this [bracelet/cuff] (fig. 1). This is a different kind of representation of relations to the land. It is a bracelet, made of smoked tanned moose hide, dyed caribou fur, and beads...This is the kind of work that women in my family do. I would say that this is an articulation of our land relations, but it's not the kind of simplification of understanding or just reducing land to its own image that we project out to the world. It's something very different from that. I think this is a much more complex thing than a painting of land.

JR: So that kind of blends into the next question, because there's criticism around what I would call the whole ecological movement at present. Thank you for sharing your example of the tanned moose hide bracelet, it is a beautiful piece, it is just exquisite. It's interesting because that piece does represent a kind of environment in and of itself. I think this has probably been one of the most difficult concepts to grasp. We all have some kind of cosmological way that we continue to articulate the

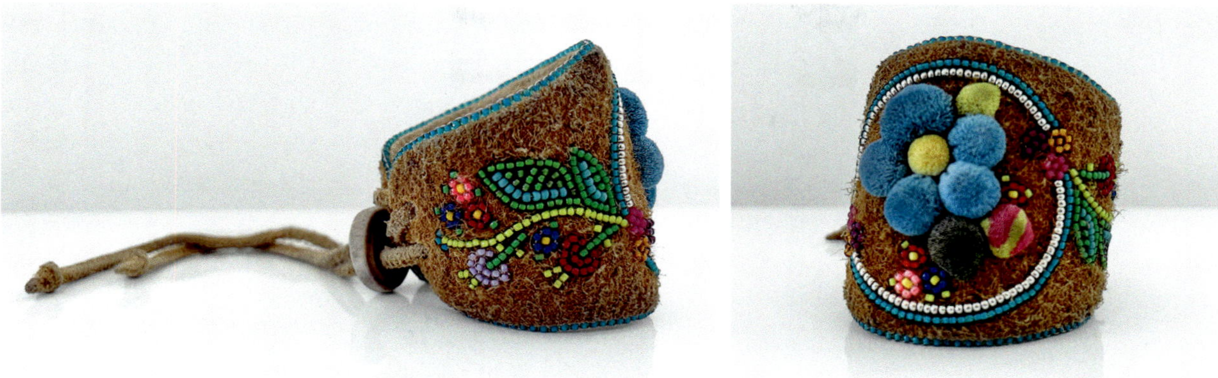

Fig. 1 Carmen Miller (Metis), *Smoked Moosehide Cuff*, 2022, caribou fur tufting, hide, beads, antler, thread, Photograph courtesy: Candice Hopkins

relationships between ourselves and all other living things. For the Haudenosaunee, it's the recitation of *Haˀ Kanęherathę̌creh*, or The Thanksgiving Address, and it's just an acknowledgment, it's a way that we remind ourselves that we are one of many living things in this world, and this is our relationship to it. When I see that bracelet, that's what that reminds me of... It's like a visual articulation of that idea. Maybe the question could be almost revised. Like instead of our relationship to land, it's about our relationship to place.

CH: Exactly. As soon as you start to parcel it out, it's something that is either represented or represented for certain kinds of desires that are projected onto it.

JR: This is one of the things that I'm questioning. This is still one of the most difficult things to insert into the arts dialogue. I've been thinking about this comparatively, globally across Indigenous communities, because there's a lot of action going on now in this area. But in the United States, the difference between race and acknowledging the ongoing structures of colonization, I think is yet to be understood. This is a big issue in the arts, because the discussion around race is very robust, but I do think that [there's] an understanding...that, for me, I argue that racism is nested within the broader structure of colonialism...Overall, I haven't seen this broader uptake, that we really have to deal with the settler and colonial condition of the hemisphere of the Americas in order to really tackle these other issues.

CH: Arguably, this is actually the fuller history of the land, whatever land we are on, whether you're talking about what is now the state of California or what is now the US—these are all obviously artificial borders, because that will immediately bring up the discomfort, Jolene, which you already put your finger on—and that is the fact that almost every treaty in the United States has been broken. If you are a settler and you're living in a place where there's a treaty, I think a lot of people don't know what those relations are. So how do we also make that longer trajectory known? For me, when I'm thinking about land, my question is always about the ways in which land has been transformed, and the capital. The reason that I spend so much time thinking about that and writing about that is because I want to find ways to interrupt it. I think you do this in your own work, Jolene, through your family's history of sovereignty treaty-making political diplomacy.[1] This isn't always well known either—that is the roles that Native communities have played in sovereign nations in the articulation of not only land rights and land agreements, but also sovereignty. I would say that the inherent right to land is deeply embedded in our culture, our ceremony. You could argue it's not just a cultural right, but it's an inherent right.

As soon as we start talking about that, then all of these things start to become an issue in terms of the way that land has been transformed...the reason that the Black Hills have never been given back, speaking of the Lakota people, is because the argument was made that they had been transformed—first by the discovery of gold, then by the carving of the faces of White presidents on them. So, therefore, it was not seen as in the best interest of the United States to give them back. That happens to our land all the time. So, I always think about what do we do to disrupt that chain of commodification? What do we do to situate, not just inherent rights, but the rights to our land?

JR: It's a really important observation. And the question of capital or capitalism in relation to the extractive nature of capitalism is always a foil in a sense. In Haudenosaunee territories, we often contend with the assertion of the reclamation of our land and the assertion of sovereignty; we often contend with the critique around the Beaver Wars or the fur trade, and that's used as an example to suggest that, given the opportunity, the Haudenosaunee and Indigenous Peoples of the Northeast were as capitalistic as any other society and hunted the beaver to exhaustion.

CH: Is that also just because they're really good hunters? [laughter]

JR: Recently I saw a quote by a woman who's on the Haudenosaunee Environmental Task Force (HETC), who said, we have to acknowledge that we did engage in this extractive, and ultimately destructive process. But that part of our culture is about acknowledging when we do things that are not life sustaining and that we have to apologize for this and we have to learn from it, in order to continue to practice the principles of the *Kayanre ̨ hstì·yu·*, or The Great Peace. I think that a lot of our communities are at this precipice of either we commit to these teachings that have been handed down to us, and we commit and understand and translate them into the way in which life expresses itself today. Or we really have to question how we situate ourselves, then, as Indigenous peoples. I don't think...We can't shy away from the complex questions that our communities have to face in this discussion.

CH: Yes, I think that what you're calling attention to, too, is Traditional Ecological Knowledge or TEK, as it is called. I felt that TEK, when it was first being introduced, was a way for scientists to acknowledge the fact that they had been ignoring the voices of those who were living in the lands that they were studying. One of the critiques is that it is an assertion after the fact that has become the norm. What it starts to represent, right now, [is] so called "Indigenous thought," when we all think differently. We all have different practices. Some of them are also extractive at certain moments in time, but only under capitalism. And so, the fur trade happened because capitalism happened to our people. The gold rush happened, and we were complicit in that, too. Sometimes, not only complicit but personally benefiting as communities. I feel like sometimes Indigenous knowledge is upheld as a solution to ecological crises, and it's not that simple. I turn to the Indigenous in times of colonial crisis, but that knowledge is often only included in ways that still benefit the scientists who are writing the papers.

So, when we're speaking about land, we're speaking about the environment. If we're truly to think about sustainability, which might mean removing the human factor altogether, if we're truly to think about land, we have to link it to what a lot of younger generations are using, I think, as a provocation. And that's Land Back. But my thoughts around things like Land Back is then, what do we do with that land? Do we have to have a plan in terms of [the land's] health as a whole? It's not just about personal benefit, but about the rights of the land. I think that that's a conversation that should be happening in relation to any conversation around Land Back. And we're often put in this position now because I feel like not only science, but a lot of fields are understanding what voices have been left out. But I think the bigger question is, who has the power? Who's writing the papers? Who's making the cases? Who's actually representing "land" in the end? And it's not always us.

JR: Recently I've been writing about artworks, and I've made a lesser-known work (fig. 2) on the *Guswenta* or the Two Row Wampum. It's interesting how much work is going on or how much [it focuses on] the Two Row, which was that initial agreement between the Haudenosaunee, specifically the Mohawk, and the Dutch. It is a date that is contested, but the oral history in Haudenosaunee communities suggests 1613. This early contact and the Two Row is both a treaty, it's a wampum, and it's also about principles of respect. It would be interesting to know if there were other forms of agreements between Indigenous peoples and other Indigenous peoples, or Indigenous peoples and settlers, because more recently around the northern part of Lake Ontario, there's a kind of awakening in the relationship between the Haudenosaunee and the Anishinaabe, through the recognition of the wampum belt called the One Dish, One Spoon. I think that our ancestors actually thought about this a great deal. And I look at the Two Row and the One Dish, One Spoon as an interesting template for a way to actually go forward, and think about coexistence.

Within a university or academic space right now, there's a lot of focus on the question of how research is conducted and the term co-creation. Co-creation in a research practice, one could argue, is a kind of theoretical expression, but maybe it's a precursor to preparing society to think about a way in which we need to think about the presence of Indigenous peoples and all other peoples who've arrived here. And that the Two Row makes clear that we're welcoming them, that we're going to share this space, but we're going to share it respectfully. We're not going to interfere with each other, but we're going to maintain our autonomous spaces. After five hundred years of violent and brutal contact—and violence and brutality continue to express themselves in the twenty-first century—against our people, I mean, Indigenous peoples across the hemisphere and globally have maintained and prevailed. We are not letting go, and we are not disappearing, and we're not doing any of the things that were wished upon us and forced upon us by this moment. It needs to be addressed, and it's no longer something that can be ignored. I think that Canada, as a settler state, and the Commonwealth, with the exception, of course, of Great Britain, which doesn't really have the same kind of physical Indigenous population—but certainly in the broader spectrum

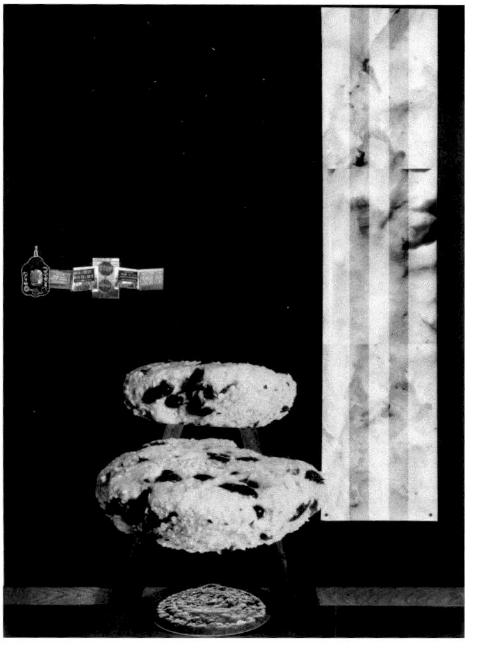

Fig. 2 Jolene Rickard, *Cornbread Room*, Courtesy the artist

of the Commonwealth. At least on the surface, there is some kind of acknowledgment that this needs to be addressed. But we have not reached that point in the United States. Part of what I observe, and this is where some of the Haudenosaunee separate themselves out from Indian country at large, because we insist upon the traditional governance of the Haudenosaunee; we insist upon autonomy and sovereignty and nationhood, as discrete political, geopolitical locations and formations. Some Haudenosaunee communities are moving in this direction, but other communities, certainly in the United States, are seeing themselves now as an extension of the United States government, and not really seeing themselves as politically autonomous. So, in a sense, they're agreeing to be an extension of the settler state, whereas the people that I was raised with have continued to maintain this demand for discrete borders...When we're talking and writing about art, how do you put this into the formula? How do you put this into the discussion?

CH: What you've just spoken about is a very particular kind of grounding. I would say that even Wampum can be understood as a declaration of a treaty, but also representations of our relations, and land and water—water, too, not to be divorced from land, thinking about physicality of what's represented in those images, but then moving to what I would call a ground zero of settler projection, which is the Mahicannituk Valley, the Hudson Valley—Mahicannituk for Mohican folks, which is an area of mass displacement—the forced removal of people over not only generations, but hundreds of years. What you're left with is really the success of what the [Hudson River School] paintings were trying to picture—and that was a land ripe for the settlement of others, but without any evidence of the people who lived and tended to these places. That's something that is really important to note—and I think people know this now—is that the reason that a lot of the paintings of the painters of the Hudson River School, the reason that those vistas were so beautiful, is because they had been tended for tens of thousands of years by Native folks, who were practicing agroforestry, seeding, harvesting—very particular kinds of plots of land were being farmed and harvested. So, there were a lot of land relations that aren't always visible in those images because it's the representation of another person.

Jolene, do you have particular feelings about these kinds of representations? I know I have lots, and I also have a lot of feelings as to why for the most part, you don't find a lot of paintings by Native folks, especially from that era, that we're doing the same thing because it's a mindset that is projected onto that space.

JR: I think that it is often ignored that those paintings are part of a disciplinary space of art history that is really about affirming the centrality of the West, or affirming the space of nationalism. I see those paintings as about confirming the way in which, to use language that might be considered too didactic, how the philosophical or cosmological construct of the West is anchored in Christianity, and this is part of the work of those paintings. When we look closely at initial contact, it was all about erasing Indigenous understandings of the world, worldview, and imposing Christian ideology.

CH: Including Manifest Destiny.

JR: This is all over the hemisphere; it wasn't unique to any particular place. It's consistent, along with the multiple, various ways in which they claim the right to this land and territory, and then set on a project to construct us as either other than human, not fully human, or intended to be enslaved or subjugated. The possession of land and then the ideological apparatus of Christianity are tandem in the colonial project. Until we began to critique that work from this perspective, and I do think there's some of that critique that goes on, but I think it stops at the border of looking at the philosophical lament of Christianity, as the construction of the sublime, or the angst around the loss of the natural world, or the desire—all of those things that you've mentioned earlier. Knowing how those paintings function is really important. There's a lot of work to be done to rethink how we ought to educate ourselves to see those paintings differently.

This exercise of expressing land acknowledgments, that began in universities—even though it's fraught with all kinds of perhaps empty gestures—there is something really important that's happened though: it provides an opportunity for our own people, in the least, to begin to learn the geography of dispossession through these acknowledgments. I guarantee that most of our own people don't know about the history that you just laid out. They might experience the Mohican or Delaware diaspora in Oklahoma, or Wisconsin, or Minnesota, but they're not really fully locating the home they were displaced from—the southern Hudson Valley, and the region adjacent to Pennsylvania and New York State. —this was their homeland. So, I do think there's an interesting function to the acknowledgments that operate in a different way within our communities, maybe an inadvertent advantage to it, which can be a completely empty gesture for the most part.

CH: At best, land acknowledgments should always be understood as a living document, a living articulation of an agreement. At their most powerful, they talk about the institution's relationship with the people on those lands that they occupy. And they can also talk about future relations, so they're almost like a form of treaty-making. You are right, that is one value in hearing them. I think that when they became almost rote or they became performative, in Canada, where people started saying this a little before places in the US did, but what you would hear are all of these professors who are well-educated but still can't pronounce Haudenosaunee properly...I would think, you've maybe only ever seen this in print, but you've actually never heard this or read it. So, in a way it would become a performance of a lack of knowledge, but it might start to produce new kinds of relations, and I think that that's a good thing.

My question is, in this area where I live now, in the Mahicannituk Valley, a place where there has been such displacement—sometimes what comes to fill those spaces is either complete projection or the feeling of comfort that some people probably get from looking at paintings of the Hudson River School. We can understand them as images of violent dispossession. And in actuality, they are the aftermath of that.

JR: It's interesting, because many of those paintings reflect the way in which the British approach North America—those paintings were a really important part of creating this sort of pastoral, safe, nurturing environment, that their citizens could feel comfortable to migrate to. They don't gesture towards any sense of violence or rupture. This is why artists like Kent Monkman have really caught the attention of the art world, because his work begins to open up that space. There are many artists that have opened up that space, but I think because his work also deals with queering the space, it is particularly legible to the art world. Just to go back to the beautiful piece you showed earlier (fig. 1), I don't think that piece is legible to even the most sophisticated of art viewers. They might still see that piece as something that, if they are part of this fine folk divide, or using the language of craft, they wouldn't understand that we see this as an evolved, aesthetic, conceptual statement, as an expression of being in multiple levels, which is really what art does. But they might not see it that way, because they have yet to understand how to read it.

CH: I should have mentioned that [the bracelet I showed earlier] does represent land. It represents things from the land—it represents flowers, and it's a motif which is common, especially in works made by women. But one thing that I was thinking, and one of the questions that we were meant to address, is how have Indigenous women engaged in or interpreted land in the nineteenth century and earlier? And this goes back earlier, even though it is practiced now. The reason that I wanted to bring this up, too, is because it shows the limits of art. Art is a field and a practice that you can't always perfectly project onto our cultural work, because our practices are more complex. This bracelet shows the relationship to sustainable harvesting, which is hunting—the hunting of the moose, the ability to prepare the hide. This hide is smoked by hand, so it is traditionally prepared, which means that it won't stretch and it retains its smell over the course of however long it will last, and it should last for decades. Then the knowledge that to use the underbelly fur here because it will dye better and make these really bright colors. Then often the patterns here will be passed down—you can tell this in the beadwork that you work with too, Jolene, which family has made a certain piece, often because the patterns will be the same. So, there's a kind of genealogy to the making as well. We're both making the same point—that when we think about the relationship between Indigenous women and land and its representation, it's through things like this, I would argue, that are far more complex than a landscape painting from the nineteenth century.

JR: Well, complex in really different ways. I agree. So it seems there are pieces occurring within the academy or within intellectual, artistic circles that we both intersect or travel in, that suggest that there's some curiosity about this, or this sort of emergent discussion of materiality.

CH: New Materialism, as it's called.

JR: The discussion, the still completely misunderstood discussion of ontologies, and the theoretical space of the establishment of colonialism, but then the discussion of a kind of post- to neo-colonial theorization. I mean, all of these things are kind of like necessary elements that could lead to an understanding. But if there isn't some kind of a reckoning of the question of the West as understanding itself, as always in charge or centered, that all of that knowledge then just becomes appropriated into their continued version of the way in which reality works. I think we're kind of at that moment where we're asserting that our way of thinking about the world is really equally, if not more, important. This is where there is some intersectionality, with TEK or Traditional Ecological Knowledge, or some sort of nod to it in this discussion. But it doesn't mean that we will have the authority to activate, to be recognized in this way in the future. We've gone through all these phases of decentering and trying to come to terms with, or at least acknowledging, multiple knowledge systems. But how do you make an intervention on a knowledge system that, inherent to its construct, consistently privileges its humanness above all of the living things?

CH: I think what we're arguing for, even in this conversation around land and art, is not only an expanded form of understanding of land, but, Jolene, what you're talking about is an expanded theoretical framework or a methodological framework as well. Perhaps what's beneficial for this conversation, in this framing, when I think about what Indigenous women were doing in interpreting land in the nineteenth century or earlier, why not include, for example, a seal gut parka? I'm thinking about that because of work that I've done with artists from the Arctic. That shows a very good demonstration of Traditional Ecological Knowledge—like how to make a waterproof stitch, for example; how to make something perfectly shaped and formed for someone's body so they can go out and potentially hunt a whale, which is an incredibly dangerous thing to do; how you're making that entirely out of things of the land and what is it telling you about those relations at the time, whether it's decorated with the feathers of a certain kind of duck. I think a rereading of all of those cultural belongings, as representations of land, water—Traditional Ecological Knowledge is needed. Our things incorporated worldview and esthetics in highly complex ways, just differently.

JR: I think about it within the context of our languages, often described as having multiple temporal expressions or different spatial and temporal expressions, which is not unique to Indigenous languages. There are many languages in the world that functioned in this way. But as an indicator of what became so much a part of Western philosophy are the hard boundaries that were drawn between the sacred and the secular, the hard boundaries that are drawn between the life of the mind and the life of the body. We've resisted those hard boundaries and actually continue to insist upon permissions to move between the past, the present, and the future in a single moment. We resist letting go of this idea that as physical beings we're the only life force in the world, but that we're acknowledging constantly these other forms of life.

Sometimes what I feel I'm doing is resisting translating, not wanting to be a translator. I often think back to the conference that you and Dylan Robinson put together, on multiple sovereignties and careful listening.[2] I think about how there seems to be more interest in what Indigenous people are thinking and saying, but there isn't a mechanism yet to shift the authority, and a validation, that thousands of Indigenous peoples across the world have been making this point about a rethinking of our relationship as human beings to land and to all of the beings other than human, or more than human beings. There hasn't really been this sort of turn or affirmative acknowledgment of "okay, this is what we're all going to do now, we all have to learn this." We're at the very early phases of this. I studied with this important literary scholar who's involved in literature and anthropology, Professor Dennis Tedlock (d. 2016), who spent a great deal of time with the Maya. He would shake his head and say: "The colonizer has understood all of this from the beginning. So, it really isn't about acknowledging these ways of knowing...it's really that they don't want to. They really don't want to think about life in this way. They really want to continue with the hierarchical expression of thinking about life in terms of wealth and ownership."

CH: I was even thinking, would a radical turn in land acknowledgments be less about acknowledging the original people of a certain place, and what might happen when those acknowledgments actually turn to acknowledging the land itself? Which is common in the Thanksgiving Address. That's how you do it. That's what that acknowledgment is. It's decentering us, it's decentering people. I think you're totally right. That's the hard part of this thing to perhaps acknowledge, this has been known all along. Certainly, the chorus is perhaps getting louder and certain others are paying attention, but I really wonder what the rupture is. A leader in my community, Carcross/Tagish First Nation, former Chief Mark Wedge, wanted to name this moment actually the "Indigenous Spring." I thought that was interesting because it implies that term. And I thought it was quite good.

JR: But even though there was the Arab Spring, it hasn't really changed much for the lives of people from the Middle East. I do think that these kinds of moments of reckoning or recognition are significant, but there has to be then, accountability.

CH: It needs to go beyond the politics of recognition.

JR: Yes. We've been recognizing it for 500-plus years. And now we need to really look at accountability. I was just talking with this new hire at the University of Buffalo, a new faculty member there, and he comes from people whose homelands are in the Louisiana Delta. They're among the first people that are now displaced by the impact of climate change. There's no kind of acknowledgment that this has really happened to them, it's seen as just sort of like rural people being displaced, and that they all just have to deal with it individually. This is what we're faced with across the world. Actually, many Indigenous peoples are in the front line with the impact of environmental change and degradation. Yet there's no accountability. There are lots of opportunities for people who have benefited from this centuries-long period of irresponsible extraction to make good or balance. But is that happening? Where is that happening?

CH: I think recognizing that this extraction has roots and colonialism, gentrification has roots in colonialism—we need to acknowledge that. It's often women who are on the front lines. To point to one example, my sister-in-law was involved in a delegation of five women who, after the forced closure of the water protector camps at Standing Rock, went to European banks (they started in the US and then went to European banks—in Norway and then in Switzerland) to ask them to divest. They were there in front of them, and saying this is affecting the health, not just of a community, but the health of women and children. And we're standing in front of you as evidence of that. Because often what capital does is it tries to obscure. Their accountability was to go to the people on the other end, the people who don't realize the impact of their actions of [their] investment. And given that these investments in things that now exploit the land are often multinationals, it becomes that much harder to follow the money. It was one way of putting a face to that, and foregrounding with the impact that it was having.

JR: What were the results of that?

CH: The Norwegian bank divested. I am speculating, but Norway has a history of Indigenous activism going all the way back to the Sixties with the Sámi Action Group, and others, making campaigns that were successful in the late Seventies and early Eighties in terms of bringing what would be the equivalent of a Sámi Bill of Human Rights. But in Switzerland, they got a diplomatic answer saying, we'll do our research, and we'll look into it. This was a non-action answer.

JR: It's interesting because in 2024, the Haudenosaunee Confederacy is getting ready to acknowledge the 100-year anniversary of our first attempt at being recognized internationally, because we sent a Gayogho̱:nǫ (Cayuga) Deskaheh, Levi General, the person who held the title, to the League of Nations (Geneva, Switzerland) in 1924 to advocate for the recognition of our nations and our autonomy. And it's interesting because that was the exact same treatment that we received in 1924. I'm working on an exhibit with the community of people here in the Haudenosaunee Confederacy to raise the profile of this work, because we have a few organizations that we continue to work with in order to advocate for this kind of recognition. There's been a lot of work on this idea, and well maybe we're asking for the wrong thing, or we're plumbing the wrong construct by thinking in terms of nation. But the question is, how do we make ourselves visible or legible when that's the system of organization that we're dealing with? I think that we need to think about what form we should adopt, that we should make our own, that provides this sort of safe harbor or at least a dynamic space for our people to continue to consider these ideas. And for me, this gets into another thing, and it's that I don't really understand, Candice, when people think of themselves or want to maintain a relationship to their Indigenous identity, but at the same time have no responsibility or really don't seek to understand the philosophical principles that these identities are based in. That opens up just a whole other conversation about the criticality in which artists from our communities are assessed. How is their discussion informed? I think that all of these things are components or part of this discussion.

CH: Yeah, you might even be talking about protocols, knowledge of the protocols and how you enact those as part of the community. But also, certainly where I'm from, like land- and water-based, and you could even consider them almost like methodology.

JR: For me what this conversation has really foregrounded is that landscape is very much a trope of Western artistic practice. I think there are Indigenous peoples and artists [for whom] that framing is not generative. So, artists that inherently practice as constructing landscape as such, they're influenced by this modality of making. I guess I'm more interested in Indigenous artists that are pressing up or resisting that trope. To return to Candice's evocative use of the cuff link made by the woman; it identifies a single artist, but if we shift the way that we're seeing and thinking, we would find there are many artists that are engaging with this process. But I don't know if we've really named it or marked it in this way.

CH: It's kind of like expanded form. I was thinking of someone like Natalie Ball, who's now a councilwoman in her tribe, and advocated as part of her work for Land Back and the health of the Klamath Watershed. She incorporates in some of her work things like Sweetgrass. But that to me goes beyond representations of land because it simply *is* land. When we make work, it's less about representing it and it's more about bringing it in, into the work that people are making. But I was also thinking about how more recently Jaune Quick-to-See Smith is using maps of the United States but turning them on their side. When you turn them on their side, to me anyway, they start to look like hides. A hide is something that has a lot more function, in my mind, than a map of the United States, because you can make something out of it. You can sew it, you can tend it, and you can use it to clothe your family. You can use it as shelter. It has utility. So, in a way that simple act of turning that map, starts to wash away all of these negative associations of nationhood and the imposition, the way that maps and landscapes have been impositions onto us. I think there's a lot of artists working right now who are engaging with that in ways that are, again, about these kinds of openings. There are more openings to understand art as part of a broader ontology, let's say, to bring that work to bear.

JR: What's important for me is that we're both saying that we feel that these expressions or the expressiveness of this is really important, that isn't the issue. It's really about how we can read these works and make them work in ways that aren't reinforcing these older framings. So, this work actually has to work in conversation with conversations just like this or opportunities to talk about it, write about it, express these ideas in other ways. It's difficult to get here without actually the collaborative process of dialogue.

1 Jolene Rickard's paternal grandfather, Clinton Rickard was part of an early twentieth-century assertion of sovereignty in support of the work of Gayoghó:nǫ (Cayuga) title holder, Deskaheh Levi General. The Haudenosaunee or Six Nations petitioned the League of Nations in 1923-24 to be recognized as sovereign nations. The League of Nations in Geneva, Switzerland was the precursor to the United Nations, the other locations being in New York City.

2 *Listenings* was a gathering and series of public events at the Agnes Etherington Arts Centre and Isabel Bader Centre for the Performing Arts that took place March 20–24, 2019 in Kingston, Ontario and was organized by Dylan Robinson. The format provided time for listening and discussion: each participant presented a sound/song/piece of music which was collectively heard then responded to.

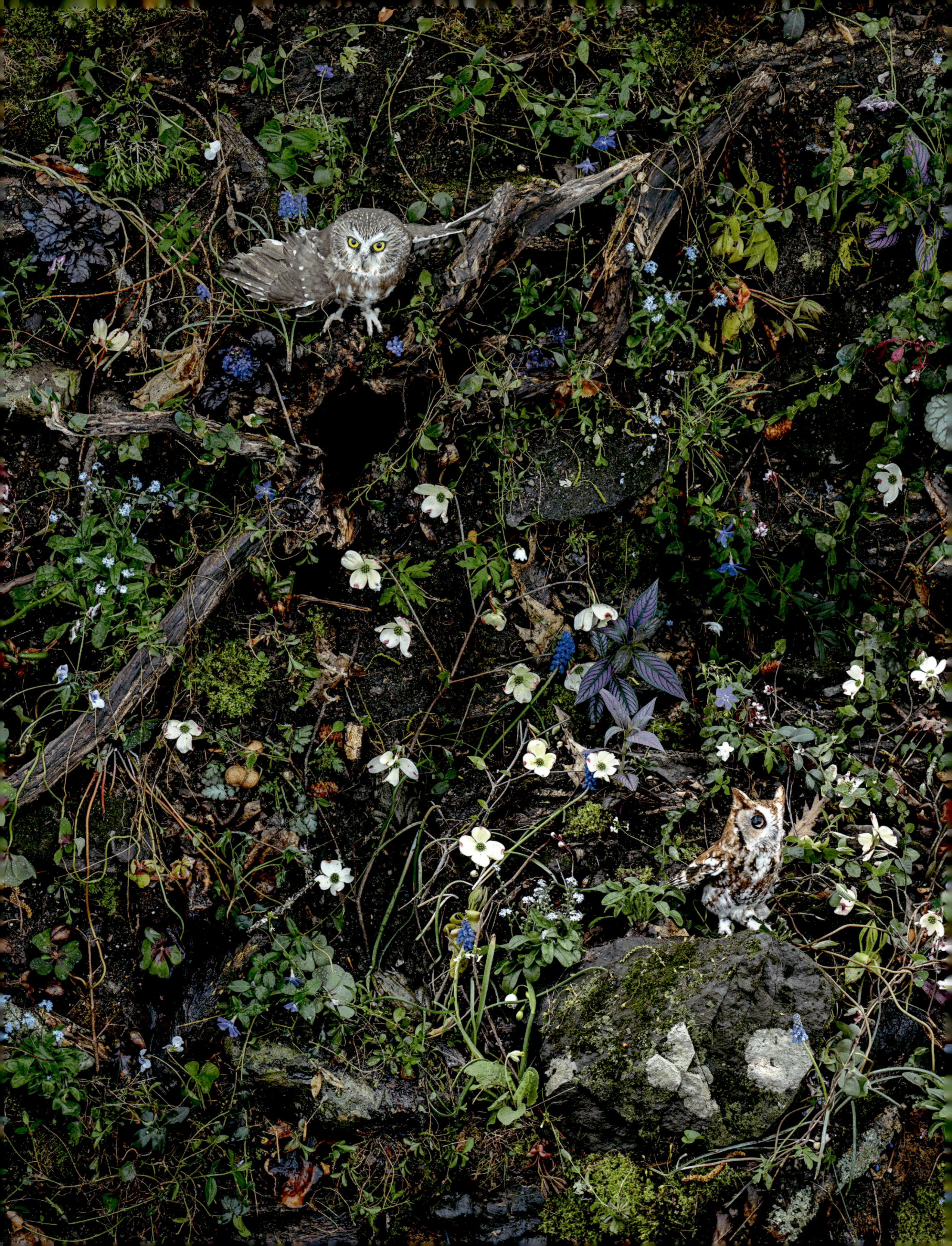

ARTIST TEXTS AND PLATES

TERESITA FERNÁNDEZ

ARTIST AS ARSONIST: BURNING DOWN THE MYTH OF THE AMERICAN LANDSCAPE

Before the sixteenth century, when only Indigenous tribes inhabited what is now known as the United States of America, the life-giving waterway known as the Hudson River was referred to by the local Lenape tribes as *Mahicantuck*, "the river that flows two ways." I'd thought a lot about this when in 2017 I was invited by the Cisneros Foundation to create a collaborative project at Olana, the historic house museum and grounds of Frederic Church in Greenport, New York. When I first started to ponder what it would mean to have my work shown alongside historic paintings made by so-called "traveler artists" or "Hudson River School" painters, I kept asking myself, "Where am I?" When I stand here, overlooking this astounding river, where am I geographically, historically, economically, racially? Who built this house? Who dug out the reservoir? What happened here? Who lived here 2,000 years ago? How does this place linger in our collective imagination? And with this questioning I started to mentally set fire to any preconceived ideas of the Hudson River or Hudson River School painting, and instead began to imagine *Mahicantuck*.

Being asked to write for this publication by the Thomas Cole National Historic Site further ignited this burning down of conditioned terminology and ultimately brought me to this question: What does it mean to think about American art, or the American landscape, or even the very notion of the term "American"? This was especially urgent in relation to the deep-seated colonialist constructs inherent in these ideas, which push us to reconsider our understanding of the concept of landscape. What happens when we shift the word landscape to land? One must wonder if a place like Olana, itself a colonial construct, situated next to the Hudson River, a site in the land "defined" by colonists, is doubly offensive and dangerous when juxtaposed, as though more than the sum of its parts.

For the resulting exhibition *Overlook: Teresita Fernández Confronts Frederic Church at Olana*, the works exhibited (both mine and those that I chose from the Cisneros and Olana collections) challenged associations with the word "America." The historic selections included paintings by Church, Cole, and their contemporaries that specifically depict what we think of today as Latin America and the Caribbean: a sampling of the many places these "traveler artists" visited throughout the "Americas" to create the epic landscape views that are taught to art students as fact. As I researched hundreds of images of historical works I was given access to for the exhibition, it struck me that the landscapes, while technically exquisite, showed us almost nothing about the people who lived there, how they may have lived, or even how these painters interacted with them. Distinct from these, and seemingly unrelated in the way they were organized archivally, were dozens of revelatory portraits by Auguste Morisot that I culled from the Cisneros collection. These portraits consisted mostly of small, rapid sketches of Indigenous individuals that the French artist encountered on his eight-month journey through the Guayanas and Amazonas regions along the Orinoco River. The titles give us a glimpse into Morisot's own bias, and how he both objectified and categorized these individuals: *Mulatta in the Market of Pointe-a-Pietre in Guadeloupe*, February 1886; *Carib Indian, Ciudad Bolívar*, May 1886; *Nicacio Tumaki*, October 20, etc.

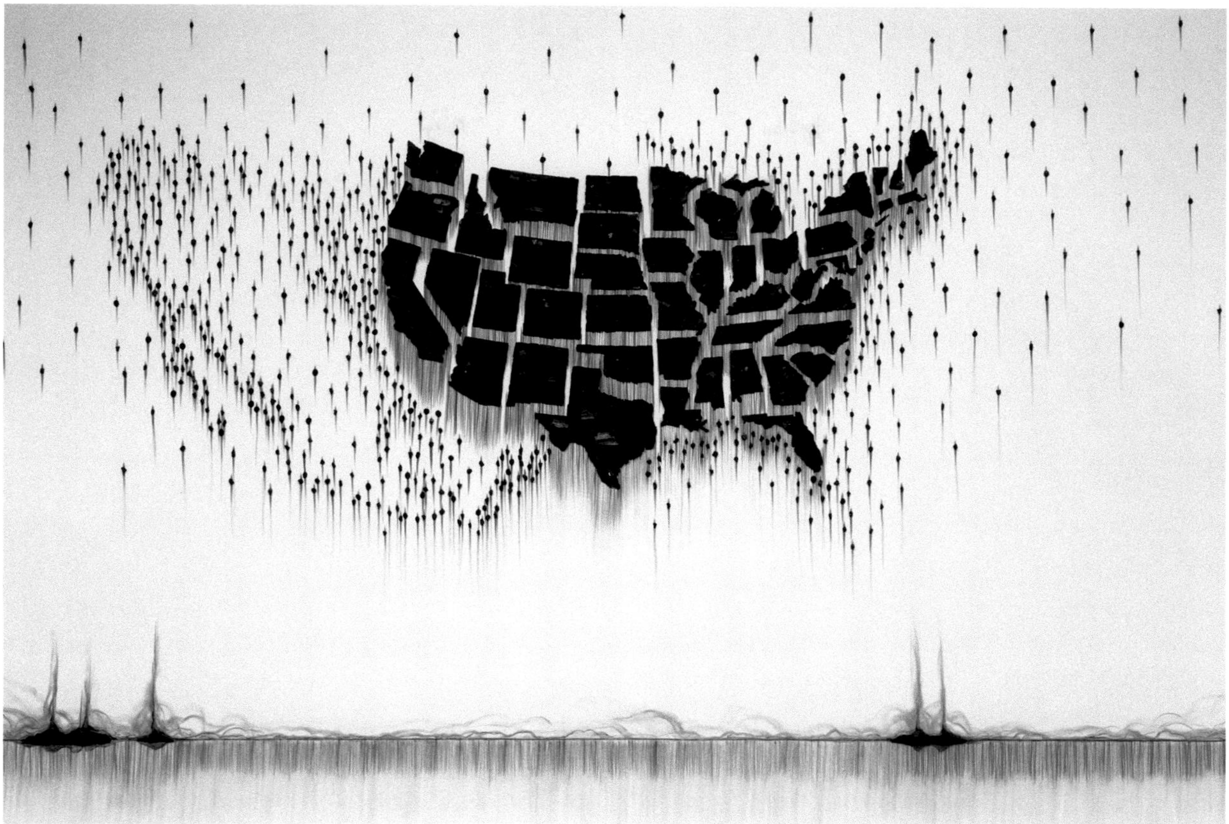

Teresita Fernández, *Fire (United States of the Americas) 2,* 2019, charcoal, 137 × 442 × 1 in., Installation view from *Teresita Fernández: Elemental,* 2020, Phoenix Art Museum, Courtesy the artist and Phoenix Art Museum, Phoenix, AR, Photograph: Airi Katsuta

My own contributions to the project sat carefully nestled within these histories, like undercover agents that had infiltrated this space by posing as passive landscape paintings and portraits. These subtle interventions were rooted in the particularities of how I see the landscape in an anthropomorphized and reciprocal way. If you look at the landscape, the landscape must, it seems, also look back at you. This premise of looking and being looked at has shaped my practice for two decades. Indeed, it seems that the connections between seeing and not seeing are actually very important; to be dazzled and to be blinded are, optically, very similar. To show one view means completely blocking or obliterating another. It's hard to see something if you're too close to it, but it's just as hard if you're too far away. Seeing, both physically and metaphorically, depends on a human presence—a toggling, a constant adjustment, both pulling out and zooming in, in order to reveal what is being distorted or erased. It is as though seeing resides not in looking, but in the saccadic movements of the eye, flickering between what is visible and invisible, named and nameless—a constant filling in that requires a different kind of "seeing," with robust imagination and a willingness to peel back the layers. Erasure is always deliberate, and therefore seeing, it seemed to me, must also always be intentional.

In the main gallery at Olana, the installation consisted of a densely packed wall of small portraits staring at a wall covered with landscape paintings. The subjects here returned their gaze to the painted, empty landscapes that perhaps depict the lands of their origins. The irony, of course, is that these landscapes are devoid of human presence. In these fabricated renderings of "the Americas," landscape painters were more concerned with creating the myth of virgin, unpopulated wilderness than they were with depicting the ravaging effects of colonization, industrialization, the displacement of multitudes of Indigenous populations, and the forced labor of enslaved people. Visitors to the gallery stood in between these two views, becoming implicated as stand-in figures in the landscape. When looking at the landscapes, 36 pairs of eyes stared at the viewers' backs, and when turning to look at the wall of faces, the landscapes became an out-of-sight backdrop, denied to viewers.

In the end, *Overlook* sought to rescript the conditioned reading of landscape painting traditions in order to question the self-anointed authority of what gets called "American art," instead proposing that landscape is not a fixed vista in front of our eyes, but rather an ever-changing portrait of the history of people living in, and being banished from places. While the term "landscape" suggests images, the term "land" more concretely suggests the history of power, greed, and conquest. What would happen if we taught landscape painting alongside the socio-political and historic events that framed each scene? What if landscape became a way of looking at images of sites as being not just about what is depicted topographically, but also about how we imagine narratives about what has been omitted? The installation of mostly nameless portraits confronting empty landscapes, and the viewer's bodily inability to engage both walls simultaneously, somatically illustrated how when one story is being told, another is being omitted.

Across the river from Olana is the Thomas Cole National Historic Site. Cole was Church's mentor and teacher. It is in this area that the story (and branding) of Hudson River School Painting was invented. When we walk through museums and look at historic works by Cole or Church, we think of the expansive, romanticized landscapes they portray as being images of "America," and by default of "America" as being just the United States. The corresponding moral and cultural ideals of the sublime were not just about painting—they were about constructing a national myth of beauty and nature that was deeply entrenched in tactics of domination and erected on a foundation of violence; this idealized American story has been insidiously used to justify the decimation of Indigenous populations and the enslavement of Africans. Passed by Congress on January 31, 1865, and ratified on December 6, 1865, the 13th Amendment, which abolished slavery in the United States, occurred 17 years after Cole's death and at the height of Church's career. This singular, disturbing fact makes it crucial to reframe the continued celebration of American landscape painting as intricately tied to violence.

Contrary to popular belief, the land we call America was not a virgin landscape at first European contact, much less the unpopulated Eden that the Hudson River School painters depicted it to be. It was a place where Indigenous people had lived for thousands of years, and where they had carefully managed the land in sophisticated ways, including traditional "slash-and-burn" agricultural techniques, which keep land healthy and fertile in cycles of rest and renewal. Through this sustainable practice, the cyclical burning of select forested areas significantly shaped the landscape for millennia, long before European contact. Today, there is a pervasive notion that fire is a negative, destructive force, which completely ignores the history of how this very place was shaped precisely by humans skillfully setting deliberate fires.

Under this directive of violence and conquest, the idealized myth of America that Cole and his contemporaries were depicting was rapidly, tangibly expanding. There are obvious, carefully crafted parallels between the invention of the American myth as noble and rooted in freedom, and the aggressive land grab that persists. Cole died on February 11, 1848, just nine days after the United States devised a forced treaty that claimed more than half of Mexico's territory following a brutal invasion and war. The Treaty of Guadalupe Hidalgo dramatically altered the topography of the United States, tripling its size (after the doubling of size with the Louisiana Purchase) and extending its borders to the shores of the Pacific Ocean, fulfilling the insidious ideas behind "manifest destiny," a phrase that had been coined only three years earlier following the admission of Texas as the 28th state in the Union. This forced treaty was not a unique, historical exception—since the nineteenth century, the United States has consistently backed coups throughout Latin America. It has militarized right-wing groups; intervened in elections, civil wars, and revolutions; and spearheaded massacres and gang violence that have left deep scars on the land, forcing the impoverished and imperiled to move north seeking asylum. The details surrounding stories of this other "American" history are largely unfamiliar to many United States citizens, and this societal amnesia insidiously shapes and continues to enable the hateful anti-immigrant sentiment so pervasive in this country.

The work of Cole and other Hudson River School painters very often omits the many horrific events that were happening simultaneously, rendering them invisible, much like the blind space between the two walls of my installation at Olana. We do not look at these historical works as historical peoples, we look at them in the present. When we think of the sublime and the supposedly beautiful representations of the "Hudson River Valley," we must contextualize them against the brutal drive for westward expansion, the massacres of Indigenous peoples, and the enslavement of African people, all of which were intricately woven into these warped ideas of beauty. As we face current immigration bans, mass incarceration, and deportation, we cannot look at Cole or Church's paintings without contending with all the ideas of place, travel, landscape, land, boundaries, and nation-building myths bound up in them.

Anywhere we are, we are actually in many places at once—a concept I refer to as the idea of "stacked landscapes." Anywhere I am in the world, the matter that surrounds me—the mountains, rocks, trees, and streams—all hold a great deal of information and knowledge. The landscape remains witness to all the atrocities that have been committed in that place. We live on haunted land, just as Cole's home sits on haunted land that remembers everything that has happened there. If we step outside of what we think about landscape, we can allow ourselves to recognize that thought and place are deeply connected; that geography is a colonial invention; and that land and memory are deeply intertwined. Place is the vehicle for understanding who we are, and by extension who we are in relation to one another, both historically and in the present.

Back to setting it all on fire: while the act of burning is often connected to destruction, it simultaneously offers the possibility for renewal and reinvention. I have always loved the word "plot"—a reference to a demarcated section of land but also a word meaning the ability to mentally plan and strategize. To plot how to burn down the myth of America, the American landscape and all its derivatives is to create fertile ground, to become active participants in re-shaping history and cultivating possibilities. It seems all too appropriate that we are given sticks of charcoal in art school, a humble tool made from trees that have been burned, in order to conjure up radical images out of shameful injustices and scorched earth: artists as arsonists.
—Teresita Fernández

GUERRILLA GIRLS

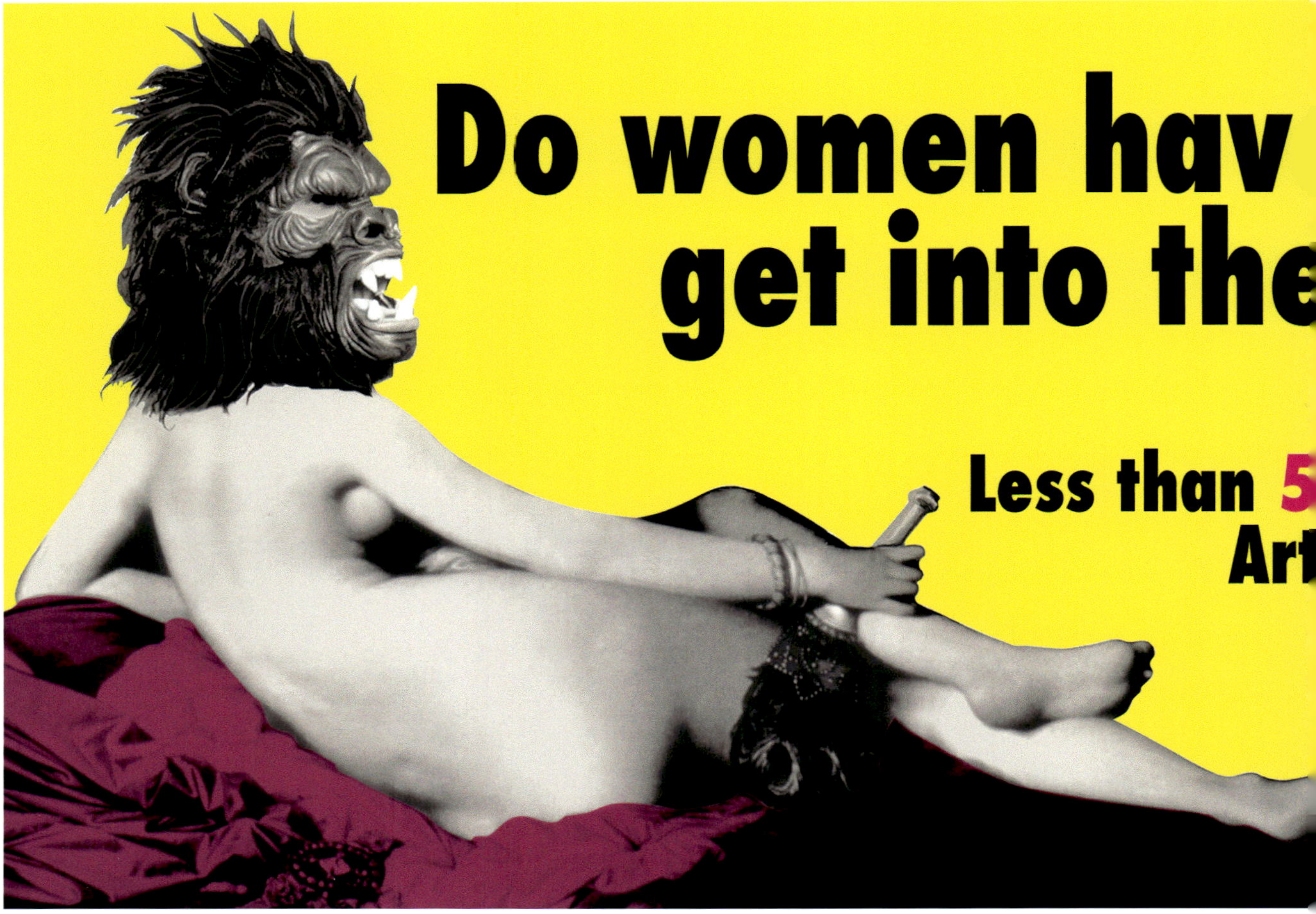

Guerrilla Girls, *Do women have to be naked to get into the Met. Museum?*, 1989, digital poster,
Copyright © Guerrilla Girls, Courtesy guerrillagirls.com

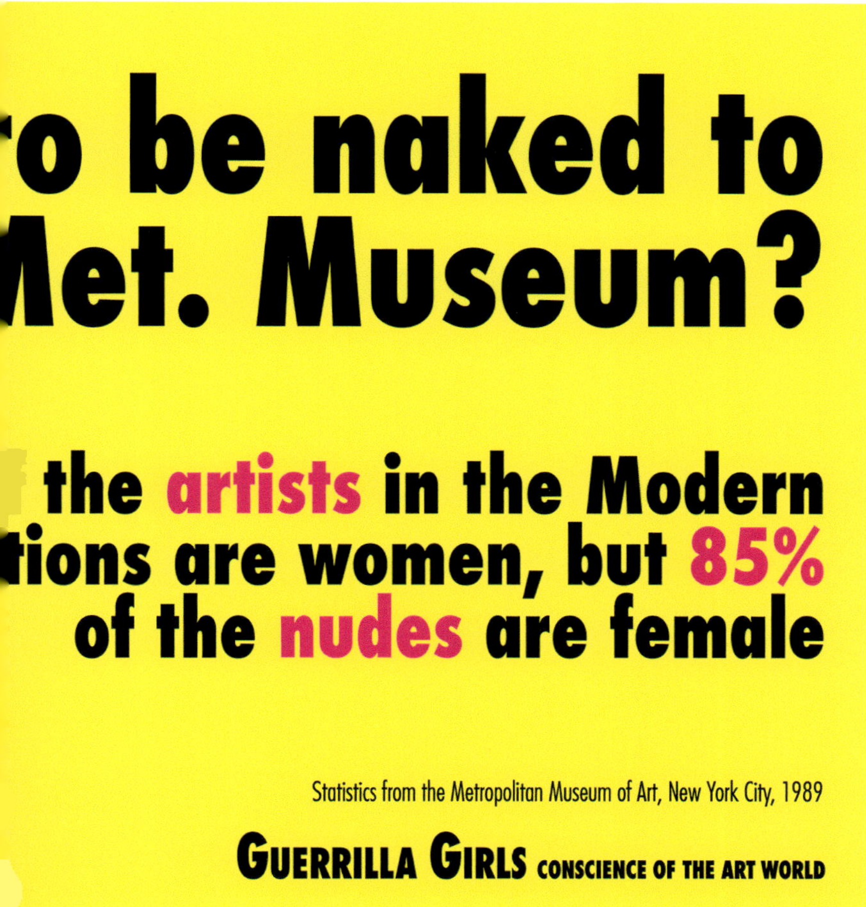
o be naked to
Met. Museum?
the artists in the Modern
tions are women, but 85%
of the nudes are female
Statistics from the Metropolitan Museum of Art, New York City, 1989
GUERRILLA GIRLS CONSCIENCE OF THE ART WORLD

ANNA PLESSET

Value Study 1: A View of the Catskill Mountain House / Copied from a picture by S. Cole copied from a picture by T. Cole / 1848 (2020) is the first in a series of paintings that are part of *American Paradise*, my project that reframes the history of the Hudson River School to give visibility to the many women who were affiliated with this iconic movement but who have been largely omitted from the art-historical canon. The title—invoked critically—takes its name from *American Paradise: The World of the Hudson River School,* an exhibition catalog published in 1987 by the Metropolitan Museum of Art that perpetuates the mythology of the Hudson River School as being founded by, and exclusively comprised of, men. In fact, as early as 1818—seven years before its ostensible founding in 1825—women were painting scenes of the Catskills and beyond in styles ascribed to the movement's "founding father," Thomas Cole, and its other male members.

This painting and the others in my *Value Studies* series reference works created by women—Sarah Cole, Louisa Davis Minot, Susie Barstow, and Julie Hart Beers, among others—who hiked and painted alongside and separately from the men associated with this movement. I call these paintings *Value Studies* because it's a play on a basic painting and drawing exercise while simultaneously referring to the content of my work: these paintings give value and visibility to the many women and works that have been largely absent from the dominant narrative of the Hudson River School.

The first painting in this series, *Value Study 1: A View of the Catskill Mountain House / Copied from a picture by S. Cole copied from a picture by T. Cole / 1848* (2020), references a painting made by Sarah Cole in 1848 titled *A View of the Catskill Mountain House* that was copied from an 1845–48 painting by Thomas Cole, her brother, titled *A View of the Catskill Mountain House*. Only a handful of Sarah Cole's paintings have survived and most of them are copies of her brother's works. After learning this, I started thinking about the historical tradition of copying "important" paintings—another basic painting exercise that functioned both as a learning tool and as a way of paying homage—and began creating "unfinished" copies of paintings by the women who had been pushed to the margins of the Hudson River School history.

Like Thomas Cole's original painting on canvas, Sarah Cole's painting measures around 15 × 23 inches and is also an oil on canvas. In keeping with this and the tradition of copying, my painting is the same size and facture as its two precedecessors. However, in my version, the copy is in progress and is being painted from what looks like a printed screenshot of Sarah Cole's painting taped to the upper right corner of the canvas. In fact, this "source material"—the ostensible reference for the "unfinished" painting—is painted in *trompe l'oeil,* making it the "true copy" of Sarah Cole's painting. Together, the two painting modes make visible the act of historical recovery and acknowledge that act as always in progress and never finished. —Anna Plesset

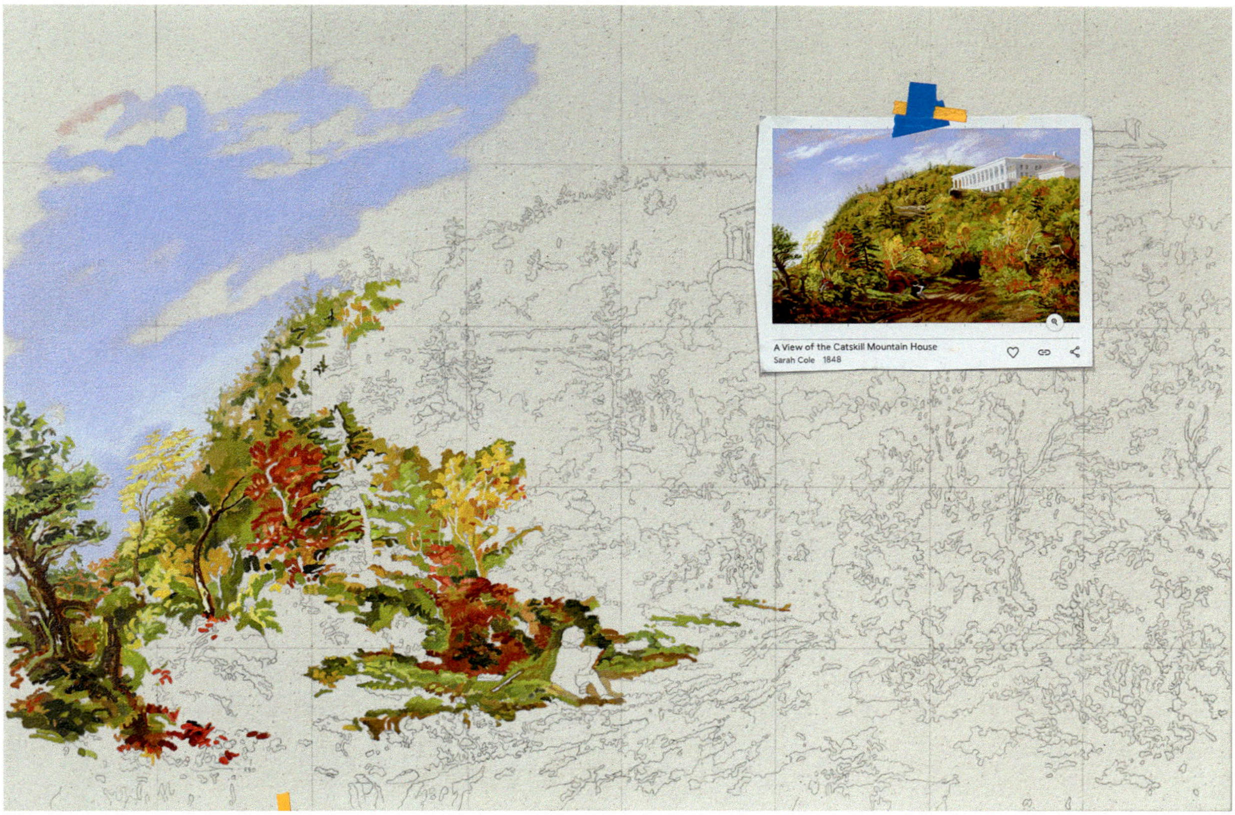

Anna Plesset, *Value Study 1: A View of the Catskill Mountain House / Copied from a picture by S. Cole copied from a picture by T. Cole / 1848*, 2020, oil and graphite on canvas, 15⅜ × 23 7/16 in., Sundeep Mullangi and Trissa Babrowski Collection, Courtesy the artist and PATRON Gallery, Chicago, IL, Photograph: Etienne Frossard

TANYA MARCUSE

The ancient Greeks imagined the machinery of fate as three women, weaving the lives of humans and gods into an enormous tapestry, killing or giving life by snipping or knotting a thread. Through the medium of photography, in my series "Woven," I imagine myself introducing time, and thus mortality, into the lush flora and fauna which make up the millefleurs backgrounds of medieval hunting and falconry tapestries. The 5 × 10-foot photographs in this series sometimes take weeks to compose, and during this process of composition, of collecting, arranging, burning, painting, and transplanting, there is change. Flowers wither, spiders build webs, new shoots emerge, and corpses decay.

The wooden structure on which I composed the scene is like a garden bed tilted up at a 45-degree angle, terraced to hold dirt, plants and rocks. A shallow diorama that is living and dying. Each *Woven* piece is constructed on this same frame, the remains or ruins of one piece becoming the foundations of the next.

Most of the works from the "Woven" series feature dead and decaying flora and fauna; they foreground the cycles of growth and decay. But for *Woven № 33* I wanted to create an image filled with life. I composed a living woodland scene, or stage set, for the rescue owls (Leo the Saw Whet and Linus the Screech owl) I'd arranged to have brought in on the day of the shoot from Ravensbeard, a wildlife rehabilitation center in Saugerties, NY. I transplanted forget-me-nots from my garden, borrowed frogs from nearby swamps, composed mossy branches and designed a small stream bed to trickle down the left side of the frame. An artifice of naturalism.

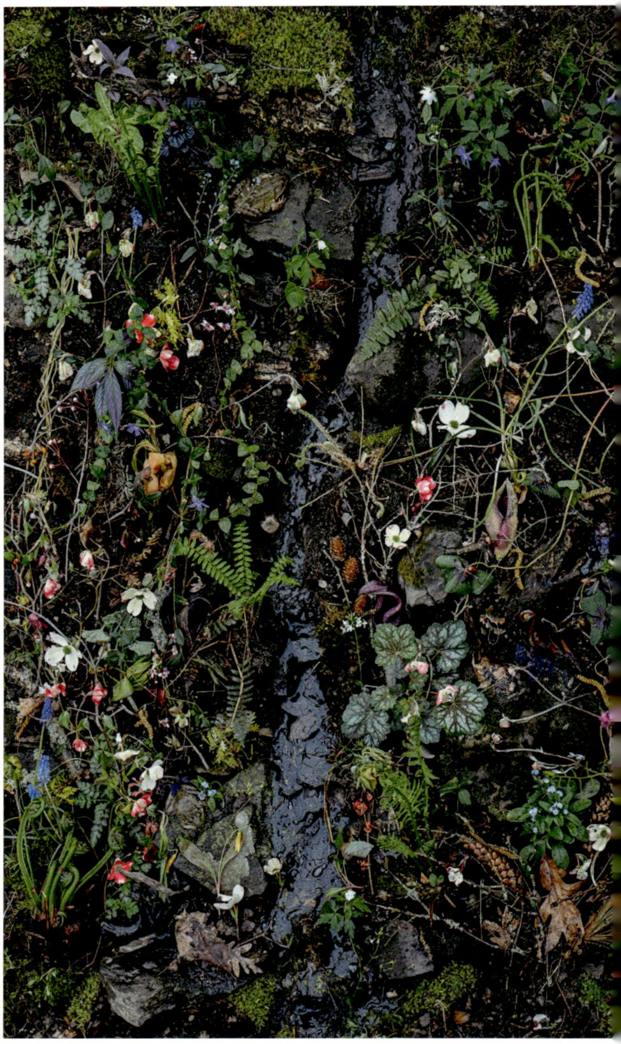

Tanya Marcuse, *Woven № 33*, 2019, inkjet print, 62 × 124 in., Courtesy the artist

The scale and intricacy of the "Woven" series suggest a reverence and majesty akin to the landscape paintings of the Hudson River School artists. But there are no horizons in *Woven*; my sense of landscape is intimate, tactile, experiential. Not a far-off vista, but the ground we're standing on, a place both fabled and real. I photographed this elaborate tableau from up on a scaffold, beneath a

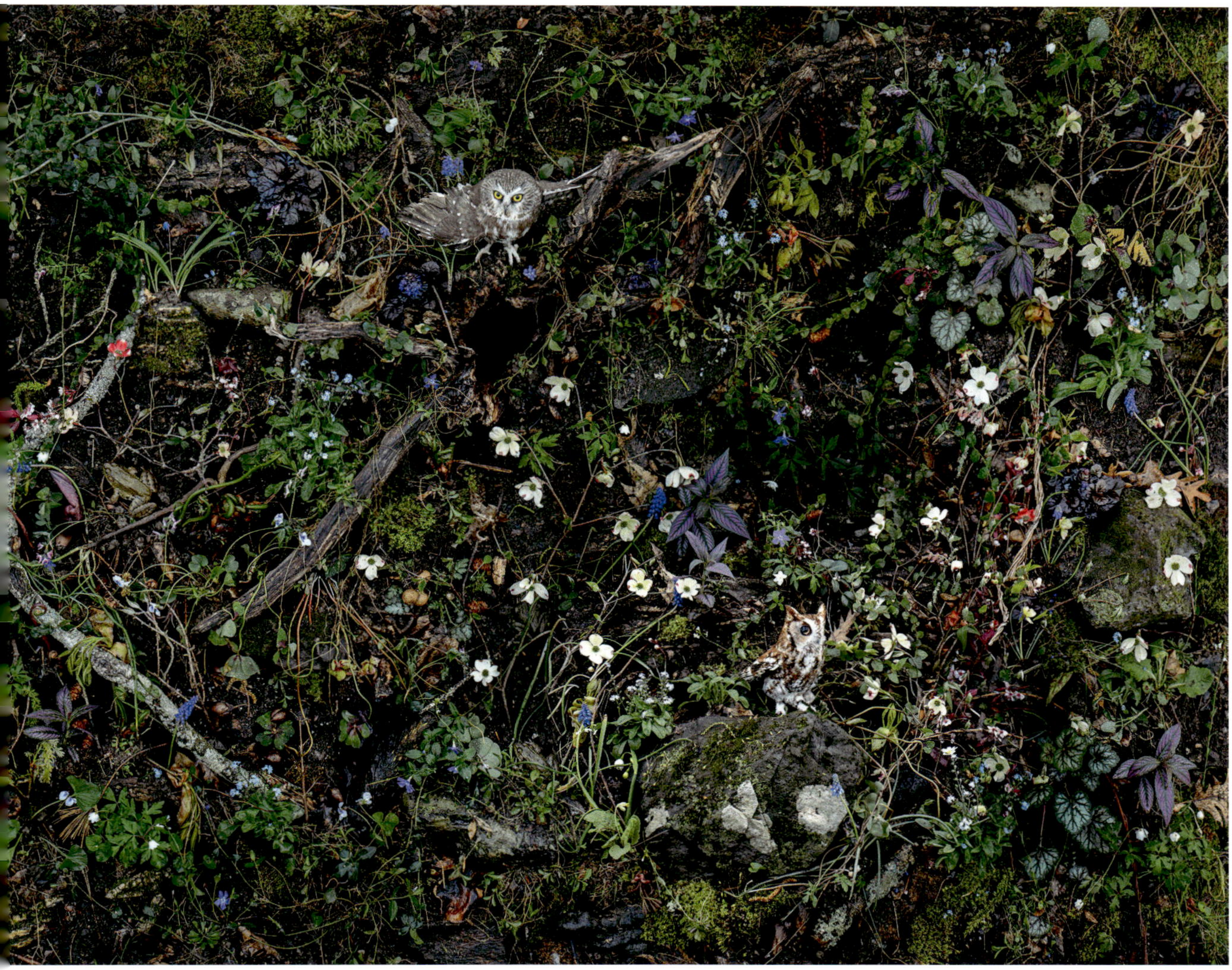

huge canopy in my backyard. Transformed into a photograph, its scale slightly larger than life, I hope to convey a sense of immersion and awe.

What is common to all works in the series is an opulence which verges on excess, a plenty which verges on plunder; all within a space where the inexorable movements of nature are shown forth, and growth and decay, beauty and terror, life and death are woven together. —Tanya Marcuse

SAYA WOOLFALK

We believe in Hudson River School paintings as historical documents of American land and life, and I want to shift these paintings for you. These paintings contain the desires, hopes, fears, and love of a certain population of a nascent country.

Although I love these paintings, there is much about them that I find alienating and problematic. They present America as a kind of Eden that naturalizes the displacement of Native populations, celebrates agrarianism without the acknowledgment of the constant precariousness of the lives of tenant farmers, while erasing the enslaved Africans who worked farms all over the country to produce unprecedented wealth for America.

I spent a year as an artist in residence at the Newark Museum thinking about how these paintings continue to shape our vision of what America is...During this time, I created the installation *Tumbling Into Landscape,* which includes a collaged self-portrait silhouette in the center of, and composed with, fragments of the paintings that flank it—historic American landscape paintings from Newark Museum's collection, made between 1840–1900 and associated with the Hudson River School. These illusionistic windows onto pristine landscapes from the northeastern United States, hang in museums all over the country and communicate a specific version of the American creation myth.

I wanted to explore how Hudson River School paintings could be used in the service of alternative narratives, outside the bounds of the expected...In *Tumbling Into Landscape,* the central figure stands up straight, feet facing forward and arms by her sides, palms out. The stance is a variation on the mountain pose in yoga, taken to ground oneself on the earth and in the present. Together, this composite silhouette with the group of paintings forms a single artwork, an altarpiece to an alternative creation myth.

Being an American today is different from being one in the era of the Hudson River School, yet the way these artists taught us to think about the United States has left an indelible mark. Even today, it is not uncommon for strangers to ask me where I am from. When I respond that I am from New York, some of these strangers, dissatisfied with my answer, follow up with, "Where are you from originally?" The question implies that I am not of this place, somehow not quite American. My response to such questioning has been in part to focus on the notion of hybridity in my art practice, to create artworks that defy classification. Working across media and conceptual boundaries, I create bodies of work that seem to constantly shift and evolve—a series of modular parts that stabilize for a moment, then separate again, with the potential to become something else.

Swirling around the figure are life-size wilting leaves based on tracings of medicinal plants from the Newark Museum's herbarium collection...The figure is also encircled by stylized gold flames, a reference to the elaborate frames of the historical paintings. By using the gold within the body, I wanted to imply a different kind of frame, one that moves, that is molten and shifts its boundaries.

One space where I disrupt the boundary between interior and exterior worlds is a double ribbon of words by Sojourner Truth, handwritten across the figure's sternum and lower torso. Almost obscured within a dark field of shrubbery and clouds, these words read "give her a chance to set

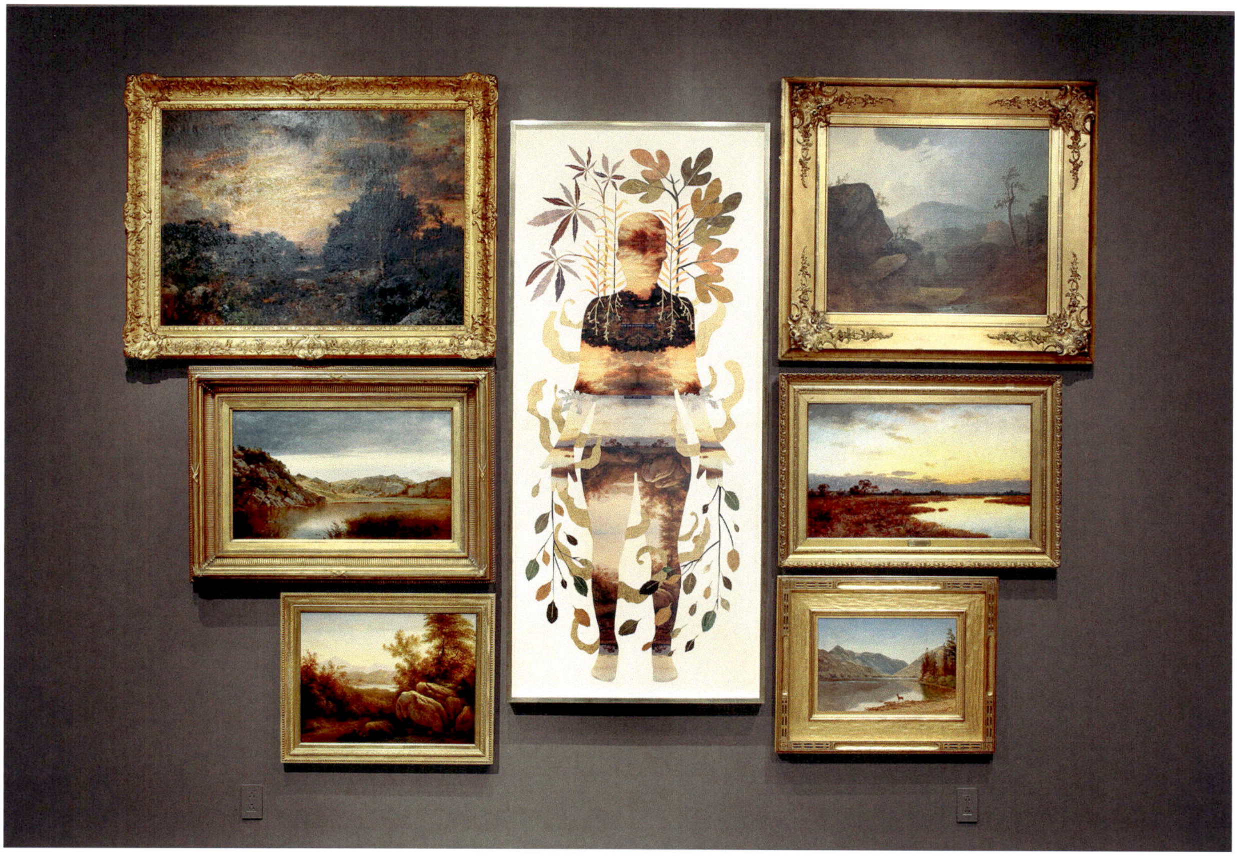

Saya Woolfalk, Installation view from *Saya Woolfalk: Tumbling into Landscape* with *Self-Portrait (Words by Sojourner Truth)*, 2021, hand-painted stained rice paper and Bristol paper, Japanese gold foil paper, watercolor, gouache, gudy glue, acrylic gel medium, digital print on Hahnemühle paper, methyl cellulose, gum arabic, and Nepalese Lhakpa paper, chine colléed on Arches paper, 32 × 74 in., Courtesy the artist and The Newark Museum of Art, Newark, NJ, Photograph: Richard Goodbody

it" and "right side up again." Sojourner Truth grew up in slavery on a farm in the same area represented in the Hudson River School paintings, yet there is little trace of her, or people like her, in most of the art of this period.

The six landscape paintings that inspired my inquiry act as found objects flanking the figure, and the composition of the elements together looks alternately like pelvic bones or a set of wings. To me this implies that the assemblage is only one part of a more monumental body. This fragment, made up of other fragments, suggests the potential for a larger figure, one that is not defined or contained by a traditional frame. —Saya Woolfalk (This text is an edited excerpt from the artist's writing for *Saya Woolfalk: Field Notes From The Empathic Universe* and the catalog of the same title, commissioned by the Newark Museum.)

EBONY G. PATTERSON

She is soil
She is the memory
She is land
She is home
She is the burial
She is mother
She is aunt
She is sister, cousin, friend
She is the birthing
She is nourishment
She is time
She is the...waiting
She is the...............blessing
She is the mourning
She is love
She is care
She is the bellying
She is protest
She is our warning.

[In] *when the land is in plumage...*, I was thinking about the relationship between a landscape and a peacock's tail. Here, we see the plumage of the peacock's tail that appears to be the land creeping up the wall, but there is a molting happening. There is a changing, an oozing, a shedding that seems to be happening from this white peacock. I made this work thinking about the idea that somehow the land holds the secrets. That the land also holds the truth. And what if we were able to pick up the land and to look underneath it, to look in between it, to see all of the mysteries that the beauty on top holds. What would that, then, tell us about the truth of the spaces that we live in, sit in, and exist in? What would that tell us in terms of the truth of the histories that have been erased because of this molting? When I made this work [in 2020] a number of protests were already beginning to sweep the nation, but at the same time a number of fires in California had also started. It made me think about the slash-and-burn agricultural practices that the farmers used to clear the land, that somehow fire becomes a purifier in removing things. That somehow witnessing these burnings, I couldn't help but think about how the molting in a peacock's tail is also related to this moment. There was a change that was happening on and across the land that was going to create a regenerative moment. This moment is by no means new, but the question is what are we learning through the process of regeneration? Here in this work, the peacock is looking back at its own tail, witnessing its own molting, its own collapsing, its own growing, its own oozing. —Ebony G. Patterson

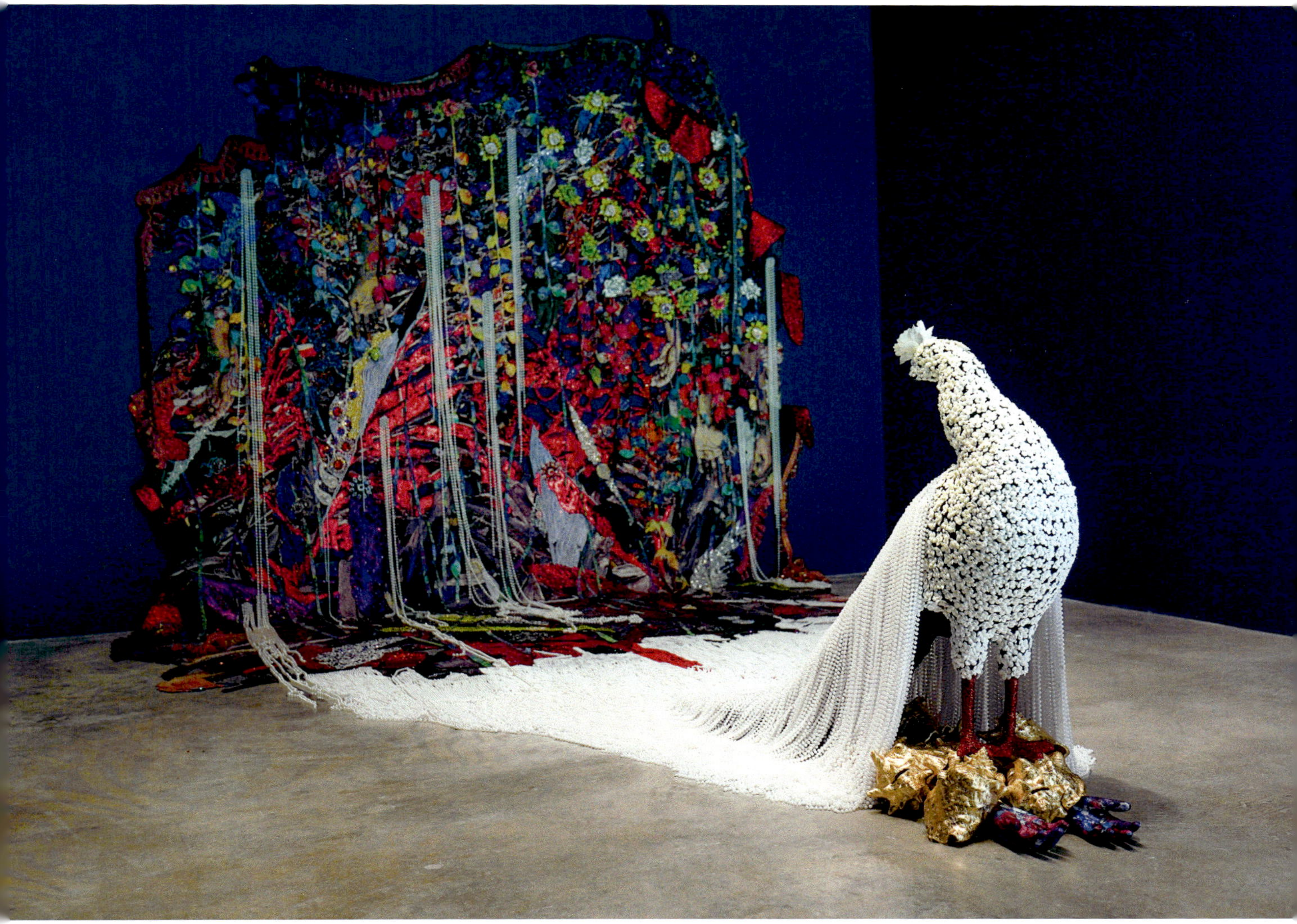

Ebony G. Patterson, *when the land is in plumage...,* 2020, glitter, glue, beads, plaster, conch shells, gold leaf, porcelain, paint, trimmings, jewelry, embellishments, fabric, jacquard tapestry, and paraffin wax, 108 × 134 × 140 in., Courtesy the artist and Monique Meloche Gallery, Chicago, IL

WENDY RED STAR

Red Star's early self-portrait series, *Four Seasons* (2006), signals a point of departure for several serial photographic projects that followed. This is one of the earliest series in which Red Star used herself as a subject, and it captures the humor and playfulness integral both to Crow culture and to her artwork. In the series, Red Star poses within constructed dioramas filled with inflatable animals and artificial materials, a project that pokes fun at the boundaries between conceived authenticity and stereotypical portrayals of Native subjects. The portraits encourage self-reflection, making viewers aware of the deeply ingrained stereotypes of Native Americans in popular culture. By staging herself in artificial scenes, Red Star evokes precedents like Cindy Sherman's *Untitled Film Stills* from the late 1970s, in which the artist posed in fictitious scenes that make visual reference to Hollywood B movies. Like Sherman, Red Star draws on feminine stereotypes constructed and reified through popular culture. However, rather than performing the self as multiple, as Sherman does through her constantly changing disguises, Red Star is driven by the complex narrative of her identity as an Apsáalooke woman and by an awareness of the difficulties that Native women encounter navigating the art world. In this sense, her series represents a strategic mode of intervention into the conventions of portraiture and can be understood through its signifiers of race, cultural rootedness, and female agency, tying this body of work instead to self-portraiture precedents by artists like Carrie Mae Weems, Ana Mendieta, and Laura Aguilar. —Nadiah Rivera Fellah (From *Wendy Red Star: "A Scratch on the Earth,"* in: exh. cat. Newark Museum 2019, ed. by Nadiah Rivera Fellah and Tricia Laughlin Bloom)

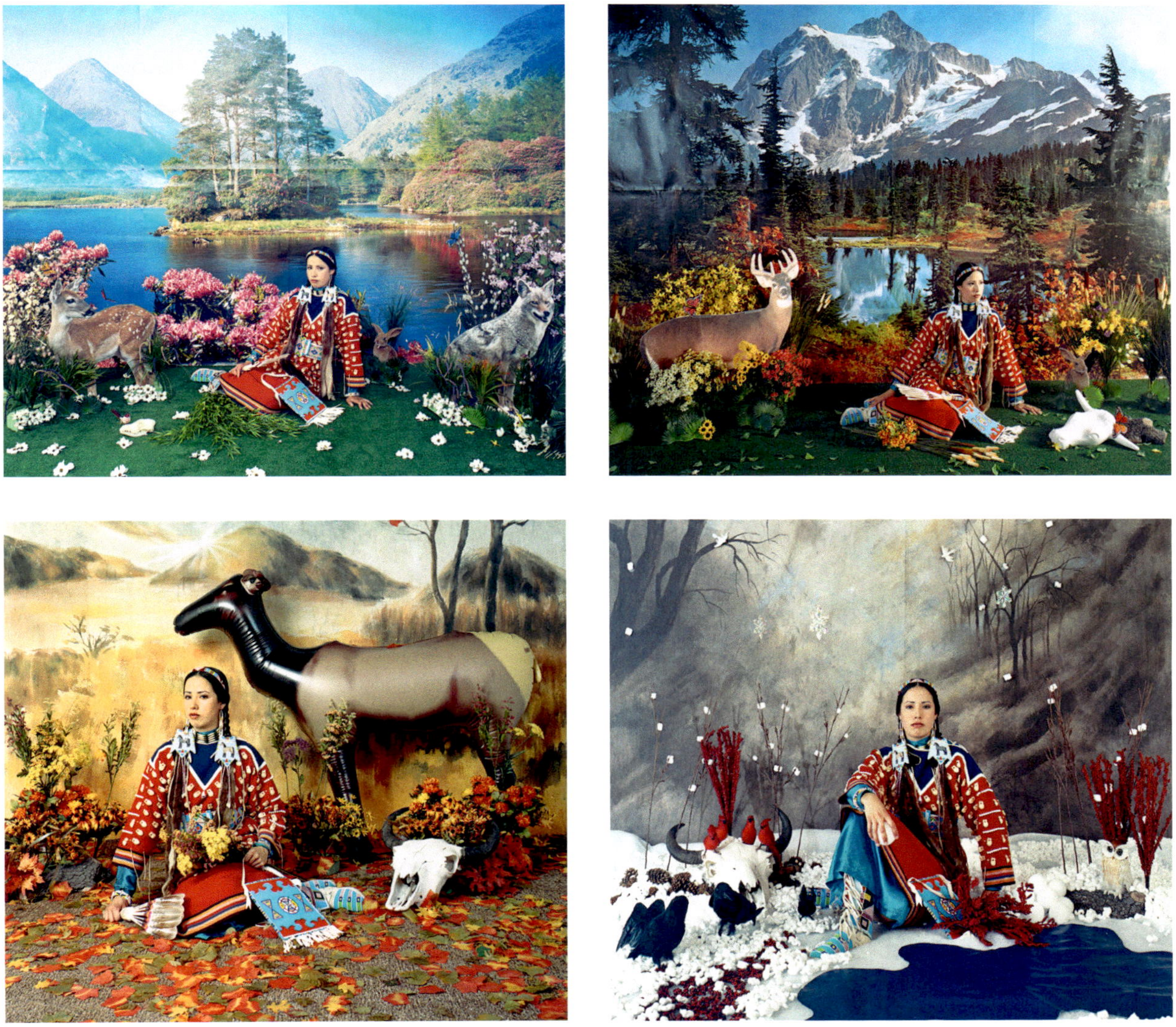

Wendy Red Star, *Four Seasons*, from top left to bottom right: *Spring / Summer / Fall / Winter*, 2006, series of four archival pigment prints on Sunset Fiber rag, 21 × 24 in. each, Art Museum of West Virginia University, Morgantown, WV, Courtesy the artist and Sargent's Daughters, New York, NY

JAUNE QUICK-TO-SEE SMITH

"A map is not an empty form for me, it's not an icon of this incredible country. It's not just a vacant idea, it's real. It's about real land—stolen land, polluted land."[1]

"In her new series of monumental paintings, Jaune Quick-to-See Smith rotates the American map, encircling the landmass in a sea of bead and basketwork patterns from the Plateau region. This simple but iconoclastic act dislodges the landmass from its contextual meaning...Maps have never been mere objective descriptions of landmasses. They have been instruments in the exercise of power and territorial expansion. Across the series, Smith hints at the map's many potential alternate meanings. Female fertility figures grace each canvas, asserting that the landmass is, foremost, Mother Earth herself. Pictographic turtles reassert America's previous title to many of its inhabitants: Turtle Island. References to 'India' recall Columbus's geographic mistake that still reverberates in our language. Through the simple rotation, Smith notes, the map becomes a 'thing of Indian power.'"[2]

"As early as I can remember, I wanted to be an artist. My father would draw little pictures of animals that I would carry in my pockets. Besides reading books, it took me into a place that didn't have violence in it, didn't have hunger, was just the most wonderful place to be...In high school I decided that I did, yes, want to go to college and take art. At the end of the year, the professor called me into his office and said, 'You can draw better than the men, but I have to tell you, you need to go into another field because,' he said, 'you'll never be able to be an artist. Women are not artists.'"[3]

1 Jaune Quick-To-See Smith, in Joshua Hunt, "Jaune Quick-to-See Smith Maps New Meanings," *The New York Times*, December 1, 2022, https://www.nytimes. com/2021/12/02/t-magazine/jaune-quick-to-see-smith.html.

2 "Jaune Quick-to-See Smith: Woman in Landscape," *Garth Greenan Gallery,* https://garthgreenan.com/exhibitions/jaune-quick-to-see-smith-woman-in-landscape/press-release.

3 Jaune Quick-to-See Smith, "Meet Jaune Quick-to-See Smith," video for Smithsonian American Art Museum, December 3, 2012, https://americanart.si.edu/artist/jaune-quick-see-smith-4505.

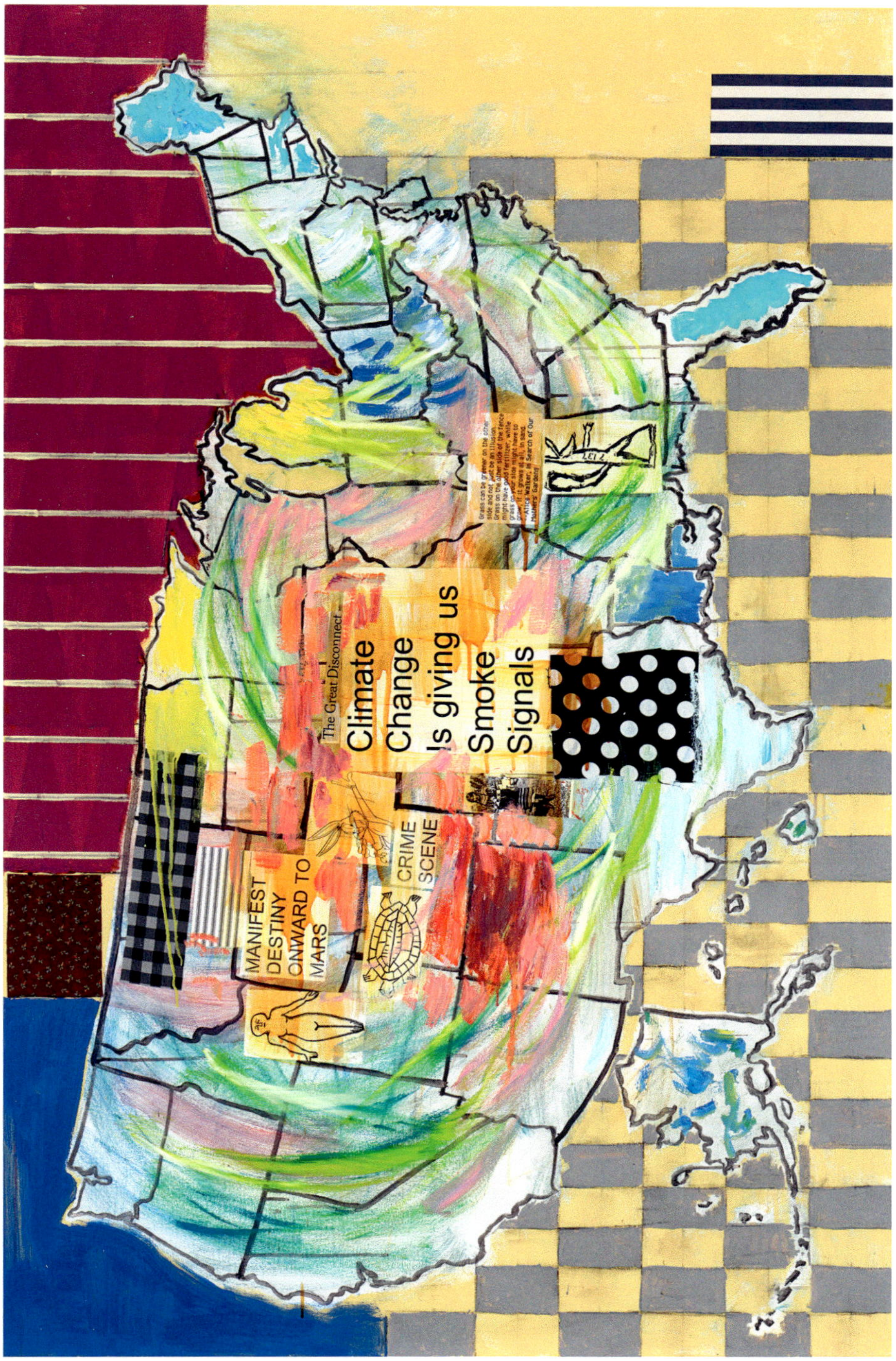

Jaune Quick-to-See Smith, *Smoke Signals Map*, 2021, mixed media on canvas, 72 × 48 in., Courtesy the artist and Garth Greenan Gallery, New York, NY

KAY WALKINGSTICK

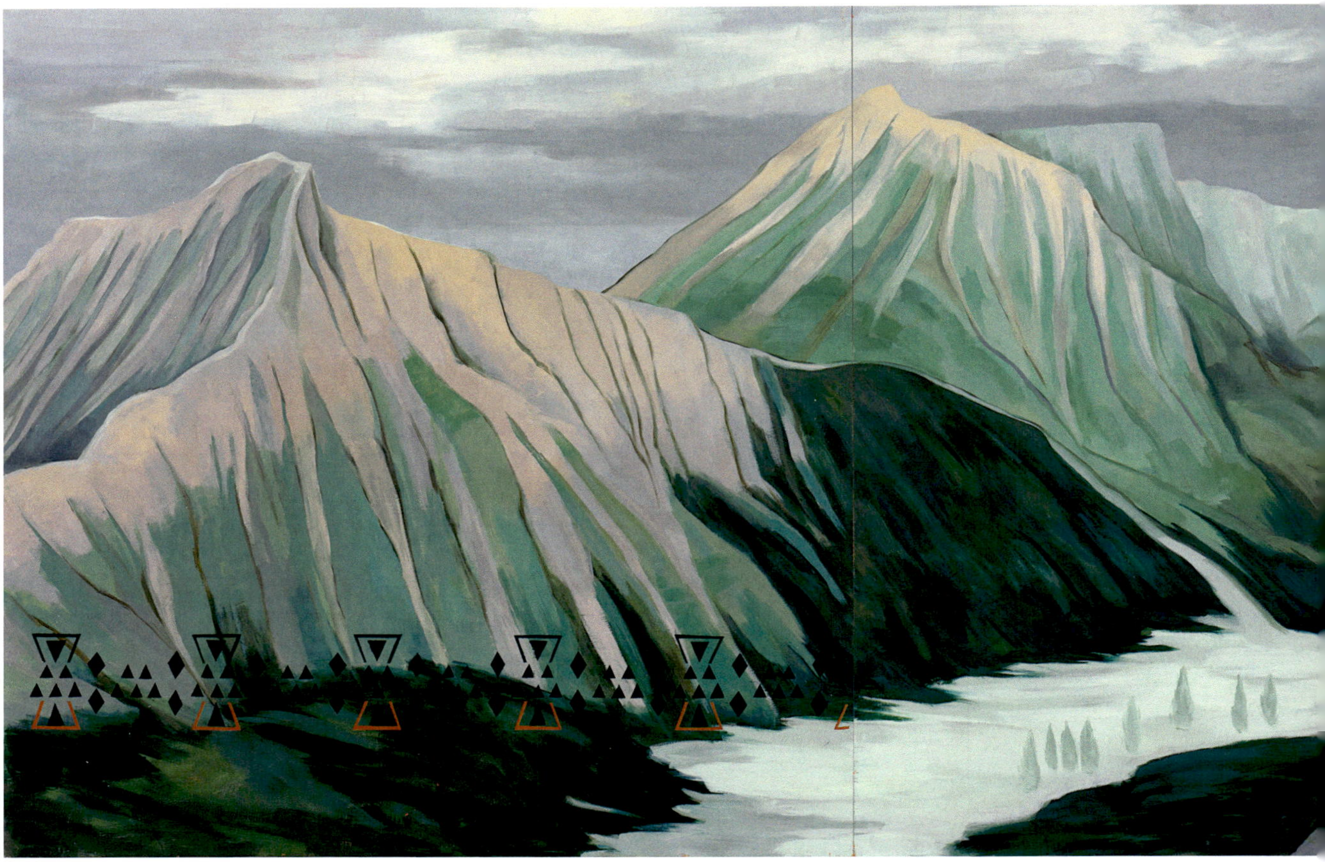

"The craft of painting is important to me...they're crafted with care...My intention is to have a thing that really is as beautiful or nearly as beautiful as the place—our beautiful planet deserves to be described beautifully...It is [also] important to me on a very deep level, on a spiritual level, that people understand that we are all living on Indian land, every one of us. Some of the projects being done in museums are beginning to recognize that, but I think that many people don't remember not-so-distant history...The fact is that we're living on Indian land. There are Indian people everywhere in this country. When I first came to New York, the view was that, well, there are no Indians anywhere in New York. Certainly, there are! Maybe not millions, but thousands of people who are Native people, Indigenous people, are living in NYC. So, it's important to me that people recognize that this land is beautiful, and this is Indian territory.

The other thing that's equally important to me, is the fact that we have this gorgeous Earth that we're going to lose. We're losing our Earth because we haven't taken care of it. And this exquisite planet is going to be drowned and gone, not tomorrow, but maybe the next day...We have a very short time here to take care of this and maybe put off losing it. But our planet is truly endangered, and I want people to understand that.

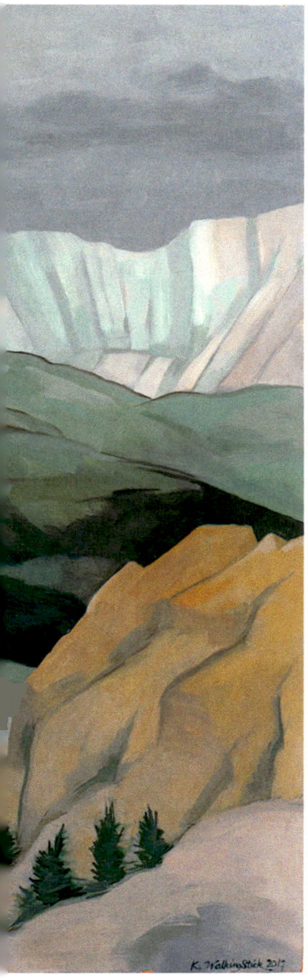

Kay WalkingStick, *Winter Passage*, 2017, oil on panel in two parts, 36 × 72⅛ × 2 in., Courtesy the artist and Hales Gallery, London and New York, NY

I want people to see my paintings as beautiful because I want them to remember that our planet is full of wonder. My goals are different from the nineteenth-century landscapes of the Hudson River School, but I want my paintings to be as beautiful, because I want people to remember what we have and what we're throwing away. So, I work at that, it's intentional...I want the works to be genuine, authentic.

The patterns presented in my paintings are not general Indian patterns (if there is such a thing). They are from very specific people and based on very specific patterns...The pattern becomes a barrier of sorts. It's almost like a fence. It's not integrated into the painting because the goal is to stop the eyes of the viewer and force them to see the pattern and to recognize that it is on top of the land. It's superimposed on the land. So, the viewer will think about that pattern when looking at the painting. If I integrated it into the clouds or something like that, it would be a decorative element. By putting it out front it becomes a barrier. They're forced to recognize that a pattern is there and it has meaning...It's a stencil that is applied differently from the way the rest of the work is painted... It becomes very different-looking in the paint surface itself and by doing this, it separates that pattern, otherwise it would just look like part of the land. So, this way it looks like a separate entity. It forces people to think about it. "What's going on?" I'd really like people to just look at the paintings and say, "Oh, I get it."

In my research for patterns, I look for artifacts and objects of the specific tribe who live in the place I am painting. The landscapes are not past; there is nothing past about any of it. I go to the locations, make drawings and photographs and come home and paint. They're not about a memory or history. They're my short-term memory of a place. They're not about what it was. They're about what it is. Indian people are here right now, living on this land and that is the subject of these landscapes.

We all know that we are destroying our land, and we have to start seriously taking care of it. Maybe there's still time. I tend to be a rather optimistic person. I really believe that we can do things successfully, and make changes if we work at it. —Kay WalkingStick (Edited excerpt from a conversation with Amanda Malmstrom and Kate Menconeri, October 3, 2022)

CECILIA VICUÑA

My father realized that I was a little reader—not only a writer, but I was, above all, a reader, that I devoured everything [laughing] that was in that house. And so he gave me a subscription to *Encyclopaedia Britannica*, and the *Encyclopaedia Britannica* had a series for youngsters, for teenagers. And every year they had a yearbook. And I remember that it was probably the year 1965 that the yearbook had an essay, an article about the Club of Rome, a gathering of scientists that warned that the world was going to come to an end if the destructive activity could go on the way it was happening. So I learned that, and I knew that my life work would be precisely about that. So I was turned into an activist as a teenager.

And so I think that operated in a sort of mysterious deep level in me because my first works when I became aware—just as I had become aware that I was a writer—that I was an artist were given to me by the ocean. And this happened in Concón. Concón is one of the most sacred sites, with culture going back 10,000 years.

And it was the site selected by the Chilean government to place the first oil refinery. So when I was growing up, playing on the beach of Concón, the soles of my feet were already black with petroleum. And we didn't think of it as pollution, but we knew it was there. We knew we would come home and have to spend hours trying to remove that black thing from our fingers, from our toes.

So this was part of my body, part of my being. And my art began one day when I felt that the sea, the light, the sun, everything was aware. I sort of dissolved, disappeared as a person, and I just became someone who grabbed a little stick lying about and I planted it as a sign that I could see that everything around me was aware. So it's a kind of activism that operates in the acknowledgement of the awareness of the world around us. Comes from the understanding that your awareness is possible because everything is aware.

Somehow I had clarity to understand that that was a new kind of art—new, perhaps, because it is ancestral; new, because it's probably thousands of years old; new, because perhaps we forgot it. And now it's coming back.

Was it ritual? Was it performance? Was it an act of awareness? It was all of that. At the time, nobody used the word "performance," and so it predates any sort of affiliation to a known category. And that's why I call it *art de precario*, creating my own category. —Cecilia Vicuña (Text courtesy Solomon R. Guggenheim Museum, New York, NY)

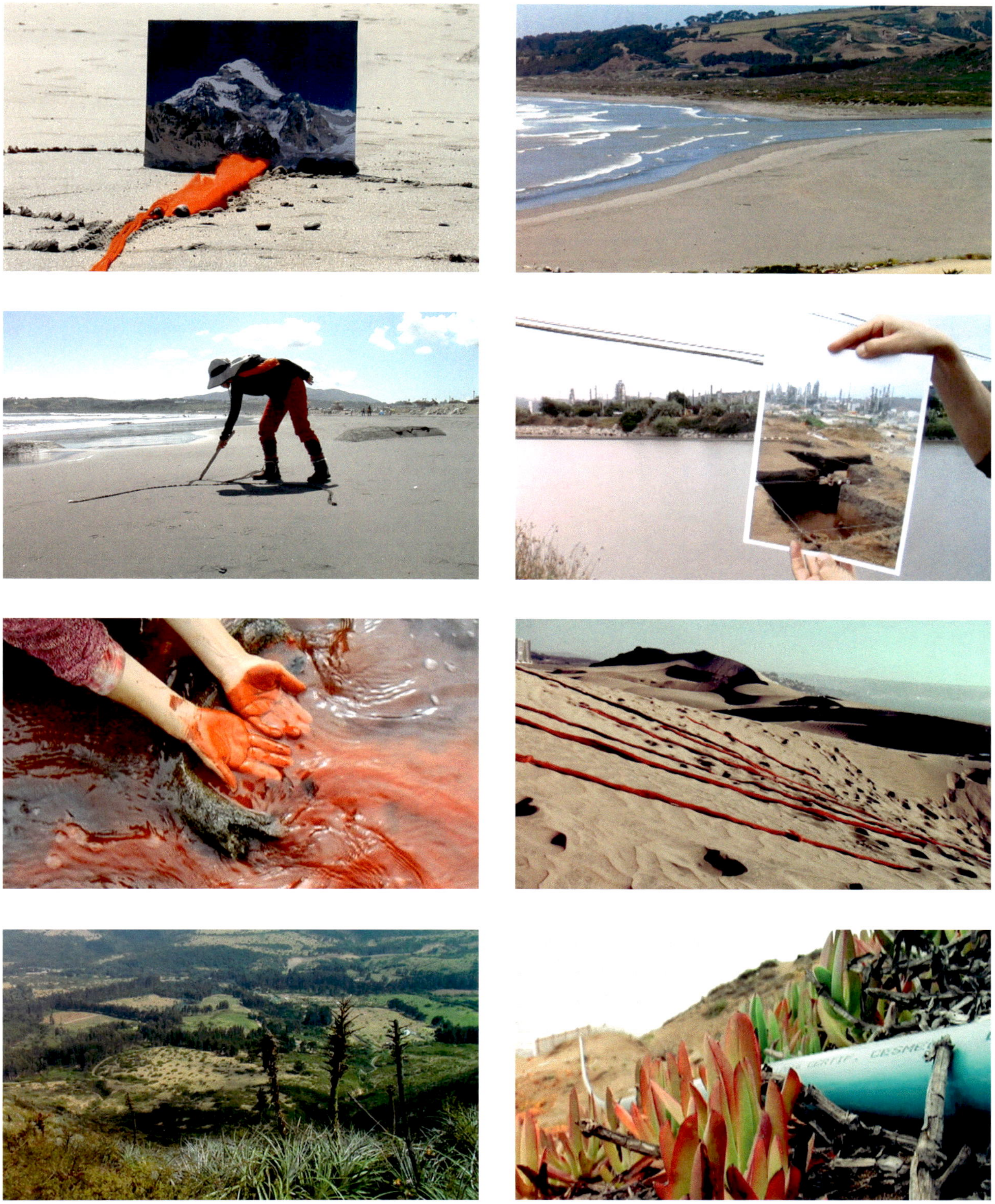

Cecilia Vicuña, *Kon Kon,* 2010, film stills, color, sound, HD video, Spanish with English subtitles, 53:55 min, Courtesy the artist, Lehmann Maupin, and Electronic Arts Intermix, New York, NY

JEAN SHIN

By situating my work outdoors, I amplify a dissected view of organic life cycles, while maintaining opportunities for close-up viewing and intimate reflection. I create imaginative installations, using cast-off materials to draw attention to everyday objects, underscoring their history of use, circulation, and cumulative impact upon our lived environments.

I recently collaborated with scientists to execute a monumental installation incorporating living species to address whole ecological systems. My commission at Cherry Street Pier for Philadelphia Contemporary presents a filtration ecosystem motored by freshwater mussels. Once abundant in the Delaware River, they now face extinction. This fountain is situated at the pier where polluted river water is pumped into the Delaware River. Made of mass produced and unused vintage pearl buttons manufactured all over the world, *Freshwater* (2022) is an urgent call to care for the mussels that are vital to our health and the health of our waterways.

Through research, I examine how extractive practices, overconsumption, and pollution from e-waste and plastics have devastated habitats and contributed to biodiversity loss in both land and water. Interdisciplinarity is fundamental to my practice that approaches materials and concepts holistically. My work is in constant evolution, never fixed. *Freshwater*, for instance, though already installed, can be expanded and rethought. Vibrant exchanges between artist and scientist underpin my practice, and will continue to, in particular through my residency at Stanford University working with infectious disease scientists conducting research on the effects of plastic pollution on planetary health. Together, we are reimagining how regenerative and circular practices can reverse harm and leave a thriving ecosystem for the next generation.

On the occasion of *Women Reframe American Landscape* at Thomas Cole National Historic Site, I am creating a time capsule and archive of waste from my past art installations. A poignant balance structures this sculptural installation. *Displaced* is simultaneously a reflexive apparatus for a given community, and a work informed by my experience as a first-generation immigrant bearing witness to racial, economic, and environmental injustices. It is a perspective that inspires me to originate meaning out of discards as a form of emotional and ecological repair; to address these inequities by reimagining the material potential of our world; to reveal forgotten histories and make visible the undervalued labor of the marginalized. This experiment in form asks that we question the value and role of preservation when confronted with the climate crisis. Working as an artist in the age of the Anthropocene, this future work brings a self-critical lens to the struggle to maintain a zero-waste art practice. How might I balance the work of repurposing and the processes of entropy and decay? What knowledge might this project bring to the complex relationship of land stewardship and art-world practices? —Jean Shin

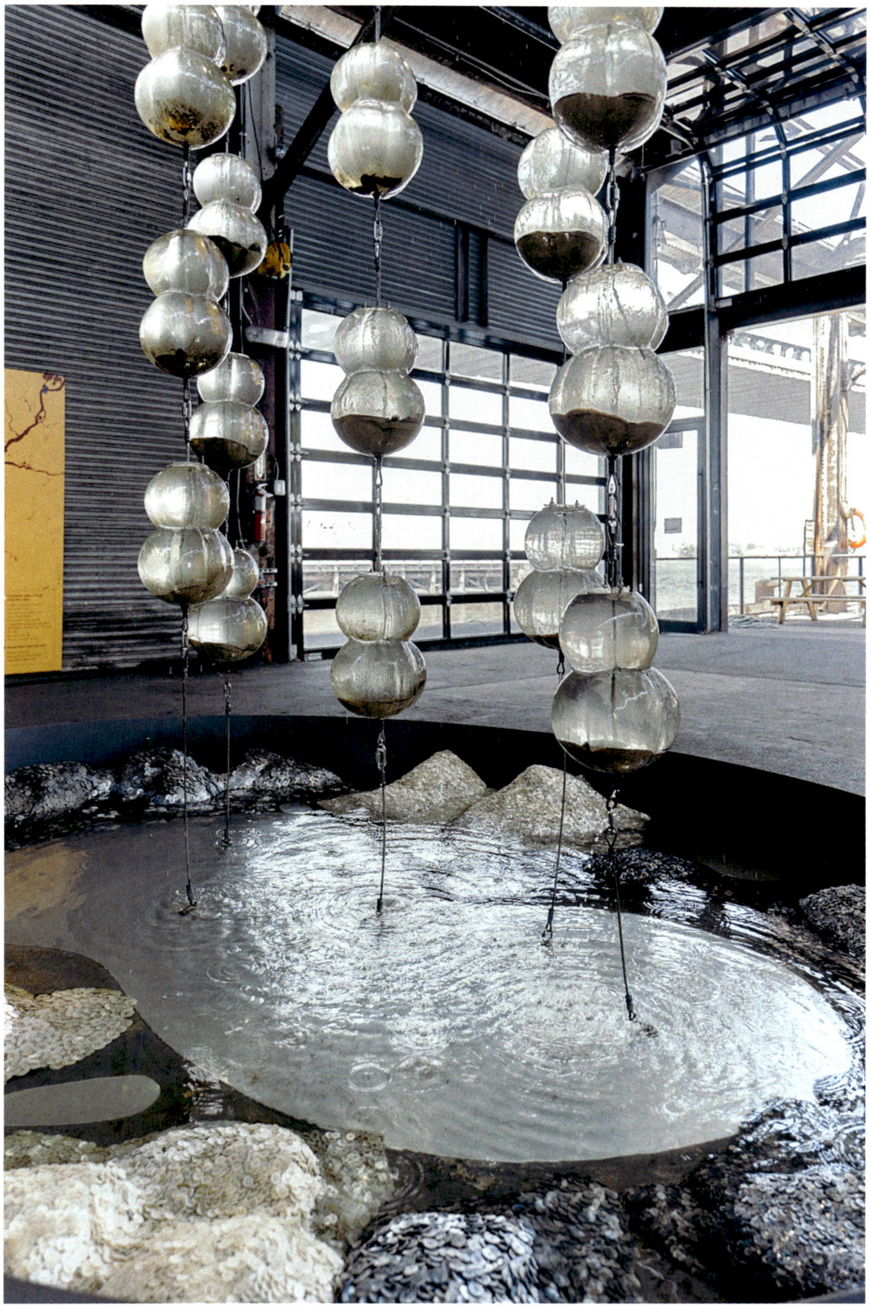

Jean Shin, *Freshwater*, 2022, freshwater mussels, glass vessels, sand, water pumped from the Delaware River, vintage mother-of-pearl shell buttons, metal basins, Perspex mirror and cables, various dimensions, Installation at Cherry Street Pier, Philadelphia, PA, Commissioned by Philadelphia Contemporary, Courtesy the artist and Philadelphia Contemporary, Photograph: David McDowell

MARY MATTINGLY

Swale was a floating edible landscape built atop a 5,000-square-foot barge that traveled to public piers in New York City welcoming visitors to harvest perennial fruits and vegetables free of charge. *Swale* docked at public piers in Brooklyn, Governors Island, and the Bronx in spaces adjacent to the city's public land. Public land in the city equates to 30,000 acres, as compared with the 100 acres of community garden space where, if you have a plot, picking food is allowed. In the ways that artist Agnes Denes's *Wheatfield* turned New York City's land value on its head, *Swale* re-valued public land by using the 'common law' of the water as a loophole to do what had been illegal on public land: legally, picking plants was considered destruction of property. *Swale* followed the insights of social scientist Elinor Ostrom and Traditional Ecological Knowledge that claimed that in a vibrant commons, people had a vital role to play not only as beneficiaries, but also as co-creators, protectors, and decision makers.

Swale was also experiential: people walked onto a barge adjacent to a city park to find that it looked, smelled, and tasted like land but felt different. As they grew accustomed to the moving vessel and their forested surroundings, their perspective shifted and soon it could feel as if the city was moving back and forth, as the structure they were on began to feel stable. People suddenly cared about everything: where the soil came from, where the water came from that watered the plants, and how this translated to the food they were eating at home. An edible forest built on an industrial barge questions land use in the city, food systems, infrastructure, public-health priorities, and whether the establishment of a commons is still possible. It can also model alternatives, request involvement, and put trust in city dwellers as agents who care for shared resources. As a direct result of *Swale* and the support of community groups, in 2017 the New York City Parks Department opened their first land-based pilot—a public "foodway" at Concrete Plant Park in the Bronx. In line with Mierle Laderman Ukeles's *Maintenance Art*, I believe in a shift towards revaluing the work of maintenance, through art and through actions that support it. —Mary Mattingly

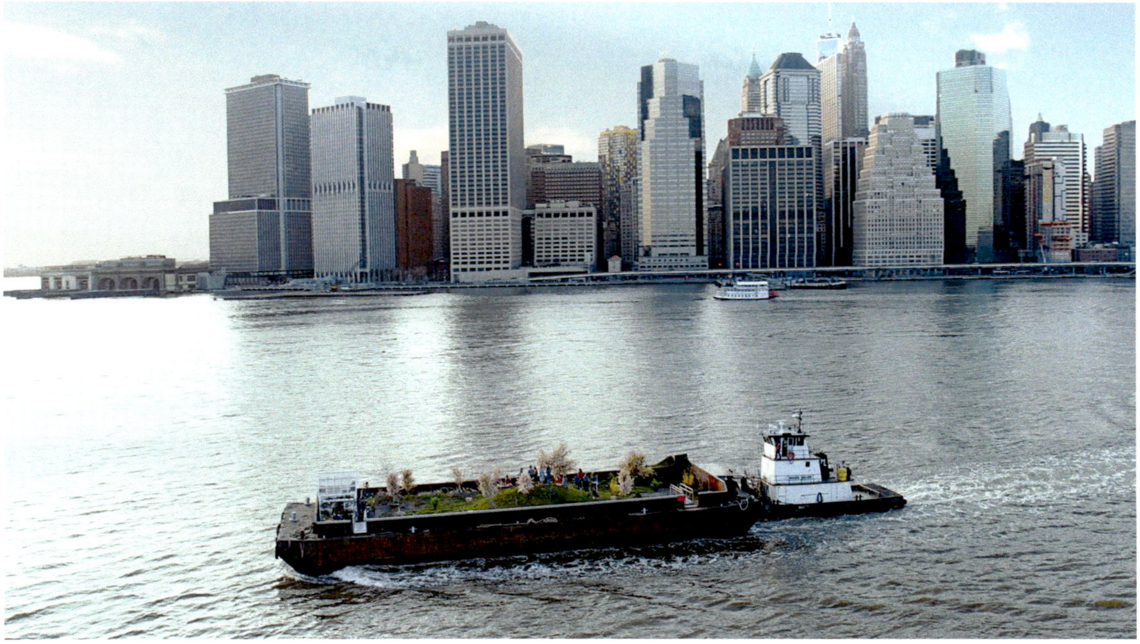

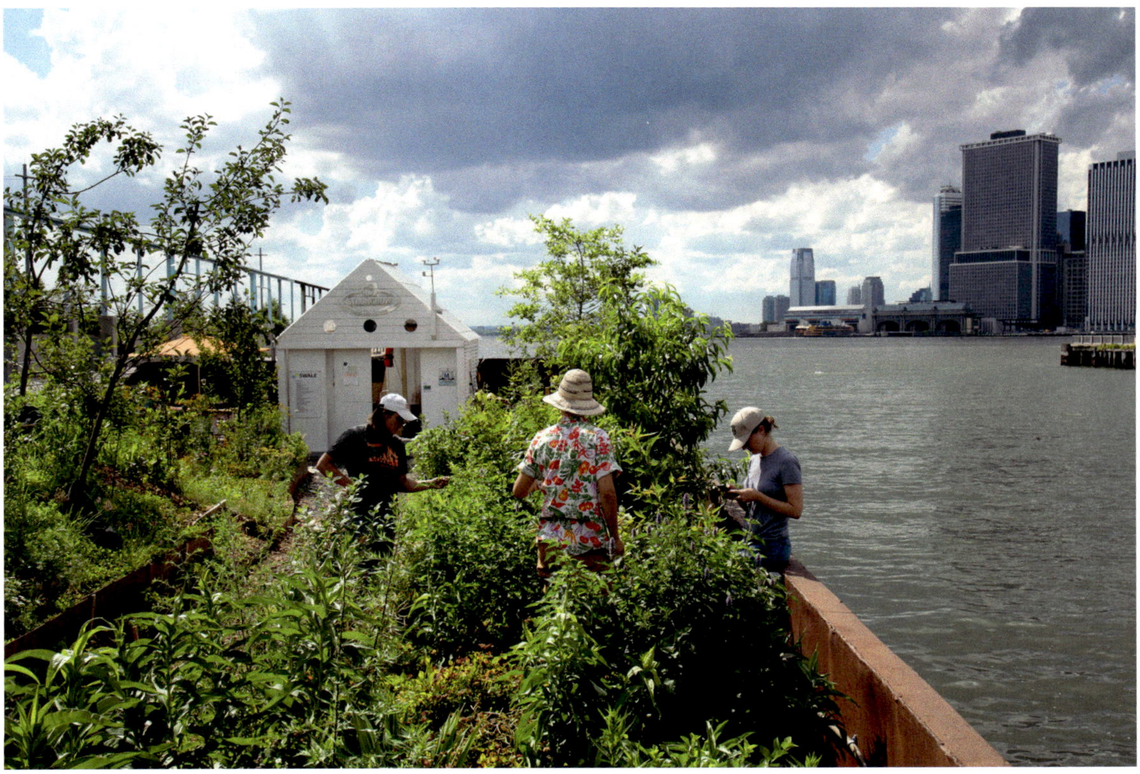

Mary Mattingly, Views of *Swale*, 2017–ongoing, floating edible landscape on a barge: steel, soil, gravel, perennial plants, water, IBC totes, wood, 130 × 40 × 20 ft., Courtesy the artist, Photograph: Cloud Factory

MARIE LORENZ

Wave Chime came out of a collaboration with the composer, Kurt Rohde in 2021. I was looking for ways that my marine debris installations could generate sound as we developed ideas for our opera. I have always been attracted to junk from the beach, collecting foam, driftwood, sea glass, and plastic for prints and sculptures. My early flotsam installations sometimes generated a didactic voice that didn't entirely resonate with me. When people saw marine debris in my artwork, they assumed I was trying to relay a sense of shame, as if I wanted the audience to feel bad that I had found this trash on the beach. But sometimes I feel quite the opposite, I feel lucky and excited to find it. I think beach foam and marine debris are magical and mysterious and I want the audience to feel the same way, at least at first. When you see a Jean Tinguely sculpture, you don't immediately feel bad that someone threw away all those flywheels and bicycle parts. Tinguely's position on waste and industry is not the very first thing that comes to mind, at least for me. It's more about some hopeful, hapless, impossible harmony. Then, gradually I might think about waste or hubris, like seeing into the hidden and inept side of futurism. That slow reveal just makes it better. So using flotsam in this new theatrical, kinetic, sound-producing way for the *Wave Chime* was a breakthrough moment, an opportunity to extend the magic and harmony I feel about waste, and open another door somehow with the same material. The *Wave Chime* was in development right when I was asked to make a piece for Catskill Creek, and it came together almost by accident. The creek is reasonably protected from wind, and the audience was able to get very close; it was a perfect water stage. Being able to engage an audience that way helped push everything along to the standing instruments that I am making now.

When I came to the Thomas Cole Site for the first time, I saw Thomas Cole's painting *Interior of the Colosseum, Rome* (1832) and read about his interest in that form. He had written at the time that the Colosseum was "stupendous, yet beautiful in its destruction." "It looks," he wrote, "more like a work of nature than of man." I perceive city infrastructure around the water in that same way, and as a kind of exercise, I try to lose the distinction between the natural and the manmade. I think the practice of blurring one's perception in that way can show the fragility of these very solid things that we take for granted. For Thomas Cole, it was the Colosseum and then his fantastical constructions in *The Course of Empire*. For me, it might be a crumbling train bridge or a cavernous sewer tunnel on the waterfront that inspires that same feeling. But then we are in a different time, just beginning to understand that man does not return to dust, or we still might, but our empire won't. So now the intentional blurring of perception has an antipodal point, when your focus slides back, the image becomes more real and more destitute. —Marie Lorenz

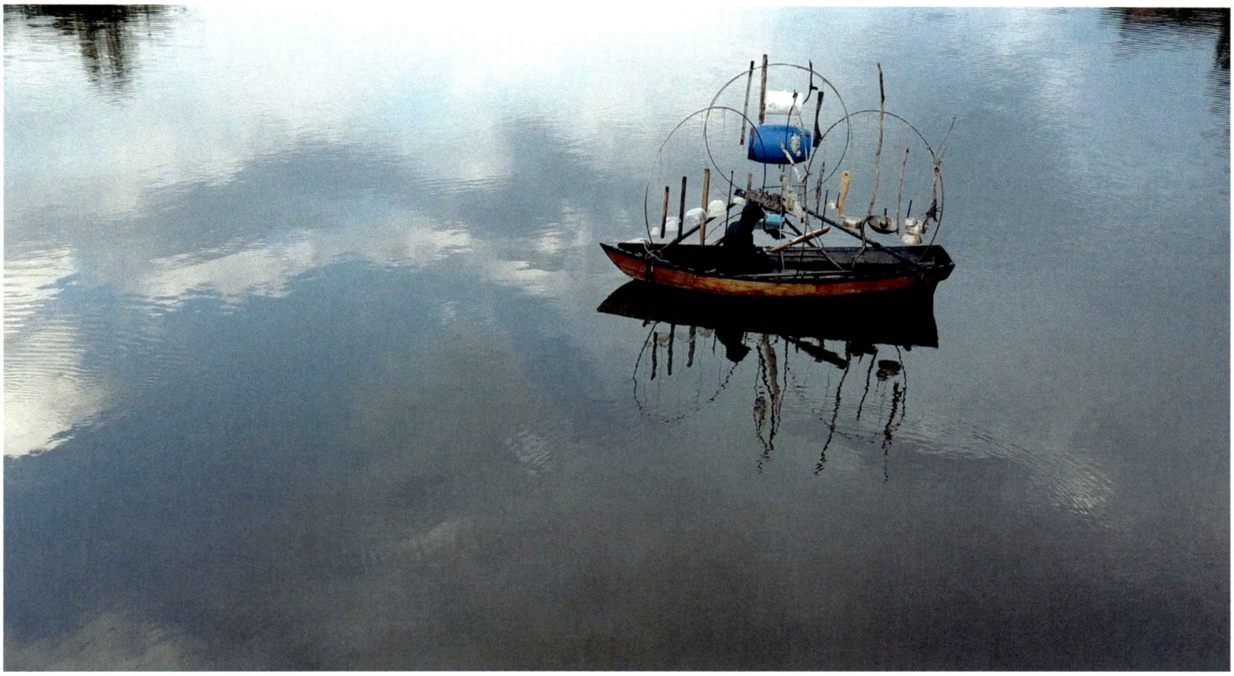

Marie Lorenz, *Wave Chime*, 2021, wood, steel, sea glass, and marine debris, 96 × 168 × 168 in., Courtesy the artist and Jack Hanley Gallery, New York, NY

WOMEN, LAND, + ART: A BRIEF AND INCOMPLETE TIMELINE

Women Reframe American Landscape includes the first large-scale retrospective of any woman artist of the Hudson River School. Why has this taken two centuries? Why have studies and exhibitions of landscape art in the United States overwhelmingly focused on art made by men? Historically, women have experienced unequal access to the art institutions, associations, schools, social spaces, and mentorships required to achieve "professional" artist status. However, women indeed produced artwork and pursued careers as artists, in alternative and evolving ways in the ongoing struggle for gender equity in the arts. This timeline explores this history, recognizing the complex interconnections between gender, art, politics, and land. The dates and events below not only mark progress within the art world, but also in legislative changes related to women's suffrage, property rights, and bodily autonomy. We hope that this timeline, while brief and ongoing, will improve and expand alongside the growing attention given to the lives and work of women.

Researched and edited by Sofia Thieu D'Amico and Heather Bruegl with Amanda Malmstrom

1670 A free Black woman, **Zipporah Potter,** becomes Boston's first Black property owner, purchasing a home at a time when women and people of color could not legally own land.

1718 In Pennsylvania, women gain the ability to own and manage property if their husband is incapacitated.

1771 In New York, the **Act to Confirm Certain Conveyances and Directing the Manner of Proving Deeds to Be Recorded** requires married women to sign the deed to her property before her husband sold or mortgaged it, and to meet with a judge in private to provide assurance that the transfer met with her approval.

1781 **Nancy Ward** (Cherokee) addresses the US Treaty Commissioners, advocating for conflict resolution between the US and Cherokee, as well as Cherokee retention of tribal lands.

1805 **Sacagawea** (Shoshone) joins the Corp of Discovery, helping lead Lewis and Clark on their journey to the Pacific Ocean.

1824 **Sarah** and **Anna Peale** are elected to the honorary position of Academician by the **Pennsylvania Academy of the Fine Arts**, established in 1805.

1826 The first session of the **National Academy of Design** is held, supervised by two Academicians and twenty students–all men–and becomes the country's leading arts institution.

1827 **Rosalba Peale** is named an **Honorary Member of the National Academy of Design**, and **Ann Hall**, **Emily Maverick**, **Maria Anna Maverick**, **Frances Platt Townsend Lupton**, and **Julia Fulton** are named Associates. The six women join 56 male members.

1830 The **Indian Removal Act** displaces about 40,000 Indigenous people from southeastern regions of the US, leading to the **Trail of Tears**.

1831 The **National Academy of Design's Antique School** begins admitting women to draw from casts.

1833 **Ann Hall** is nominated as an **Academician** of the **National Academy of Design**. She becomes the first female member.

1839 The **Mississippi Married Women's Property Act** sets the standard for American women to own property, becoming the first of a series of Married Women's Property Acts.

1842 The **Philadelphia School of Design for Women** is founded and becomes the longest-surviving school of design for women in the US.

1844 The **Pennsylvania Academy of the Fine Arts** begins organizing classes for women to sketch antique casts and statues.

1848 The **Seneca Falls Convention** meets as the first women's rights convention in the US at the Wesleyan Chapel in Seneca Falls, New York. The convention excludes non-White women and those of lower economic status.

1851 The **New England School of Design for Women** is founded in Boston.

1852 The **New York School of Design for Women** is founded by Susan Carter and others, and later becomes part of the Cooper Institute.

1853 At age seventeen, **Susie Barstow** graduates from the **Rutgers Female Institute,** in a class of nineteen women studying drawing and painting.

1858 **Anna Mary Freeman** becomes the first woman to rent studio space at the **Tenth Street Studio Building**, built in 1857 and a popular studio space for many artists of the Hudson River School. No other women would take studio space there until 1880.

1858 Susie Barstow exhibits work at the **National Academy of Design** for the first time, during Asher Durand's tenure as president.

1860 Artists **Eliza Haldeman, Mary Cassatt**, and several friends begin meeting four days a week to **model for each other,** with Pennsylvania Academy of the Fine Arts administrators allowing them to use the modeling room. At this point, its women's life classes employ **cows** as live models.

1862 The **Homestead Act** accelerates westward expansion by granting adult heads of families 160 acres of surveyed land, and makes it legal for single, widowed, and divorced women to claim land in their own names. The displacement of Indigenous peoples from their homelands escalates.

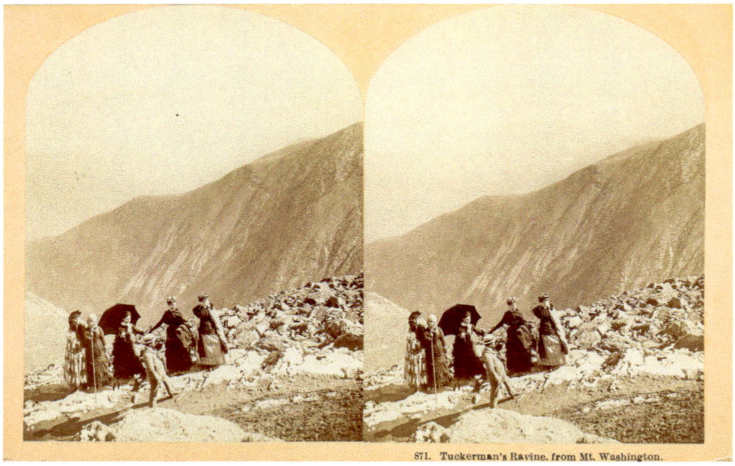

Tuckerman's Ravine, from Mt. Washington, 19th century, stereograph, 4½ × 7 in., American Antiquarian Society, Worcester, MA

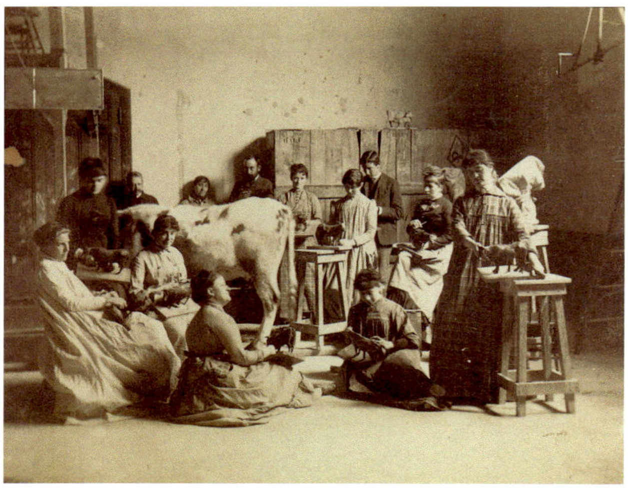

Circle of Eakins, Women's modeling class with cow in Pennsylvania Academy studio, ca.1882, albumen copy print, 3 11⁄16 × 4 15⁄16 in., Charles Bregler's Thomas Eakins Collection, purchased with the partial support of the Pew Memorial Trust, 1985.68.2.801

1862 **Mary Jane Patterson**, a teacher, graduates with a bachelor's degree from Oberlin College. She is considered the **first African-American woman** to earn a **bachelor's degree**.

1863 Under the Homestead Act, **Letitia Carson**—a formerly enslaved woman—files a claim for 160 acres in Oregon as a widow and single mother of two children. In 1869, Letitia Carson's claim was certified by President Ulysses S. Grant, making her the only Black woman in Oregon and one of the first nationally to successfully **secure a claim and legally own land**.

1866 The **American Equal Rights Association (AERA)** is formed by Elizabeth Cady Stanton and Susan B. Anthony, and includes members like Lucretia Mott, Frederick Douglass, Harriet Purvis, and Sojourner Truth, initially under universal suffrage. However, the group begins to splinter as members start to exclusively prioritize White women's or Black men's right to vote.

1867 The **Ladies' Art Association** is founded in New York, becoming the first American women's arts organization.

1868 The **Pennsylvania Academy of the Fine Arts** begins providing a **Ladies' Life Class** with a female model.

1869 Congress passes the **15th Amendment**, granting African American men the right to vote.

1869 Elizabeth Cady Stanton and Susan B. Anthony form the **National Woman Suffrage Association**, opposing the 15th Amendment's exclusion of women. Many White suffragettes actively distance themselves from abolitionist movements and Black women's suffrage in order to further support for their cause.

1871 The **National Academy of Design** begins offering a **life class** for women, with partially-nude male models for female students over twenty-one years of age.

1872 **Victoria Woodhull** becomes the first woman to run for US president.

1877 The **Pennsylvania Academy of the Fine Arts** begins employing **male models** for **Ladies' Life Classes.**

1878 The Georgia Supreme Court upholds the prohibition against African American (free or enslaved) land ownership in the case of ***Swoll et al. v. Oliver et al.***

1880 The **San Francisco Women Artists** forms out of the Sketch Club from the Pine Street Art School in San Francisco as the country's oldest continuously-operating women's arts group.

1883 **Sarah Winnemucca** (Northern Paiute) becomes the first Indigenous woman to publish a book, "Life Among the Piutes: Their Wrongs and Claims," which discusses the forced removal of the Paiute from their homelands.

1895 **Cecilia Beaux** is invited to join the Pennsylvania Academy of Fine Art faculty and becomes **the first female professor at a co-educational art school.**

1896 **Frances Morris** becomes the first woman to work professionally at **The Metropolitan Museum of Art**, founded in 1870.

1910 **Eliza Burton Conley** (Wyandot) becomes the first Indigenous woman to argue before the US Supreme Court, advocating to save what is now known as the Wyandot National Burying Ground.

1912 The **National Association of Women Artists** is founded, and becomes the most successful 19th-century club of women artists.

1920 Congress ratifies the **19th Amendment**, **granting women the right to vote**, after first being introduced to Congress in 1878. However, women of color are still barred from legally voting.

1924 The **Indian Citizenship Act** grants citizenship to all Indigenous peoples in the United States.

1924 Wyoming's **Nellie Tayloe Ross** becomes the first woman elected as a state governor.

1929 New York's **Museum of Modern Art** is founded by **Abby Rockefeller, Lillie P. Bliss,** and **Mary Quinn Sullivan**.

1930 **Gertrude V. Whitney** becomes the founder of the **Whitney Museum of American Art**.

1934 **Dorothy Canning Miller** becomes the first curator at the **Museum of Modern Art**.

1939 **Hilla von Rebay** becomes the first director and curator of the **Guggenheim Museum** in New York.

1964 The **Civil Rights Act of 1964** prohibits discrimination on account of sex, marital status, or sexual orientation.

1965 The **Voting Rights Act** outlaws discriminatory voting practices, including literacy tests as a prerequisite to voting, enabling women of color to legally vote.

1973 The Supreme Court rules in ***Roe v. Wade*** that the Constitution of the United States confers the right to abortion.

1974 The **Equal Credit Opportunity Act** prohibits discrimination on account of sex or marital status in connection with credit, allowing women to fully manage their finances and establish a line of credit without representation by a man.

1978 The **Pregnancy Discrimination Act of 1978** forbids discrimination based on pregnancy in any aspect of employment. Before this act, women could legally be fired from their workplace for going on maternity leave.

1980 The **Equal Employment Opportunity Commission** issues regulations defining sexual harassment and stating it a form of sex discrimination prohibited by the Civil Rights Act of 1964.

1981 **Sandra Day O'Connor** becomes the first woman to be sworn in as a US Supreme Court Justice.

1988 **The Century Association**, a private art and social club in New York City founded in 1847, accepts its first class of 20 women nominees including Helene L. Kaplan, Brooke Astor, and Jacqueline Kennedy Onassis.

1991 The **Civil Rights Act of 1991** adds provisions to Title VII protections, expanding the rights of women to sue and collect damages for sexual discrimination or harassment.

1994 The **Violence Against Women Act** is signed into law, providing $1.6 billion toward the investigation and prosecution of violent crimes against women and establishing the **US Department of Justice's Office on Violence Against Women.**

1997 **Annette Blaugrund** becomes the first female director of the **National Academy of Design**.

2010 ***Remember the Ladies: Women of the Hudson River School***, curated by **Dr. Nancy Siegel** and **Jennifer Krieger** at the Thomas Cole National Historic

Site, is the first exhibition ever to highlight the work of women associated with the Hudson River School.

2016 **The Century Association** in New York City elects **Susan Morrison** as its first female president after 169 years of operation.

2016 **LaDonna Brave Bull Allard** (Lakota) starts the Sacred Stone Camp, kicking off protests at the Dakota Access Pipeline.

2017 **Kiki Smith** becomes the first woman to have a solo exhibition (***Kiki Smith: From the Creek***) at the Thomas Cole National Historic Site.

2019 **Ashley James** becomes the Guggenheim Museum's first Black curator.

2019 **Sharice Davids** (Ho-Chunk) and **Deb Haaland** (Laguna Pueblo) become the first two Indigenous women elected to the US House of Representatives

2019 Congress passes the **Fairness for Breastfeeding Mothers Act** requiring certain public buildings to provide a shielded, hygienic space other than a bathroom, that contains a chair, working surface, and an electrical outlet for use to express milk.

2019 **Emily Cole** becomes the first woman from the 19th-century to have a solo exhibition (***The Art of Emily Cole***) at the Thomas Cole National Historic Site.

2019 **Joy Harjo** (Muscogee Creek) becomes the first Indigenous female Poet Laureate of the United States.

2020 **Patricia Marroquin Norby** is appointed Associate Curator of Native American Art at the Metropolitan Museum of Art, making her the first Indigenous curator and the first full-time curator of Native Art in the museum's 150-year history.

2021 US Representative **Deb Haaland** (Laguna Pueblo) becomes the first Indigenous person to serve as a Secretary of the Interior and the first Indigenous woman to serve in the US Cabinet.

2021 **E. Carmen Ramos** becomes the first person of color and the first woman to occupy the position of Chief Curator of the National Gallery of Art in Washington, DC.

2022 **Cynthia Chavez Lamar** (San Felipe Pueblo) becomes the first Indigenous woman to be named Director of a Smithsonian Museum, leading the National Museum of the American Indian.

2022 The Constitutional Federal right to abortion through *Roe v. Wade* (1973) is overturned, enabling states to restrict abortion access.

2022 **Kentaji Brown Jackson** becomes the first Black woman to be sworn in as a US Supreme Court Justice.

2023–24 *Women Reframe American Landscape* includes *Susie Barstow & Her Circle,* the **first large-scale retrospective exhibition of any woman artist of the Hudson River School.**

ARTIST AND CONTRIBUTOR BIOGRAPHIES

TERESITA FERNÁNDEZ (b. 1968) creates work characterized by an interest in self-reflection and conceptual wayfinding. Her immersive, monumental works are inspired by a rethinking of landscape and place, as well as by diverse historical and cultural references. Born in Miami, FL and currently based in New York City, Fernández received a BFA from Florida International University, Miami in 1990 and an MFA from Virginia Commonwealth University in 1992. Often drawing inspiration from the natural world, Fernández's practice unravels the intimacies between matter, places, and human beings. Her works poetically challenge ideas about landscape by exposing the history of colonization and the inherent violence embedded in how we imagine and define locations. Her work questions power, visibility, and erasure in ways that prompt reflective engagement for individual viewers. Fernández is a 2005 MacArthur Foundation Fellow and the recipient of numerous awards including a Guggenheim Fellowship, a National Endowment for the Arts Artist's Grant, and a Louis Comfort Tiffany Biennial Award. Appointed by President Obama, she is the first Latina to serve on the US Commission of Fine Arts, a 100-year-old federal panel that advises the President and Congress on national matters of design and aesthetics. Fernández is represented by Lehmann Maupin in New York City.

GUERRILLA GIRLS are an anonymous group of interdisciplinary feminist artists who use disruptive headlines, visuals, and statistics to expose gender and ethnic bias in art, film, politics and pop culture. The group formed in New York City in 1985 with the mission of bringing gender and racial inequality into focus within the greater arts community. Known for their "guerrilla" tactics, the Guerrilla Girls employ culture jamming in the form of posters, books, billboards, and public appearances to expose discrimination and corruption, often using humor as a tactical ploy. To remain anonymous, members don gorilla masks and use pseudonyms that refer to deceased female artists such as Frida Kahlo, Käthe Kollwitz, and Alice Neel. Other Guerrilla Girls projects include banners, public actions, and videos, in addition to staging retrospectives, exhibitions, and surprise interventions at art museums. Such interventions include a stealth projection on the façade of the Whitney Museum in 2015 focused on income inequality in the arts. Their recent publication *Guerrilla Girls: The Art of Behaving Badly* collects hundreds of their projects from 1985 to 2020, and was named one of the "Best Art Books of 2020" by *The New York Times* and the *Los Angeles Times*. Recently their work has been featured at the Tate Modern and Whitechapel Gallery, London, UK; São Paulo Museum of Art, Brazil; the Venice Biennale, Italy; Van Gogh Museum, Amsterdam, Netherlands; Museum of Military History, Dresden, Germany; and Art Basel Hong Kong, among many others.

CANDICE HOPKINS is a citizen of Carcross/Tagish First Nation and lives in Red Hook, NY. Her writing and curatorial practice explore the intersections of history, contemporary art, and Indigeneity. She is Executive Director of Forge Project, Taghkanic, NY, and Senior Curator for the 2019 and 2022 editions of the Toronto Biennial of Art. She was part of the curatorial team for the Canadian Pavilion at the fifty-eighth Venice Biennale, featuring the work of the media art collective Isuma; and co-curator of notable exhibitions including the national traveling survey *Art for New Understanding: Native Voices, 1950s to Now*; *SITElines. 2018: Casa Tomada*, SITE Santa Fe; Documenta 14, Athens and Kassel; and *Sakahàn: International Indigenous Art*, National Gallery of Canada, Ottawa. Notable essays include "The Gilded Gaze: Wealth and Economies on the Colonial Frontier," in the *documenta 14 Reader*; "Outlawed Social Life," in *South as a State of Mind*; and "The Appropriation Debates (or The Gallows of History)," in *Saturation: Race, Art, and the Circulation of Value* published by the New Museum / MIT Press.

MARIE LORENZ (b. 1973) is a New York-based artist who received a BFA from the Rhode Island School of Design and an MFA from Yale. Lorenz makes videos and installations that document and respond to urban waterfronts and the tidal debris and discarded objects she encounters while traveling across waterways in boats that she designs and builds herself. Through printing, casting, or videotaping, Lorenz attempts "to un-know the metropolis by continually exploring it." The resulting works act as a visual equivalent of beach-combing and tell the story of Lorenz's explorations in "collaboration" with the tide, as well as the connections she forges with her occasional passengers. In 2005, she began her *Tide and Current Taxi* project, taking participants through New York City using only the tide and her hand-built boats. Lorenz's artwork has been exhibited nationally and internationally at Ikon Gallery in Birmingham, England; Artists Space, New York City; Susanne Lemberg Usdan Gallery, Bennington College, VT; University of Buffalo Art Gallery, NY; The Contemporary, Austin, TX; and MoMA PS1, New York City, and elsewhere. Lorenz has been awarded honors including Creative Capital and Harpo Foundation grants, and the 2008 Joseph H. Hazen Rome Prize for the American Academy in Rome. She is represented by Jack Hanley Gallery in New York City.

AMANDA MALMSTROM is Associate Curator at the Thomas Cole National Historic Site, where she works closely on exhibitions, publications, and collections. She is the co-curator of the exhibition *Women Reframe American Landscape: Susie Barstow & Her Circle / Contemporary Practices*. Her research interests center on the artistic and activist labor of women from the nineteenth to the twenty-first century. Her first role at the Cole Site was as a 2018–19 Cole Fellow, for which she researched the lives and work of women associated with the Hudson River School and the women who called the historic property home. Malmstrom curated the first posthumous exhibition of the work of artist Emily Cole (1843–1913) in 2019 (*The Art of Emily Cole*). Malmstrom is a graduate of Loyola University Chicago, where she studied Art History, History, and Women's & Gender Studies. At Loyola, Malmstrom received multiple awards and grants for her original research on the women artists of *The Catholic Worker* newspaper and the Chicago feminist artists' collective, the SisterSerpents.

TANYA MARCUSE (b. 1964) began making photographs as an early college student at Bard College at Simon's Rock. She went on to study Art History and Studio Art at Oberlin and earned her MFA from Yale. Marcuse is a student of martial arts and boxing as a method of cultivating mental and physical concentration and discipline. In 2002, she received a Guggenheim fellowship and in 2005, she embarked on a three-part, fourteen-year project, *Fruitless / Fallen / Woven*, moving from iconic, serial photographs of trees in *Fruitless* to lush, immersive, allegorical works in *Fallen* and *Woven*. Her work has been shown in exhibitions at Julie Saul Gallery, New York City; the Thyssen-Bornemisza National Museum, Madrid; the Frances Lehman Loeb Art Center at Vassar College, Poughkeepsie, NY; Yale University Art Gallery, New Haven, CT; the Museum at FIT, New York City; and the International Center of Photography, New York City. Marcuse's photographs are held in collections including the Metropolitan Museum of Art, New York City; the National Gallery of Art, Washington, DC; the San Francisco Museum of Modern Art; and the George Eastman House Museum, Rochester, NY. Her recent publications include *Undergarments and Armor*, *Wax Bodies* published by Nazraeli Press, and her three-volume triptych series *Fruitless* / *Fallen* / *Woven* published by Radius Books. Marcuse teaches Photography at Bard College and is represented by Hemphill Fine Arts in Washington, DC.

MARY MATTINGLY (b. 1978) is an interdisciplinary artist based in Brooklyn, NY. Mattingly received a BFA from the Pacific Northwest College of Art and the Parson School of Design, and a Yale School of Art Fellowship in 2002. In 2016, she launched *Swale*, a free food forest docked at public piers but following waterways' common laws, circumnavigating New York's public land laws and allowing anyone to pick free fresh food. The project helped instigate the "foodway" in Concrete Plant Park, the Bronx in 2017. In 2020, she was the Brooklyn Public Library's Artist in Residence and launched *Public Water* with +More Art, a sculpture that mimicked New York City's drinking watershed while cleaning water. Also in 2020, Mattingly developed the traveling installation *Ecotopian Library*, combining the disciplines of forestry, botany, art, literature, and the sciences to build a toolkit for imagining regenerative futures within climate change. In 2021, Mattingly worked in Glacier National Park on a water clock called *Limnal Lacrimosa*, and completed a two-part public sculpture called *Vanishing Point* at Southend Pier in the UK. Mattingly's artwork has also been exhibited at the Istanbul Biennale, Turkey; the Havana Biennial, Cuba; Storm King, New Windsor, NY; the Seoul Art Center, Korea; the Brooklyn Museum, NY; the New York Public Library, NY; DeCordova Museum and Sculpture Park, Lincoln, MA; and the Palais de Tokyo, Paris, France. In 2022 her work was published in a monograph titled "What Happens After." Mattingly is represented by Robert Mann Gallery in New York City.

KATE MENCONERI is the Chief Curator and Director of Curatorial Affairs, Contemporary Art, and Fellowship at the Thomas Cole National Historic Site. She is the co-curator of the exhibition *Women Reframe American Landscape: Susie Barstow & Her Circle / Contemporary Practices*. She has organized over 100 exhibitions and publications that have spanned nineteenth-century artists, such as Thomas Cole to contemporary artists including Nick Cave, Jeffrey Gibson, Shi Guorui, Paula Hayes, Leslie Hewitt, and Kiki Smith. In her role at the Cole Site, she worked with artists Mark Dion and Dana Sherwood to realize *The Pollinator Pavilion*, a living public artwork, and co-curated the national touring exhibition, *Cross Pollination: Heade, Cole, Church, and Our Contemporary Moment,* which featured over 85 works by 25 artists. She conceived and curates *OPEN HOUSE: Contemporary Art in Conversation with Cole,* a series of artist-driven installations presented within the historic artist's home and studios. Curated exhibitions have been featured in *The Brooklyn Rail*, *The New York Times*, *Sculpture Magazine*, *Hyperallergic,* and awarded grants from The National Endowment for the Arts, Luce Foundation, and Terra Foundation. She has presented talks with the United Nations, Art Omi, Crystal Bridges Museum of American Art, The Reynolda House Museum, and the Albuquerque

Museum, among others. She earned her BA in English from the State University of New York at Albany and a MA in Art and Contemporary Culture from the Center for Curatorial Studies, Bard College.

EBONY G. PATTERSON (b. 1981) received her BFA in 2004 from Edna Manley College of Visual and Performing Arts in Kingston, Jamaica. She completed an MFA in 2006 from the Sam Fox School of Design & Visual Arts at Washington University in St. Louis. Patterson's expansive practice addresses visibility and invisibility, through explorations of class, race, gender, youth culture, pageantry and acts of violence in the context of "postcolonial" spaces. With the sensibility of a painter, Patterson works across media, using tapestry, photography, video, sculpture, drawing and installation in works united by her visual language, intricate embellishment and intention. Patterson has had exhibitions and projects at institutions including Baltimore Museum of Art, Baltimore, MD; The Studio Museum, Harlem, NY; Atlanta Center for Contemporary Art, Atlanta, GA; SCAD Museum of Art, Savannah, GA; Pérez Art Museum, Miami FL; Speed Art Museum, Louisville, KY; Nasher Museum, Durham, NC; Museum of Contemporary Art Chicago, Chicago, IL; and Kunsthal Aarhus, Denmark. Patterson's works are in the public collections of the Los Angeles County Museum of Art, CA; National Gallery of Jamaica, Kingston; Pérez Art Museum, Miami, FL; Speed Art Museum, Louisville, KY; The Studio Museum in Harlem, NY; and The Whitney Museum of American Art, New York City. In 2021, Patterson was included in both the Liverpool and Athens Biennials. Patterson currently lives and works in Chicago and Kingston, Jamaica. Patterson has taught at the University of Virginia, Edna Manley College School of Visual and Performing Arts, the University of Kentucky, and was the Bill and Stephanie Sick Distinguished Visiting Professor at the School of the Art Institute of Chicago. She is represented by Monique Meloche Gallery in Chicago, Illinois.

ANNA PLESSET (b. 1977) is a New York-based interdisciplinary artist who uses painting, drawing, and sculpture to examine how history, memory, and knowledge are mediated. She received her BFA from Cornell University and an MFA from the Rhode Island School of Design. Plesset's work has been featured in exhibitions in New York City at Yossi Milo Gallery, Jack Barrett, Marlborough Chelsea, Shirley Fiterman Art Center, and JDJ; and at PATRON Gallery, Chicago, IL, Hunter Harrison, London, UK, and Kenderdine Art Gallery, University of Saskatchewan, Saskatoon, Canada. Plesset has received awards and fellowships including The Lower East Side Printshop Keyholder Residency; Joan Mitchell Emerging Artist Grant; Abrons AIRspace Residency; and the Terra Summer Residency and Fellowship, Giverny, France. Her work has been written about and reviewed in publications including *The New York Times, Artforum, Hyperallergic, Frieze, ARTnews, Cultured, Bomb Magazine, Modern Painters,* and *The Brooklyn Rail.* Plesset is represented by PATRON Gallery in Chicago, Illinois.

JAUNE QUICK-TO-SEE SMITH (b. 1940) was raised in St. Ignatius Indian Mission and is an enrolled Salish member of the Confederated Salish and Kootenai Nation, Montana. Smith received an Associate of Arts Degree at Olympic College in Bremerton, WA in 1960, a BA in Art Education from Framingham State College, MA in 1976, and an MA in Visual Arts from the University of New Mexico in 1980. Combining appropriated imagery from commercial slogans and signage, art history, and personal narratives, Smith forges an intimate personal lexicon of developed imagery in abstract painting and prints to convey her socio-political commentary of identity. Smith has received numerous awards such as the Academy of Arts and Letters Purchase Award, the Joan Mitchell Foundation Painters Grant; the Women's Caucus for the Arts Lifetime Achievement; the College Art Association Women's Award; election to the National Academy of Art, and the Georgia O'Keeffe Museum's Living Artist of Distinction Award. Smith's work is held in the collections of the Cornell Fine Arts Museum, Ithaca, NY; Museum of Modern Art, Quito, Ecuador; the Museum of Mankind, Vienna, Austria; The Walker Art Center, Minneapolis, MN; the Metropolitan Museum of Art, New York City; and the Smithsonian American Art Museum, Washington DC. Smith is represented by Garth Greenan Gallery in New York City.

WENDY RED STAR (b. 1981) was raised on the Apsáalooke (Crow) reservation in Montana; she now lives and works in Portland, Oregon. She holds a BFA from Montana State University, Bozeman, and an MFA in sculpture from University of California, Los Angeles. Red Star's work is informed both by her cultural heritage and her engagement with many forms of creative expression, including photography, sculpture, video, fiber arts, and performance. An avid researcher of archives and historical narratives, Red Star seeks to incorporate and recast her research, offering new and unexpected perspectives in work that is at once inquisitive, witty, and unsettling. Red Star has exhibited in the United States and abroad at venues including the Metropolitan Museum of Art, New York City and the Brooklyn Museum, NY; Fondation Cartier pour l'Art Contemporain, Paris, France; Portland Art Museum, OR; MASS MoCA, North Adams, MA; Joslyn Art Museum in Omaha, NB; and the Anderson Collection at Stanford University, Stanford, CA, among others. Her work is held in over sixty public collections, including the Museum of Modern Art, New York City; the Amon Carter Museum of American Art, Fort Worth, TX; the Denver Art Museum, CO; and the British Museum, London, UK. She served as a visiting lecturer at Yale University, the Figge Art Museum, the Banff Centre, National Gallery of Victoria in Melbourne, Dartmouth College, CalArts, and IDEA Space. In 2017, Red Star was awarded the Louis Comfort Tiffany Award and in 2018 she received a Smithsonian Artist Research Fellowship. She is represented by Sargent's Daughters in New York City.

JOLENE RICKARD is a visual historian, artist and curator interested in the intersection of Indigenous knowledge and contemporary art, materiality, and ecocriticism with an emphasis on Hodinöhsö:ni aesthetics. Rickard is from the Tuscarora Nation (Turtle Clan), Hodinöhsö:ni Confederacy, and received a BFA from Rochester Institute of Technology in upstate New York and a PhD from the University at Buffalo (SUNY). Recent exhibitions include the Minneapolis Institute of Art national exhibition, *Hearts of Our People: Native Women Artists* (2019–2021) which also traveled to the Philbrook Museum of Art and Smithsonian American Art Museum, and *Art for a New Understanding: Native Voices, 1950s to Now* (2018–2020) at the Crystal Bridges Museum of Art, Memphis Brooks Museum of Art, and Nasher Museum of Art at Duke University.

JEAN SHIN (b. 1971) was born in Seoul, South Korea, raised in the US, and currently works in New York between Brooklyn and the Hudson Valley. She holds a BFA in Painting and an MS in Art History and Criticism from Pratt Institute. Shin is known for large-scale and often public sculptures, transforming accumulations of discarded objects into monuments that interrogate human relationships between material consumption, collective identity, and community engagement. Frequently working cooperatively with communities to facilitate conversation around social and economic challenges, Shin's works amass vast collections of everyday objects while researching their history of use, circulation, and environmental impact. Her body of work also includes several permanent public artworks commissioned by major agencies and municipalities, most recently a landmark commission for the MTA's Second Ave Subway in New York City. Her work has been widely exhibited and collected in over 150 major museums and cultural institutions, including The Museum of Modern Art, New York; Philadelphia Museum of Art, PA; Smithsonian American Art Museum, Washington, DC; and the Asian Art Museum, San Francisco, CA, where in 2020 she was the first Korean-American woman artist featured in a solo exhibition. Shin has received numerous awards, including the Frederic Church Award, and her works have been highlighted in *The New York Times* and *Sculpture Magazine*, among others. She is a tenured Adjunct Professor at Pratt Institute and holds an honorary doctorate from New York Academy of Art.

NANCY SIEGEL is Professor of Art History and Culinary History at Towson University and specializes in American landscape studies, print culture, and culinary history of the eighteenth and nineteenth centuries. She is the co-curator of the exhibition *Women Reframe American Landscape: Susie Barstow & Her Circle / Contemporary Practices*, which her most recent book *Susie M. Barstow: Redefining the Hudson River School* complements. This work builds upon her 2010 exhibition with Jennifer Krieger, *Remember the Ladies: Women of the Hudson River School*. She is developing a 2025 exhibition, *Curious Taste: The Appeal of British Satire* and completing the manuscript, *Political Appetites: Revolution, Taste, and Culinary Activism in the Early Republic*. She provides historical cooking demonstrations and lectures widely on landscape and culinary histories in addition to serving as a culinary consultant for museums and non-profit institutions. Dr. Siegel has authored / edited publications such as *The Cultured Canvas: New Perspectives on American Landscape Painting*; *River Views of the Hudson River School*; *Within the Landscape: Essays on Nineteenth-Century American Art and Culture*, among others. Her work has also appeared in *Gastronomica*, *The Burlington Magazine*, and *Nineteenth-Century Art Worldwide*. She has been the recipient of numerous research grants and fellowships including: the Eccles Centre for American Studies at the British Library; Omohundro Institute of Early American History & Culture – Georgian Papers Programme Fellowship at Windsor Castle, Windsor, UK; the Smithsonian American Art Museum; the American Antiquarian Society; Yale University; and Winterthur Museum & Library.

CECILIA VICUÑA (b. 1948) was born in Santiago, Chile, and received her MFA from the National School of Fine Arts, University of Chile, in 1971 and studied at Slade School of Fine Art, University College London from 1972–1973. Her extensive practice integrates poetry, performance, film, and textile craft in response to pressing concerns of the modern world, including ecological destruction, human rights, and cultural homogenization, as well as a desire to preserve and pay tribute to the indigenous history and culture of Chile. Her work has been shown in exhibitions at major institutions, including solo exhibitions at Tate Modern, London, UK, the Guggenheim Museum, New York City, and the Smithsonian National Portrait Gallery, Washington, DC. Additionally she has exhibited at Museo de Arte Miguel Urrutia (MAMU), Bogotá, Colombia; Centro de Arte Dos de Mayo (CA2M), Madrid, Spain; CCA Wattis Institute for Contemporary Art, San Francisco, CA; and Museo Universitario de Arte Contemporáneo, Mexico City, Mexico. Her work is in numerous international private and public collections, including the Berkeley Art Museum and Pacific Film Archive; Fonds Régional d'Art Contemporain de Lorraine, France; Museo de Arte Contemporáneo, Santiago,

Chile; Museo Nacional Centro de Arte Reina Sofía, Madrid, Spain; Museum of Fine Arts, Boston; Museum of Modern Art, New York City; and the National Portrait Gallery, Smithsonian Institution. Vicuña has received several awards, including the Golden Lion for Lifetime Achievement, Venice Biennale and The Andy Warhol Foundation Award. In 2015, she was appointed the messenger lecturer at Cornell University. Vicuña is represented by Lehmann Maupin in New York City.

KAY WALKINGSTICK (b. 1935) is a citizen of the Cherokee Nation of Oklahoma, and born in Syracuse, NY, she has Cherokee/Anglo heritage. WalkingStick earned a BA in painting in 1959 from Beaver College of Arcadia University, Philadelphia, Pennsylvania. In 1973, she was awarded a Danforth Foundation Graduate Fellowship for Women to attend Pratt Institute, Brooklyn, NY, where she earned her MA in 1975. Her practice is both a visual record of her life experience on earth and her attempt to come to terms with Indian history as a crucial part of America›s history. WalkingStick was a Professor of Fine Arts at Cornell University from 1988 until 2005. She had a major retrospective at The National Museum of the American Indian, Washington, DC, that traveled the United States to venues including the Heard Museum, Phoenix, AZ; Dayton Art Institute, OH; Gilcrease Art Museum, Tulsa, OK; Kalamazoo Institute of Art, MI; and Montclair Art Museum, NJ. Additionally, she has been included in exhibitions at Crystal Bridges Museum of American Art, Sacramento, CA; National Gallery of Canada, Ontario; Centre of Contemporary Art, Seattle, WA; The New Museum, New York City; and the Peabody Essex Museum, Salem, MA. Her work is held in collections of the Albright-Knox Museum, Buffalo, NY, Baltimore Museum of Art, MD, Cherokee Heritage Foundation, Park Hill, OK, Denver Art Museum, CO, Israel Museum, Metropolitan Museum of Art, New York City, the National Gallery of Art, Washington, DC, and the Southern Plains Indian Museum, Andarko, OK. WalkingStick is represented by Hales Gallery in New York City.

SAYA WOOLFALK (b. 1979) was born in Gifu City, Japan, and lives and works in Brooklyn, NY. She earned her BA in visual art and economics from Brown University in 2001 and her MFA from the School of the Art Institute of Chicago in 2004. She creates works of art that incorporate the African American, European American, and Japanese influences of her family background. Also alluding to science fiction, feminist theory, mythology, anthropology, archaeology, Eastern religion, and fashion, she re-imagines a utopian, empathic world through painting, sculpture, video, performance, multimedia installations, and public artworks. Her work has been exhibited in solo and group shows in museums throughout the US and Asia including, among many others, the Newark Museum of Art, NJ; the Nelson Atkins Museum, Kansas City, MS; Contemporary Arts Center, Cincinnati, OH; The SCAD Museum of Art, Savannah, GA; the Studio Museum in Harlem, NY; the Brooklyn Museum, NY; MoMA PS1, New York City; the Museum of Contemporary Art, Chicago, IL; the Contemporary Art Museum, Houston, TX; and the Yerba Buena Center for the Arts, San Francisco, CA. Works by Woolfalk are in the collections of the Buffalo AKG Art Museum, NY; the Baltimore Museum of Art, MD; the Seattle Art Museum, WA; the Studio Museum in Harlem, NY; the Weatherspoon Art Museum, Greensboro, NC; the Whitney Museum of American Art, New York City; and other major institutions. She is the recipient of many honors, awards, and public commissions. Woolfalk is represented by Leslie Tonkonow Artworks + Projects in New York City.